Resilient Sustainable Cities

M000114944

Urbanization is occurring at an unprecedented rate; by 2050 three-quarters of the world's people will live in urban environments. The cars we drive, products we consume, houses we live in and technology we use will all determine how sustainable our cities will be. Bridging the increasing divide between cross-disciplinary academic insights and the latest practical innovations, *Resilient Sustainable Cities* provides an integrated approach for long-term future planning within the context of the city as a whole system.

Over the next thirty years cities will face their biggest challenges yet, as a result of long-term or 'slow-burn' issues: population growth will stretch to the breaking point urban infrastructure and service capacity; resource scarcity, such as peak oil, potable water and food security, will dramatically change what we consume and how; environmental pressures will change how we live and where; and shifting demographic preferences will exacerbate urban pressures. Cities can't keep doing what they've always done and cope – we need to change current urban development to achieve resilient, sustainable cities.

Resilient Sustainable Cities provides practical and conceptual insights for practitioners, researchers and students on how to deliver cities which are resilient to 'slow-burn' issues and achieve sustainability. The book is organized around three overarching themes:

- pathways to the future
- innovation to deliver the future
- leadership and governance issues.

The book includes a variety of perspectives conveyed through international case studies and examples of cities that have transformed for a sustainable future, exploring their successes and failures to ensure that readers are left with ideas on how to turn the places where they live into resilient, sustainable cities for the future.

Leonie J. Pearson is Senior Research Fellow at the University of Canberra and fellow at the University of Melbourne, Australia.

Peter W. Newton is Research Professor in Sustainable Urbanism at Swinburne University of Technology, Australia.

Peter Roberts is Professor Emeritus of Sustainable Spatial Development at the University of Leeds, UK, and Vice-Chair of the Northern Ireland Housing Executive.

Resilient Sustainable Cities

A future

Edited by Leonie J. Pearson, Peter W. Newton, and Peter Roberts

Routledge
Taylor & Francis Group

NEW YORK AND LONDON

First edition published 2014
by Routledge
711 Third Avenue, New York, NY 10017

and by Routledge
2 Park Square, Milton Park, Abingdon, Oxon OX14 4RN

Routledge is an imprint of the Taylor & Francis Group, an informa business

British Library Cataloguing in Publication Data
A catalogue record for this book is available from the British Library

Library of Congress Cataloging-in-Publication Data
   Resilient sustainable cities: a future/edited by Leonie Pearson, Peter Newton, and
   Peter Roberts. — First edition.
      pages cm
   Includes bibliographical references and index.
   1. Sustainable urban development.   2. City planning—Environment aspects.
   3. Urban policy—Environmental aspects.   4. Urban ecology (Sociology)
   I. Roberts, Peter W.
   HT241.R47 2014
   307.1'16—dc23   2013015727

ISBN13: 978-0-415-81620-5 (hbk)
ISBN13: 978-0-415-81621-2 (pbk)
ISBN13: 978-0-203-59306-6 (ebk)

Typeset in Frutiger
by Keystroke, Station Road, Codsall, Wolverhampton

Printed and bound by CPI Group (UK) Ltd, Croydon, CR0 4YY

Contents

Notes on contributors

Pelin Arslan, Ph.D. candidate, Massachusetts Institute of Technology.

Kathy Arthurson, Director, Neighbourhoods, Housing and Health, at Flinders Research Unit, Flinders University.

Guy Barnett, Research Team Leader, CSIRO Ecosystem Sciences.

Timothy Beatley, Teresa Heinz Professor of Sustainable Communities, University of Virginia.

Janis Birkeland, Professor of Sustainable Design, School of Architecture and Planning, University of Auckland.

Edward J. Blakely, Honorary Professor, United States Studies Centre, University of Sydney.

Rebekah Brown, Professor and Director, Monash Water for Liveability, School of Geography and Environmental Science, Monash University.

Federico Casalegno, Director of Mobile Experience Lab, Massachusetts Institute of Technology.

Peter Doherty, Laureate Professor, University of Melbourne.

Robert Dyball, Senior Lecturer, Fenner School of Environment and Society, Australian National University.

Taegen Edwards, Research Fellow, Melbourne Sustainable Society Institute, University of Melbourne.

Thomas Elmqvist, Professor in Natural Resource Management, Stockholm Resilience Centre, Stockholm University.

Alex Houlston, Senior Project Manager, Department of Human Services, Government of Victoria.

Nigel Jollands, European Bank for Reconstruction and Development.

Allen Kearns, previously Deputy Chief, CSIRO Ecosystem Sciences.

Lee-Anne Khor, Research Associate, Monash Architecture Studio, MADA, Monash University.

Lewis Knight, Director of Planning Landscape & Urban Strategies Group, Gensler, San Francisco.

Thomas Kvan, Professor and Dean of the Faculty of Architecture, Building and Planning, University of Melbourne.

Kate Luckins, Research Fellow, Victorian Eco-Innovation Lab and Melbourne Sustainable Society Institute, University of Melbourne.

Neil McInroy, Chief Executive, Centre for Local Economic Strategies.

Shane Murray, Dean, MADA, Faculty of Art, Design and Architecture, Foundation Professor of Architecture, Monash University.

Peter Newman, Professor of Sustainability, Director of Curtin University Sustainability Policy Institute.

Peter W. Newton, Research Professor in Sustainable Urbanism, Institute for Social Research, Swinburne University of Technology.

Craig Pearson, Professor and Director of Melbourne Sustainable Society Institute, University of Melbourne.

Leonie J. Pearson, Senior Research Fellow at the University of Canberra, and fellow at the University of Melbourne.

Gil (Guillermo) Penalosa, Executive Director 8-80 Cities, Toronto, Canada and Urban Expert, Mobility and Citizen Engagement, Gehl Architects, Denmark.

John Rayner, Senior Lecturer, Resource Management and Geography, University of Melbourne.

Peter Roberts, Professor Emeritus of Sustainable Spatial Development at the University of Leeds, and Vice-Chair of the Northern Ireland Housing Executive.

Gilbert Rochecouste, Director, Village Well.

Rob Roggema, Professor of Design for Urban Agriculture, Wageningen University/Van Hall Karenstein, Velp, the Netherlands and Senior Research Fellow, Swinburne Institute for Social Research, Swinburne University of Technology.

Rhiannon Saward, Urban Forest Planner, City of Port Phillip, Landscape Architect and Urban Designer.

Harry Viraswamy, Ph.D. candidate, University of Melbourne.

Brian H. Walker, Research Fellow, CSIRO.

Cathy Wilkinson, Researcher, Stockholm Resilience Centre.

John Wiseman, Professorial Fellow, Melbourne Sustainable Society Institute and Melbourne School of Population Health, University of Melbourne.

Tony Wong, Professor and Chief Executive, Cooperative Research Centre for Water Sensitive Cities, Australia.

Patrik Zapata, Associate Professor, School of Public Administration, University of Gothenburg.

María José Zapata Campos, Researcher, Gothenburg Research Institute, University of Gothenburg.

Foreword

Brian H. Walker

As this book makes clear, by 2050 three-quarters of the world's people will be living in urban environments. By far the greatest number of the new urban dwellers will be in new and expanding cities in the developing world, not in the old cities of the developed world, and this will put a strong emphasis on 'urbanizing' as opposed to 'urbanized' social–ecological–technical systems (which is what cities are). The development options of the two (urbanized, and urbanizing) are different. Developing urban regions that are not yet cities have choices that are unavailable to existing cities, and there is hope that new cities can avoid some of the features of old cities that are proving to render them so vulnerable to shocks. Can new cities learn from the mistakes of the old ones? And can old cities take advantage of new sustainability opportunities?

As the sizes and densities of cities increase, and the frequency of climate-change-related shocks, energy crises, and food and water shortages rise, more and more people are concerned about the ability of cities to cope with what the future may bring. Coupled with the spectre of further global financial shocks, increasing attention is being paid to the issue of urban resilience. Using the resources available to a city government for making the city a sustainable, beautiful and pleasing place to live is very worthwhile, and is demanded by the inhabitants; but it assumes that the city will be able to continue functioning in the face of whatever shocks it might have to face. This makes (or should make) building resilience the primary, basic goal of urban planning. The question facing city planners is how to go about achieving it.

There are three important assumptions in a resilience approach to city planning and management. First, we must recognize that cities are self-organizing systems. A change in one part of the system leads to changes in others, with feedback effects from those changes to the original change, and so on. Second, this self-organizing ability keeps the city-system functioning in a characteristic way, but within limits. There are limits to how much various parts of the city can be changed and still recover – resume a trajectory back towards what it was; and once the limits are exceeded the new trajectory can be highly undesirable in terms of human wellbeing. Third, you cannot plan or manage a city by focusing on separate sectors (transport, water, power, food, health, waste, etc.) or by focusing on particular parts (scales) of the city; resilience is strongly determined by the cross-scale and cross-sector interactions.

So what makes a city resilient? What attributes of its structure, and of the way it functions (including its governance), confer resilience on a city, enabling it to cope with shocks? There have been some welcome efforts in publications to address resilience in cities, but the bulk of resilience research and writing has thus far been in regard to natural and agro-ecosystems. Hence this book is a timely and very welcome addition to the literature.

The book sets out to examine two questions:

- What is a resilient, sustainable city?
- And how can it be achieved?

It approaches these questions through a variety of practical case studies from Europe, Australia and the USA, making it an engaging read for practitioners and students interested in developing resilient, sustainable cities.

To get at what resilience in cities is all about, the book uses examples from current lifestyles and cities. The authors aim to get an understanding of the essential ingredients of resilience, the things that make a city flexible and adaptable to both slow and fast changes, like population ageing and the unwelcome shocks outlined above, and yet at the same time dynamic enough to take and make opportunities for enhancing the future for society and the natural environment. They place particular emphasis on the interactions that occur between society, the built infrastructure and the natural environment. By touching on a wide range of issues – transportation, communications, urban water, buildings and waste – the book highlights the necessity for governance, social engagement and leadership to align city development with building resilience and achieving sustainability.

The editors and authors of this book are leaders in the fields of sustainable city design and urban ecology and the book will surely make a most valuable contribution to students and practitioners alike.

PART ONE

UNDERSTANDING RESILIENT, SUSTAINABLE CITIES

CHAPTER 1

Introduction to the magic and practice of resilient, sustainable cities

Leonie J. Pearson, Peter W. Newton and Peter Roberts

Urbanization is occurring at an unprecedented rate: by 2050 three-quarters of the world's population will live in urban environments. The cars we drive, products we consume, houses we live in and technology we use will all determine how sustainable our cities will be. *So what is a sustainable city? How does it look, feel and act?* Although sustainable development is a contested concept, it is also clear that it can be envisaged and delivered in a variety of ways. For a city, sustainable development should always be subject to the test of whether key aspects of our daily lives and the urban systems within which they play out can be continued indefinitely into the future from a social, environmental and economic perspective – until or unless something emerges to underpin sustainable development in a key urban domain. Figure 1.1 illustrates these relationships as they apply to cities and adds the crucial dimensions of inter- and intra-generational equity and governance.

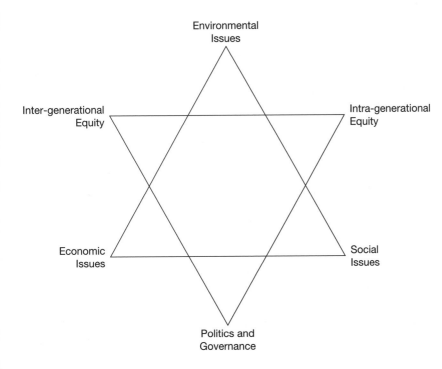

Figure 1.1 Sustainable development and cities
Source: Roberts, Ravetz and George (2009)

Not only are cities facing their current challenges of pollution, transportation, climate change and more (see Chapter 2) but they are about to experience the 'slow burns' of: population growth that will stretch to breaking point urban infrastructure and service capacity; resource scarcity (e.g. peak oil, potable water and food security) that will dramatically change what we consume and how; environmental pressures that will change how we live and where; and shifting demographic and business preferences that will exacerbate urban pressures. The type of city that can handle current challenges, including 'slow burns' and exogenous 'shocks' (e.g. climatic, financial, tectonic, socio-political, etc.), and thrive in the future is a *resilient city*.

This book attempts to maintain a dual focus on the sustainable development and resilience of cities throughout. Sustainable urbanization represents the objective for managing the dynamics of future city development to achieve desirable environmental, social, economic and political–institutional outcomes for the long term (UN Habitat 2004). Resilience is generally conceived as the ability of a system (e.g. a city system) to absorb disturbance and reorganize to retain 'essentially the same function, structure, identity and feedbacks' (Walker *et al.* 2004, p. 5). We are pluralistic in the use of the term in this collection, finding useful insights from resilience in ecology, adaptive capacity in social–ecological systems, transition studies in social–technological systems and adaptation in social systems.

We can position these two terms here as complementary but separate axes of performance that cities aspiring for longevity need to achieve: that is, where sustainable development is measured on the vertical axis (from sustainable to unsustainable) and resilience (from brittle to resilient) is on the horizontal axis to provide for a potential mapping of the states of current cities. Such dual-factor mappings are now emerging for particular dimensions of city or country performance; for example, sustainability and liveability (Newton 2012); happiness and GDP (Worldwatch Institute 2008, cited in Jackson 2009); health and income inequality (Wilkinson and Pickett 2009); and sustainability and equity (UNDP 2011), among others. However, resilience measures for cities are less advanced (UNISDR 2012) and do not yet feature on such radar screens.

This realization that the world needs sustainable *and* resilient cities is a clear message coming from governments, communities, researchers, society and the stressed environment, and it is beginning to reverberate through the media. It is the aim of this book to clarify the urban sustainability–resilience agenda as well as help in its implementation in the future planning and management of our cities by asking leading practitioners and thought leaders to provide their insights on:

- What is a resilient, sustainable city?
- And how can it be achieved?

Following the path-breaking work of the World Commission on Environment and Development (1987) and the host of government policy statements and practical actions which followed, many books and papers have been written on particular aspects of sustainable urban development (e.g. transport, housing, infrastructure, service delivery, energy and planning requirements), and risk recovery planning of cities to ensure they are more 'resilient' to crises (e.g. hurricanes, tsunamis, etc.) in the manner in which they rebound, bounce back. This sector-specific approach to planning and risk management of current city life constrains urban futures to sub-optimal performance outcomes and does not necessarily position cities to be better able to cope with holistic 'slow-burn' or 'sudden-shock' issues. This is the distinguishing feature of this collection compared to current offerings: an attempt to provide a more integrated approach for long-term future planning within the context of the city represented as a whole *socio-technical–built–environmental system*.

Our book is in four parts. Part One provides an introduction to the need, theory and practice of resilient, sustainable cities. It does this through three chapters: this introduction followed by a chapter highlighting the increasing exogenous (e.g. resource constraints, climate change and financial uncertainty) and endogenous (e.g. socio-demographic change and infrastructure uncertainty) stressors to our city systems (Chapter 2). The third chapter focuses on the leading-edge theory in resilient and sustainable cities – providing clarity in the meanings of: social-ecological systems, resilience and sustainability as well as frameworks for understanding how these terms may be used.

Part Two takes a systems perspective to investigate issues for achieving resilient and sustainable cities focused on economic (Chapter 4), social (Chapter 5), environmental (Chapter 6) and built (Chapter 7) sub-systems. This part is conceptual and identifies within the different sub-system opportunities, blockers and ways forward to achieving resilient and sustainable cities. A synthesis of the four sub-systems and their priorities is pulled together in Chapter 8.

Part Three takes a sectoral perspective to highlight innovative ideas and opportunities associated with city sectors. This part is wide ranging and covers the sectors of: urban technology, biophilic design, food security, transport, water, waste, buildings, energy, network technology, social inclusion and urban design (Chapters 9–20). Each chapter provides examples from the developed world on best practice with insights of where our current cities are innovative and delivering 'parts' of a resilient and sustainable city. It also highlights areas where we could do more.

The final part provides insights for leadership and governance that could deliver a city that we can be proud to pass on to our children – in better shape than the one we inherited. Its six chapters start with academic (Chapter 21) and practitioner (Chapter 22) insights into city governance, then touch on leadership (Chapter 23) and policy (Chapter 24). The book then provides its own leadership in the area by a practitioners' chapter which examines how to make all the changes in the book happen and some great examples of where they have been successful (Chapter 25). Lastly, a conclusion pulls together the whole book and offers suggestions of priorities for the future.

Whilst the book is a selection of commissioned chapters, taken together they weave a complex and comprehensive web of opportunities and ideas for the *design* of our cities capable of delivering a future that is resilient and sustainable (where 'design' covers built infrastructure, policy, governance, societal and economic institutions).

This is a positive, optimistic story about change, opportunity and challenge for a better world. We use case studies and examples from around the world to explore opportunities, successes and failures. It is a collection of work that draws out the leading-edge thinking in research and practice; therefore, relevant references and links are provided. It reflects current best practice thinking and knowledge about the challenges and opportunities for transforming our cities: from degraded failing places to resilient, successful urban centres. The need for such books will last as long as our desire for progressive change endures. The innovative approaches and novel ideas contained in this book are contributions to this end.

While the idea for this book started with a unique conference in Melbourne in 2011 (Sustainable Urbanization: A Resilient Future), the ideas have grown, matured and flourished to produce a more international and holistic work. We thank the conference sponsors: the Australian Academy of Sciences, the University of Melbourne's Melbourne Sustainable Society Institute, and Swinburne University of Technology's Institute for Social Research. Also the conference organizers Professor Craig Pearson and Dr Leonie Pearson – a truly intergenerational partnership that worked!

Key link

Sustainable urbanization: A resilient future: http://tedxcarlton.com/Home.aspx

References

Jackson, T. 2009. *Prosperity without growth: Economics for a finite planet*, Earthscan, London.
Newton, P. 2012. Liveable *and* sustainable? Socio-technical challenges for twenty-first-century cities, *Journal of Urban Technology*, 19(1), 81–102.
Roberts, P., Ravetz, J. and George, C. 2009. *Environment and the city*, Routledge, London.
UNDP. 2011. *Human development report 2011*, New York.
UN Habitat. 2004. *Urban indicator guidelines*, Kenya.
UNISDR. 2012. *Making cities resilient report 2012*, New York.
Walker, B., Holling, C. S., Carpenter, S. R. and Kinzig, A. 2004. Resilience, adaptability and transformability in social–ecological systems, *Ecology and Society*, 9(2), 5.
Wilkinson, R. and Pickett, K. 2009. The spirit level: Why more equal societies almost always do better, Penguin, London.
World Commission on Environment and Development. 1987. *Our common future*, Oxford University Press, Oxford.

CHAPTER 2

The challenges to urban sustainability and resilience

Peter W. Newton and Peter Doherty

2.1 Introduction

Perhaps the single most important challenge for the twenty-first century is to work towards a more resilient and **sustainable urbanized world**. In this global strategic urban context, *resilience* concerns the capacity of an urban system – including its natural, built, social and economic elements – to manage change, learn from difficult situations and be in a position to rebound after experiencing significant stress or shock, while *sustainability* questions whether or not certain aspects of our daily activities, and the systems within which they operate, can be continued indefinitely into the future, again from a social, economic and environmental perspective.

With a prediction that by 2050, around 75 per cent of an estimated global population of 9 billion will live in urban environments (UNDESA 2012), cities will clearly play a large role in determining whether the world will be a more sustainable place. An ever-growing catalogue of reports (UNEP 2012; UNCSD 2012; Franklin and Andrews 2012) highlights a list of critical issues for cities that will inevitably intensify by mid-century. The need is to start confronting these now with a process of concerted, well-considered actions.

In this chapter we seek to highlight briefly some of the pressures – both exogenous (external origin) and endogenous (local origin) – that impact urban areas and what might be done as a context for framing the urban challenge: *what cities need to prepare for*. Other sections of the book will focus in more detail on specific interventions designed to enhance resilience and sustainability.

2.2 Exogenous pressures

As cities become increasingly connected in a globalized world, sets of exogenous pressures are likely to exert greater impact than has been the case in even the recent past. Pressures can also be categorized along a 'slow burn' versus 'fast moving' continuum. For example, climate change, ageing infrastructure, ageing population, resource consumption and quality of human capital can be seen as slow-burn issues that change almost imperceptibly year by year and are often ignored by short-sighted planning, but have significant cumulative impact over decades. In contrast, sudden, fast-moving events such as a financial crisis, earthquake, any extreme weather event, breach of biosecurity, unexpected surge in population, as well as a major infrastructure disruption, to name a few, have immediate impact. How well a city's long-term planning strategies, management processes, urban system efficiency and redundancy and emergency response capacities are developed for a particular jurisdiction will be key indicators of local resilience and sustainability.

Resource constraints

The social and economic repercussions of living in a finite world are increasingly evident. Cities in high-income societies have built their acknowledged profiles of liveability on what are now known to be unsustainable and inequitable levels of resource consumption (see Figure 2.1). As developing countries industrialize and modernize, and developed countries maintain their consumption patterns, these resource pressures are intensifying. Current estimates indicate that natural resources are being consumed annually at a rate 50 per cent higher than the planet can replenish (WWF 2012). If our vision for twenty-first-century living is limited simply to

Figure 2.1 City liveability and resource consumption *circa* 2010 Source: Newton (2012)

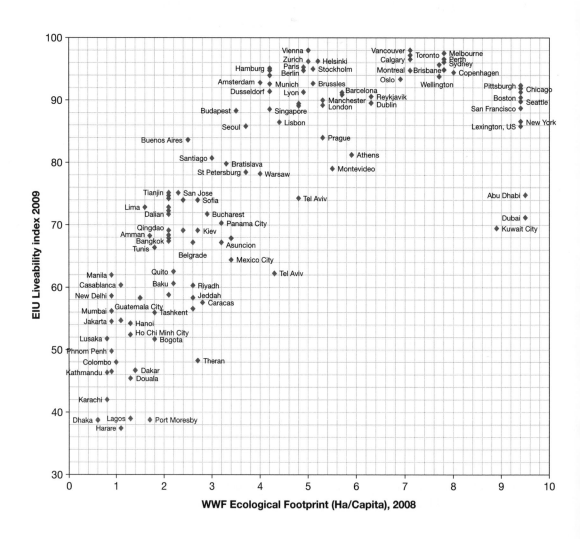

continuing down the present path, there are obvious resource constraints that will influence future urban development. Principal among these are:

- Petroleum: globally, the growth in demand for oil is exceeding that of new supply from readily accessible sources (see Newman *et al.* 2009 for a discussion on peak oil) – a looming challenge for urban populations that are car dependent (Dodson and Sipe 2008). The uptake and/or development of alternatives to the internal combustion engine (ICE) vehicle in the form of hybrid, electric and hydrogen cars remains some way off (in Australia, petrol/electric hybrids comprise less than 0.5 per cent of all new vehicle registrations). Used in combination with the more active transport (walking, cycling) being redesigned into cities, such initiatives provide some optimism for a more resilient and sustainable future for urban travel.
- Arable land: land on the urban fringe of cities, often among the most productive for intensive agriculture, continues to disappear under slabs of concrete and bitumen in all continents, often at a rate exceeding that of population growth (Roberts 2007; European Environment Agency 2011; Sobels *et al.* 2010). The negative consequences for a range of ecosystem services such as fresh food, biodiversity, recreational green space, air quality and heat island effects seem blindingly obvious to all except the less sophisticated property developers and local politicians. A new logic for more intensified forms of urban redevelopment is now emerging in response to demands for more compact cities (Newton *et al.* 2012b).
- Water: the supply of water, especially where dependent on diminishing (and increasingly contaminated, e.g. with arsenic or salt) aquifers, also looms as a threat to urban development in low/variable rainfall regions unless augmented by integrated urban water systems (recycling of stormwater and wastewater) and desalination or inter-basin transfers, each having a different triple-bottom-line (TBL) outcome (Hoekstra and Chapagain 2007).

Climate change

Significant and sustained growth in anthropogenic greenhouse gas (GHG) emissions has long been scientifically linked to climate change at a global level, ushering in a new source of instability for twenty-first-century society linked to the challenges posed by severe and unpredicted weather events, increased incidence of both extreme heat and cold, rainfall variability and rising sea levels due to both temperature-related expansion of the oceans and the melting of land-based ice masses. Impacts on food production and low-lying human settlements are of particular concern. A recent Australian government report (Department of Climate Change and Energy Efficiency 2011), for example, identifies more than $226 billion of coastal commercial, light industrial, residential and road and rail assets potentially at risk by 2100. Insurance companies have begun to factor these risk elements into their premiums.

Until quite recently, human settlements have not been required to take account of the effects of rapid climate change on either their location or their design.

That was understandable in the past, but it is unforgivable if we now ignore the growing potential for catastrophic economic and human displacement from vulnerable regions. The whole march of civilization from the beginnings of agriculture to the industrial age has occurred through the relatively mild weather systems of the Holocene. Before that, the small numbers of hunter-gatherers who were our distant ancestors would simply relocate to more hospitable regions. Now, both the human population size and our reliance on the 'hard' infrastructure of ports, housing, roads and the like make any such move extraordinarily difficult, if not impossible.

Responsible for more than 80 per cent of the world's GHG emissions (Zoellick 2011), cities are both the current villains and the future white knights as they hold the key to GHG *mitigation* (Newton *et al.* 2012b). Currently, the application of the precautionary principle (in this context, *adaptive* planning and urban redesign in response to climate change scenarios) is highly variable for different regions, as reflected in the diversity of municipal government practices identified in recent surveys (Doogue and Bardsley 2012). This lack of awareness and commitment, combined with a culture of denial, constitutes a major impediment to developing community resilience and sustainability in the event that GHG emissions are not capped at present levels.

Extreme events

Some categories of extreme events – such as prolonged drought, flash flooding, cyclones (hurricanes), storm surges, coastal inundation and megafires – can be seen as harbingers of more frequent (than has historically been the case) return periods under projected climate change scenarios. Other extreme events, such as earthquakes, can have equally devastating consequences. To minimize the consequences to life and property that follow when an extreme event impacts a city (given the scale effect), or a smaller settlement for that matter, it is necessary for *planning* to limit the extent of built environments in high-risk areas and *design* to ensure codes and standards for building are aligned to the level of threat identified. We need to change the rules, but there are strong pressures against both from the property development and property owning sector. Governments should legislate now to ensure that there is no future taxpayer-funded commitment to cover insurance, replacement or adaptation costs for those who insist on building in vulnerable areas. Those who deal with such matters might also look at establishing a legal framework for ensuring that those who do foster such developments will, at a minimum, be financially liable in the very long term.

Population change

Population change can be reflected in fast-growing cities such as those in the Asia-Pacific (including Australia and some US regions) versus the shrinking numbers in some European, Japanese and other US cities. Both create challenges for future urban planning, as outlined by Roberts and Kanaley (2006) and Hollander (2011), respectively. For fast-growing cities, the problem is that the planning and delivery of accessible housing and urban infrastructure increasingly lag demand. Greenfield developments continue to be viewed by both government and industry as an easier option compared to brownfield and greyfield redevelopment. Consequently, the increasing blight of treeless, car-dependent suburbs with 'zero lot mega-mansions' represents a measure of our collective unawareness. Similar trends have been observed in Asian (Roberts and Kanaley 2006) and European cities (European Environment Agency 2011). Ireland, Spain and the US, for example, are currently dealing with the consequences of massive over-building in greenfield sites, with the likelihood that some of these developments will have to be bulldozed. Signs are emerging that mortgage stress and collapse of the housing sector could become more widespread in an uncertain global financial climate.

Where the numbers of (particularly young) people are decreasing, the challenges lie in dealing with distressed neighbourhoods, an ageing population and how to (re)direct investment in infrastructure and services to these areas. The sustainability of urban development in either setting will depend significantly on the extent to which principles of *green urbanism* can be encapsulated in the process and practice of metropolitan planning – in particular, the regeneration of inner- and middle-ring suburbs (Newton *et al.* 2012a).

Urbanization and intensification of urban development

Cities are the principal demographic absorbers of global population growth. For many developed countries, the urbanization process (i.e. population shift from country to city) has matured, but for others, particularly in Asia, the process is highly active, resulting in the rapid growth of megacities. Urban growth in the developed countries continues to occur, fuelled by high levels of immigration which, as global population pressures grow and vulnerable cultures are overwhelmed by events, can be expected to increase in the future (south to north, east to west). As a conse-quence of this continued urban growth, intensification processes are being explored in the context of urban redevelopment, with the objective of building more compact cities (OECD 2011a). The most recent phase of urbanization and city building (i.e. post-1950), which has found expression in North American, South American, Asian, Australian and a selection of Gulf State cities (but less so in Europe), unfolded in an era when planning practitioners, politicians and populations alike acknowl-edged few, if any, resource or environmental constraints on urban development (Rees and Roseland 1991). This era has now ended – liveable cities must also be sustainable and have a globally equitable ecological footprint (Newton 2012). Here again, green urbanism has been advanced as a new paradigm for sustainable city planning (Lehmann 2010; Beatley 2000).

Biosecurity

Crowded urban environments are more vulnerable to various forms of biosecurity attack as a consequence of malevolence (bio-terror, military action) or from natural events. Indeed, 'The question is not whether a new pandemic will emerge, but when and how the world will respond' (Howard 2012, p. 27). The most recent pandemic to sweep the globe (H1N1/swine flu in 2009) is thought to have caused around 1,600 deaths in Australia, more than eight times the number officially recorded (Cresswell 2012). According to recent estimates from the US Centers for Disease Control and Prevention, as many as 570,000 people may have succumbed globally, despite the fact that the elderly (normally the most vulnerable group) were apparently protected by prior exposure to a similar virus that circulated prior to 1950 (Dawood *et al.* 2012). In this relatively mild pandemic, however, there was still a problem with metropolitan emergency rooms being crowded by the 'worried well', an ideal situation for maximizing transmission. Furthermore, critical care beds are generally at a premium even when the more familiar 'seasonal' influenza strikes.

In this context, it is essential that the responsible public health authorities are appropriately resourced from the tax base (this can never be covered primarily from the private sector) and that their emergency planning is regularly updated in ways that lead to awareness at the grassroots level. During the recent 'bird flu' scare, for example, planning in the US went down to the level of local municipalities and school districts. In some ways we are better off when it comes to this type of emergency than in the past, because modern mechanisms of communication (mobile phones, the internet) allow greater physical separation combined with the benefits of telepresence. Communication delivered by electronic means is obviously safer in a biosecurity context than face-to-face interaction.

Apart from planning, improving the capacity for rapid vaccine development and production, and increasing awareness on the part of the broader population, the economic realities are such that there is no sure-fire strategy for minimizing the consequences of a novel pandemic. Previous experience tells us that people in the poorer countries will be most vulnerable, particularly those living in crowded conditions with many underlying health problems. Such issues relating to poverty and under-development need to be addressed in other contexts, and are not restricted to the present topic (Doherty 2013).

Financial uncertainty

The volatility in international financial markets that has characterized the period since the global financial crisis of 2007–08 appears likely to continue in the short to medium term. As the recent (July 2012) Libor scandal in the City of London has shown, there is still much that needs to be put right. Government rescues of key financial and business organizations and massive pump-priming of national economies have combined to expose sovereign risk and its tentacles as a major threat to a wide spectrum of supply-side private and government investment. From the demand side, high household indebtedness that existed prior to the crisis, combined with significant reductions in returns from property, equity and superannuation investments and stalled employment opportunities in many countries, mirrors anxieties on the supply side. It all adds up to a difficult environment for investment in sustainable development, where the business case for achieving TBL outcomes remains a challenge for most firms.

2.3 Endogenous pressures

Many of the endogenous stresses of a city emerge as a result of the (in)adequacy (quantity and quality) of key urban *stocks*: physical infrastructures such as housing, energy, water, transport and communication; and social infrastructures such as health and education, as well as social and human capital. The performance in each of these urban domains across cities is difficult to assess and generalize within one nation, much less internationally. There are, however, a number of persistent challenges for the built environment professions globally.

Vulnerable infrastructure

Significant components of the physical infrastructure of cities in developed, developing and under-developed societies are nearing the end of their design life performance, and, with increasing demand, pressure is mounting on the standard of service they are meant to provide. The low ratings now being reflected in 'infrastructure scorecard' studies testify to their decline. Given both the national and local significance of infrastructure (typically a nation's greatest asset) in delivering economic and social benefits, continued under-investment in capital works is a common feature in many urban economies (Regan 2008). The idea prevalent among, for example, much of the US electorate that infrastructure can somehow be provided in the absence of tax revenue (or some appropriate system of charges for use) is clearly unworkable, though attractive to political ideologues. Another class of threat to critical urban infrastructure elements like energy, water, transport and telecommunications (in addition to obsolescence and climate change) is cyber-terrorism and cyber-crime (Brenner 2011). The level of vulnerability to malevolent or natural (earthquake, floods) disruption is also greatly enhanced by the reliance that all infrastructures now have on increasingly integrated computer-communications networks.

Socio-demographic change

A raft of issues related to population demographics and change are represented in cities. Each major age cohort ('generation'), for example, tends to introduce a different set of demands. The 'baby boomers' have been a classic example as they have redefined demand for a wide range of urban services since the late 1940s, spanning health (maternity) care, primary–secondary–tertiary education, housing and leisure. As they age, this cohort continues to exert a major impact on urban cityscapes via new demands on housing, transport and health services geared to the needs of a more elderly population. What might be the housing and locational preferences of the cohorts that follow? Will they favour different living and working environments? The preferences held by particular population segments will also be influenced by the impact of the increasing income inequalities (between rich and poor, young and old) that are characterizing wealthy societies and the extent to which they can be constrained or redressed (OECD 2011c). Financial inequality translates into spatial inequality (segregation) via the operation of urban housing markets and is reflected in the variability in neighbourhood amenities evident in today's cities. The greater social complexity of twenty-first-century cities adds to the challenges and costs of urban service delivery and is ultimately reflected in the levels of wellbeing among resident populations.

Social and human capital

Stocks of human and social capital play significant roles alongside natural capital, financial capital and built environment capital as key pillars of a resilient and sustainable society. 'Bowling alone' (Putnam 2000) became the metaphor symbolizing a decline in social capital within the world's wealthiest nation, marked by a reduction in active engagement in civil society and social/community networks. These findings have been mirrored elsewhere (Ferguson 2012). There are complexities associated with measurement of social capital that inhibit spatial and temporal comparison, but there is broad agreement regarding its significance in the social and economic functioning (especially resilience) of cities and society (Allen Consulting Group 2002). Human capital is more readily defined in terms of attributes involving level of education and training and human health (critical social infrastructure linkage) and their connection with workforce productivity and income (Banks 2010). International league tables (such as the United Nations' Human Development Index) indicate how particular countries perform (see Figure 2.2), with clear implications for national economic and social wellbeing.

Urban economic base

The green economy has been advanced as the sixth major socio-technical transition to emerge in human history, with a capacity for major urban transformation to create the eco-cities of the future (Newton and Bai 2008; OECD 2011b). This follows logically in the wake of earlier post-industrial transitions: to a service economy, information and knowledge economy and creative economy, each of which displays a different spatial logic in its operation compared to its predecessor. These different

Figure 2.2 Human Development Index 2011
Source: UNDP (2011)

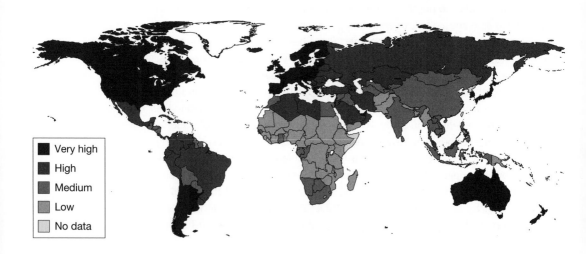

- Very high
- High
- Medium
- Low
- No data

locational preferences by both employer and employee groups need to be understood on an industry-by-industry basis by those charged with the responsibility for shaping the future of metropolitan regions. To enable this latest major sectoral and spatial transformation – to a green economy and eco-cities – there needs to be an associated critical mass of new enabling technologies capable of being linked to a clearly recognizable and pressing need in the marketplace; in this instance, the challenge of sustainable urban development. Part of the problem in instituting such advances is that old, powerful interests can be threatened and act to inhibit the necessary process of change. A major challenge can be to get the business community to think in terms of new opportunities.

Urban environmental quality

Urban environmental quality – an aggregate of ambient air quality, water quality, noise levels and the provision of open space – is a major contributor to a city's *liveability* as well as its economic competitiveness in attracting international capital and skilled labour. There is a significant difference between cities in developed, developing and under-developed societies in relation to urban environmental quality – what some see as the Kuznets effect in operation: 'cities start poor and clean, then they industrialize and get rich and dirty, and then they are rich enough so that they can afford pollution control so that they ultimately end up rich and clean' (von Weizsacker 2005, p. 1). Transition to a green economy and green growth is being strongly promoted as an opportunity for emerging and established economies alike. The former have the opportunity to adopt clean technologies as a mechanism for avoiding the 'dirty industry' phase, while the latter are seeking to be innovators in clean technology development.

2.4 Conclusion

While all these exogenous and endogenous drivers have been recognized by academics, informed communities, industry leaders and governments for years, little has been done to truly manage their emerging impact. Delay in transition to more sustainable and resilient cities and regions will be reflected in future *cost*: to the environment, the economy and societal wellbeing. Achieving sustainable, resilient cities requires a commitment to innovative long-term planning and design, appropriate regulation, nation building, global cooperation and community engagement – things that currently bedevil governments in both pluralist liberal democracies and the more controlled, rapidly industrializing societies in regions such as Asia. There are entrenched regimes from the twentieth century and myriad powerful vested interests that will resist change. Foremost among these are the massive energy companies that control fossil fuel resources.

A number of urban change initiatives are emerging that have potential for progressing the sustainability and resilience of cities. One of these involves the Dutch experiment in transition management (illustrated in Grin *et al.* 2010). This represents a process that devises alternative routes for future urban, industrial and community development by engaging with thought leaders in 'shadow arenas' that mirror the traditional operating environments of key stakeholder groups to the point of creating implementable solutions without being prematurely torpedoed by regime gatekeepers. Does this represent a viable way forward?

Another quite different initiative involves the 'spontaneous interventions' recently catalogued by the United States Institute for Urban Design (http://www.spontaneousinterventions.org/) involving hundreds of innovative 'bottom up' projects undertaken by individual citizens or local communities to enhance fragments of their built environments. Can they mushroom to achieve the necessary impact more broadly?

Irrespective of the innovative pathway followed, urban transformation also requires the assignment of targets capable of being used in performance assessment of cities across the set of challenging domains outlined in this chapter. Peter Drucker's management dictum for business, 'what's measured improves', demands wider application beyond some of the pioneering attempts of local communities (Seattle), NGOs (WWF), major corporations (Siemens) and governments (OECD), to name but a few. Measuring progress in our cities requires that we understand the rate at which they are decreasing their non-renewable resource use, reducing their waste and emissions, improving urban environmental quality, implementing more effective and efficient urban systems and processes, delivering enhanced liveability and creating greater resilience to exogenous and endogenous pressures. Having a clear understanding of the magnitude of the challenge provides the context within which informed, responsible and visionary leadership – wherever it resides – can contribute towards achieving a sustainable and resilient future for the world's population that lives in cities.

To quote former US Republican President Teddy Roosevelt in 1916: 'The "greatest good for the greatest number" applies to the number within the womb of time, compared to which those now alive form but an insignificant fraction' (Roosevelt 1920: 300–301). That is clearly a big ask for the unimaginative, narcissistic and self-indulgent trajectory that seems to dominate much current human activity. The challenges of the *anthropocene* must be confronted if humanity is to have a bright, long-term future.

References

Allen Consulting Group. 2002. *Recapitalising Australia's Cities*, Allen Consulting Group, Sydney.

Banks, G. 2010. *Advancing Australia's 'Human Capital Agenda'*, Productivity Commission, Melbourne.

Beatley, T. 2000. *Green Urbanism: Learning from European Cities*, Island Press, Washington, DC.

Brenner, J. 2011. *America the Vulnerable: Inside the New Threat Matrix of Digital Espionage, Crime and Warfare*, Penguin, New York.

Cresswell, A. 2012. 'Swine flu death toll may be revised up', *Australian*, 27 June, p. 5.

Dawood, F. S., Iuliano, A. D., Reed, C. *et al.* 2012. 'Estimated global mortality associated with the first 12 months of 2009 pandemic influenza A H1N1 virus circulation: A modelling study', *Lancet Infectious Diseases* S1473-3099(12)70121-70124, 26 June [Epub ahead of print].

Department of Climate Change and Energy Efficiency. 2011. *Climate Change Risks to Coastal Buildings and Infrastructure*, Department of Climate Change and Energy Efficiency, Canberra.

Dodson, J. and Sipe, N. 2008. 'Energy security and oil vulnerability', in Newton, P. W. (ed.), *Transitions: Pathways towards Sustainable Urban Development in Australia*, Springer, Dordrecht.

Doherty, P. C. 2013. *Pandemics: What Everyone Needs to Know*, Oxford University Press, New York.

Doogue, J. and Bardsley, D. 2012. 'Evaluating the adaptive capacity of local government in South Australia', paper presented to National Climate Change Adaptation Conference, Melbourne, June.

European Environment Agency. 2011. *Analysing and Managing Urban Growth*, European Environment Agency, Copenhagen, http://www.eea.europa.eu/articles/analysing-and-managing-urban-growth.

Ferguson, N. 2012. *Civil and Uncivil Societies*, BBC Reith Lectures, Part 4.

Franklin, D. and Andrews, J. (eds). 2012. *Megachange: The World in 2050*, John Wiley, Hoboken, NJ.

Grin, J., Rotmans, J. and Schot, J. 2010. *Transitions to Sustainable Development: New Directions in the Study of Long Term Transformative Change*, Routledge, New York.

Hoekstra, A. Y. and Chapagain, A. K. 2007. 'Water footprints of nations: Water use by people as a function of their consumption pattern', *Water Resources Management*, 21(1), 35–48.

Hollander, J. B. 2011. *Sunburnt Cities: The Great Recession, Depopulation and Urban Planning in the American Sunbelt*, Routledge, New York.

Howard, C. 2012. 'The health of nations', in Franklin, D. and Andrews, J. (eds), *Megachange: The World in 2050*, John Wiley, Hoboken, NJ.

Lehmann, S. 2010. *The Principles of Green Urbanism: Transforming the City for Sustainability*, Earthscan, London.

Newman, P., Beatley, T. and Boyer, H. 2009. *Resilient Cities: Responding to Peak Oil and Climate Change*, Island Press, Washington, DC.

Newton, P. W. (ed.). 2011. *Urban Consumption*, CSIRO Publishing, Melbourne.

Newton, P. W. 2012. 'Liveable *and* sustainable? Socio-technical challenges for twenty-first-century cities', *Journal of Urban Technology*, 19(1), 81–102.

Newton, P. W. and Bai, X. 2008. 'Transitioning to sustainable urban development', in Newton, P. W. (ed.), *Transitions: Pathways towards Sustainable Urban Development in Australia*, Springer, Dordrecht.

Newton, P. W., Newman, P., Glackin, S. and Trubka, R. 2012a. 'Greening the greyfields: Unlocking the redevelopment potential of the middle suburbs in Australian cities', *Proceedings of the International Conference on Urban Planning and Regional Development*, Venice, 14–15 November.

Newton, P. W., Pears, A., Whiteman, J. and Astle, R. 2012b. 'The energy and carbon footprints of housing and transport in Australian urban development: Current trends and future prospects', in Tomlinson, R. (ed.), *The Unintended City*, CSIRO Publishing, Melbourne.

OECD. 2011a. *Compact City Policies: A Comparative Assessment*, draft report, Paris, 17 June.

OECD. 2011b. *Towards Green Growth*, OECD, Paris.

OECD. 2011c. *Why Inequality Keeps Rising*, OECD, Paris.

Putnam, R. 2000. *Bowling Alone: The Collapse and Revival of American Community*, Simon & Schuster, New York.

Rees, W. E. and Roseland, M. 1991. 'Sustainable communities: Planning for the 21st century', *Plan Canada*, 31(3), 15–26.

Regan, M. 2008. 'Critical foundations: Providing Australia's 21st century infrastructure', in Newton, P. W. (ed.), *Transitions: Pathways towards Sustainable Urban Development in Australia*, Springer, Dordrecht.

Roberts, B. 2007. 'Changes in urban density: Its implications on the sustainable development of Australian cities', paper presented to State of Australian Cities Conference, Adelaide, 28–30 November.

Roberts, B. and Kanaley, T. (eds). 2006. *Urbanization and Sustainability in Asia*, Asian Development Bank, Manila.

Roosevelt, T. (1920) 'Bird reserves at the mouth of the Mississippi', in *A Book-Lover's Holidays in the Open*, Charles Scribner's Sons, New York.

Sobels, J., Richardson, S., Turner, G., Maude, A., Tan, Y., Beer, A. and Wei, Z. 2010. *Research into the Long-Term Physical Implications of Net Overseas Migration: Australia in 2050*, report for Department of Immigration and Citizenship, National Institute of Labour Studies, Flinders University, Adelaide.

UNCSD. 2012. *Sustainable Cities*, Issues Brief No. 5, Rio+20 UN Conference on Sustainable Development, Rio de Janeiro.

UNDESA. 2012. *World Urbanization Prospects: The 2011 Revision*, Department of Economic and Social Affairs, United Nations, New York, http://www.slideshare.net/undesa/wup2011-highlights.

UNDP. 2011. *Human Development Index 2011*, United Nations Development Programme, Geneva, http://hdr.undp.org/en/data/map/.

UNEP. 2012. *21 Issues for the 21st Century: Results of the UNEP Foresight Process on Emerging Environmental Issues*, United Nations Environment Programme, Nairobi.

von Weizsacker, E. 2005. 'Buildings technology in the vanguard of eco-efficiency', keynote speech, World Sustainable Buildings Conference, Tokyo, 27 September, http://www.sb05.com/plenary/WeizsaeckerKeynote.pdf.

WWF. 2012. *One Planet Living*, WWF International, Gland, http://wwf.panda.org/what_we_do/how_we_work/conservation/one_planet_living/.

Zoellick, R. B. 2011. *Opening Remarks at the C40 Large Cities Climate Summit*, World Bank, São Paulo, 1 June.

CHAPTER 3

Exploring urban sustainability and resilience

Thomas Elmqvist, Guy Barnett and Cathy Wilkinson

3.1 Introduction: a changing arena for urban sustainability

As global centers of production and consumption, urban areas are reliant on resources and ecosystem services, from construction materials to waste assimilation, secured from locations around the world. These distal flows of resources that connect urban and non-urban regions are important drivers of global land-use change (Seitzinger *et al.* 2012, Seto *et al.* 2012b). The classical definition of sustainable development focuses on how to manage resources in a way that guarantees welfare and promotes equity of current and future generations (such as the UN's *Brundtland Report on Sustainable Development* (1987)). Although cities can optimize their resource use, increase their efficiency, and minimize waste, they can never become fully self-sufficient. Therefore, individual cities cannot be considered 'sustainable' without acknowledging and accounting for their dependence on resources and populations from other regions around the world (Andersson 2006, Seitzinger *et al.* 2012). However, the research and application of urban sustainability principles have till now rarely looked beyond city boundaries and are often constrained to either single or narrowly defined issues (e.g. population, climate, energy, water, etc.). As such, the local scales of most urban sustainability responses have so far failed to match the magnitude required of the global sustainability problems (Seitzinger *et al.* 2012). Consequently, there is a need to revisit the concept of sustainability, as its narrow definition and application may not only be insufficient, but can also result in unintended consequences such as the 'lock-in' of undesirable urban development trajectories (Ernstson *et al.* 2010).

We suggest that a more appropriate conceptualization of urban sustainability is one that incorporates a complex systems perspective of urban areas and their global hinterlands, with a focus not just on sustainability goals or aspirations, but also on the resilience of the urbanization process which constitutes the journey for getting there. An urban resilience perspective is important, because cities are classical examples of complex adaptive systems (Batty 2008), dynamic, connected, and open – constantly evolving in many and varied ways to both internal interactions and the influence of external factors (Bai 2003). As noted by Batty *et al.* (2004), we have barely scratched the surface when it comes to understanding the complexity of cities, as evidenced by the many signals that indicate surprise, novelty, innovation, and emergence in the way that cities develop and are able to adapt to change. Therefore, instead of conventional sustainability strategies that are based on a linear and predictable view of the world, a new set of strategies is needed, based on capacity to address non-linearity, uncertainty and abrupt change, integrating natural capital in planning and development (Wilkinson 2012a, Elmqvist *et al.* 2013). While vulnerability has a long history of use in the sustainability discourse in addressing risks in urban regions (e.g. natural hazards), the concepts of resilience and transformative capacity have only recently been applied in the context of cities and their relationship to sustainability (e.g. Ernstson *et al.* 2010, Chelleri and Olazabal 2012; but see early notions in Alberti and Marzluff 2004, Pickett *et al.* 2004).

3.2 Exploring the concept of urban resilience

Resilience is a multidisciplinary concept that explores the recovery, adaptive and transformative capacities of interlinked social and ecological systems and subsystems (Holling 2001, Walker *et al.* 2004, Brand and Jax 2007, Biggs *et al.* 2012). In the urban context, resilience has been defined as the ability of an urban system either to adjust or adapt in the face of change (Alberti *et al.* 2003, Alberti and Marzluff 2004, Pickett *et al.* 2004).

When most people think of urban resilience it is generally in the context of response to sudden impacts, such as a hazard or disaster recovery (see Vale and Campanella 2005, Cutter *et al.* 2008, Wallace and Wallace 2008). However, the resilience concept goes far beyond recovery from single disturbances and there is often a distinction made between general resilience and specified resilience (Table 3.1). General resilience refers to the resilience of a system to all kinds of

Table 3.1 Definition of concepts

Term	Definition
Sustainability	Manage resources in a way that guarantees welfare and promotes equity of current and future generations.
Resilience	The capacity of a system to absorb disturbance and reorganize while undergoing change so as still to retain essentially the same function, structure and feedbacks, and therefore identity, i.e. capacity to change in order to maintain the same identity.
General resilience	The resilience of a system to all kinds of shocks, including novel ones.
Specified resilience	The resilience 'of what, to what'; resilience of some particular part of a system, related to a particular control variable, to one or more identified kinds of shocks.
Coping strategy	The ability to deal effectively with, e.g., a single disturbance, with the understanding that a crisis is rare and temporary and that the situation will quickly normalize when the disturbance recedes.
Adaptive strategy	Adjustment in natural and human systems in response to actual or expected disturbances when frequencies tend to increase.
Transformative strategy	The capacity to transform the stability landscape itself in order to become a different kind of system, to create a fundamentally new system when ecological, economic, or social structures make the existing system untenable.

Sources: After Folke *et al.* (2010) and Tuvendal and Elmqvist (2012)

shocks, including novel ones; specified resilience refers to the resilience 'of what, to what', i.e. resilience of some particular part of a system, related to a particular control variable, to one or more identified kinds of shocks (Walker and Salt 2006; Folke *et al.* 2010). While sustainable development is inherently normative and positive, this may not necessarily be true for the resilience concept. Although (general) resilience is sometimes interpreted in a positive normative sense, this should be done with caution. The desirability of specified resilience, in particular, depends on careful analysis of resilience 'of what, to what' (Carpenter *et al.* 2001) since many examples can be found of highly resilient systems (e.g. non-democratic political systems) locked into an undesirable system configuration or state.

It has often been pointed out that one of the basic principles of resilience and systems thinking (Janssen *et al.* 2006) is that too large an emphasis on system efficiency (i.e. maximizing the output from a given set of inputs) can erode resilience by reducing important system attributes such as redundancy and connectivity. For example, increasing dependence on a few resource sources will reduce backup capacity and overlap in functions, which may render the system unstable if some fail in the face of unexpected and abrupt changes (see Elmqvist *et al.* 2003).

Another important dimension is the idea that adaptation and transformation may be essential to maintain resilience (Folke *et al.* 2010) (Table 3.1). Although this may at first glance seem counter-intuitive, as change is viewed as a condition to persist, the very dynamics between periods of abrupt and gradual change and the capacity to adapt and transform for persistence is thought to be core to the general resilience of social-ecological systems (Folke *et al.* 2010).

Coping with disturbance is here used to describe the ability to deal effectively with, for example, a single disturbance, with the understanding that a crisis is rare and temporary and that the situation will quickly normalize when the disturbance recedes (see also Fabricius *et al.* 2007; Table 3.1). *Adapting* to change is defined here as an adjustment in natural and human systems in response to actual or expected disturbances when frequencies tend to increase (e.g. Parry *et al.* 2007; Table 3.1). A *transformation* is defined as a response to disturbance that differs from both coping and adaptation strategies in that the decisions made and actions taken change the identity of the system itself (Table 3.1). Folke *et al.* (2010) defined transformability as the capacity to transform and become a different kind of system, to create a fundamentally new system when ecological, economic, or social structures make the existing system untenable.

When the frequency/intensity of a disturbance increase, for example a successive increase in frequency and intensity of heatwaves, the coping and adaptation strategies will be less likely to maintain a system in a desired state, and when a transformation strategy is used, this is a consequence of a recognition that coping strategies, as well as available adaptation strategies, are insufficient and outcomes perceived as highly undesirable (Tuvendal and Elmqvist 2012). The attributes of transformative capacity have much in common with those of general resilience (Folke *et al.* 2010), including diversity in ecosystems, and of institutions, learning platforms, collective action, and support from higher scales in the governance structure. There are numerous examples of urban regions already engaged in developing both coping and adaptive strategies in response to, for exmaple, sea level rise, demographic changes, and shortage of natural resources. However, the opportunities are enormous for transformative changes, for example totally redesigning resource production, supply and consumption chains through to stewardship of ecosystem services within and outside city boundaries (Elmqvist *et al.* 2013).

If we view sustainable development in a more dynamic way we can define it as a form of development which fosters adaptive and transformative capabilities and creates opportunities to maintain equitable long-term prosperity in complex interlinked social, economic, and ecological systems. However, with this definition it could be argued that there is a substantial overlap with the definition of resilience (Table 3.1). One suggestion given so far to resolve this issue is that resilience can be seen as a necessary approach (non-normative process) to meet the challenges of sustainable development (normative goal) (Chelleri and Olazabal 2012).

3.3 Framework for urban resilience and sustainability analyses

While in the historical past there are some cities that have actually failed and disappeared (Redman 1999), modern-era experience is that cities rarely disappear, but rather they can enter a spiral of decline, becoming non-competitive and losing their position in regional, national, and even global systems of cities. Urban resilience is therefore about navigating a desirable system trajectory and state rather than avoiding abrupt change and collapse. Here, we will introduce what we argue are three essential dimensions of urban resilience:

1   Metabolic flows sustaining urban functions and quality of life.
2   Social-ecological systems connecting people with nature.
3   Adaptive governance enabling learning and planning under uncertainty.

Metabolic flows sustaining urban functions and quality of life

All urban inhabitants depend on the productive capacity of ecosystems located well beyond their city boundaries to produce the various flows of energy, water, material goods, and non-material services that sustain human wellbeing and urban quality of life (Folke *et al.* 1997, Seitzinger *et al.* 2012). These flows enter an urban system either actively through human effort (transport) or passively via processes such as solar radiation, precipitation, and various other hydrological, meteorological, or ecological means (Decker *et al.* 2000). Barriers to trade and investment are being reduced or removed by many nations, and this is encouraging greater flows of goods, capital, and information across ecological, social, and political boundaries.

Since cities are highly dependent, connected, and open systems, urban resilience is contingent on the resilience of other places to maintain a supply of goods and services. The concepts of 'resilience of cities', as opposed to 'resilience in city' (Ernstson *et al.* 2010), may be useful in this context. The message that emerges is that virtually every city and its urban landscape depend on an integrated global network of production, supply, consumption, and disposal. If resilience is built in one city, it is likely to be eroded elsewhere. This is related to the notion of specified resilience where increasing resilience of particular parts of a system to specific disturbances may cause the system to lose resilience in other ways (Cifdaloz *et al.* 2010).

Strengthening linkages between both upstream and downstream components of the chain, for example linking producers with end-users through extended producer responsibility and consumer feedback mechanisms, are hypothesized to enhance the resilience of urban systems. There is also an important role for the field of industrial ecology which aims to increase the flow from production and consumption processes to recycling. That is, the byproducts from various processes are identified as potential inputs into other industrial processes and/or recycled.

Social-ecological systems connecting people with nature

A social-technological approach has up to now been the traditional way of analysing urban complexity, particularly regarding vulnerability of, for example, public transport systems, energy supply, etc. (Geels 2004). This approach will be important in the future, but when dealing with new and complex challenges such as climate change, an urban social-ecological approach holds great potential (Ernstson *et al.* 2010, Chelleri and Olazabal 2012, Elmqvist *et al.* 2013).

The urban social-ecological system is represented by a diverse mosaic of different land uses, such as parks, gardens, green roofs, urban farms influenced by biophysical and ecological drivers, on the one hand, and social and economic drivers, on the other. These urban social-ecological systems are often highly patchy and dynamic (Grimm *et al.* 2008) and generate ecosystem services, which are the direct and indirect contributions of ecosystems to human wellbeing (TEEB 2011). Examples of such urban ecosystem services include climate regulation, protection against hazards, prevention of soil erosion, and opportunities for recreation and cultural inspiration (Gomez-Baggethun *et al.* 2013). Recently, urban resilience has been suggested to represent the capacity of a city to continue to provide ecosystem services under conditions of growing resource scarcity and climate change impacts (Ernstson *et al.* 2010).

Despite the fact that the world is increasingly urban, the ways in which cities influence and are influenced by climate change have been considerably less explored than other areas of research on global warming (Wilbanks *et al.* 2007, Leichenko 2011, Kates *et al.* 2012). It is projected that many cities will experience more frequent and severe heatwaves in the future as well as risks of flooding and sea level rise (IPCC 2007). The role of urban vegetation in reducing heat stress and risk of flooding is likely to become an increasingly important part of urban adaptation. For example, urban parks and vegetation reduce the urban heat island effect. Urban temperatures can be further lowered when the building envelope is covered with vegetation such as green roofs and green walls (Pataki *et al.* 2011). The cooling effect of trees in cities may contribute significantly to reduce energy needs from fossil fuels and cut carbon emissions. Interception of rainfall by trees, other vegetation, and permeable soils in urban areas can be critical in reducing the pressure on the drainage system and in lowering the risk of surface water flooding (Pataki *et al.* 2011). Ecosystems, particularly forests, wetlands, and floodplains, represent important buffering systems for reducing peaks in water flows and also in nutrient retention and water purification (Opperman *et al.* 2009).

Adaptive governance enabling learning and planning under uncertainty

As the world's cities continue to grow in size and complexity, we increasingly witness the unintended consequences of poor urban design and management, the rise and fall of urban institutions, and the shifting of power and influence (Pickett *et al.* 1997). However, since the dynamics of cities are non-linear, their problems cannot be addressed by traditional linear planning methodologies. New, innovative means of planning that deal with urban complexity and sustaining urban ecosystem services are needed. While planning theory so far has paid surprisingly little attention to human–nature relations (Wilkinson 2012a), insights into urban resilience and social-ecological theory nonetheless provide planning with a new language and metaphors for the dynamics of change in complex systems and new tools and methods for analysis and synthesis. However, most importantly, it confronts modes of governance based on assumptions of predictability and controllability (Wilkinson 2012b). On the other hand, resilience thinking and social-ecological theory provide planning with little guidance in prioritizing or addressing tradeoffs between different strategies, drawing attention to uncertainty when decision-makers want to feel more, not less, secure (Wilkinson 2012a, 2012b).

   To move forward, experimentation and learning are central, and treating cities as laboratories and innovation hubs is important for addressing the complexity and uncertainty of urban challenges (Felson and Pickett 2005, Ernstson *et al.* 2010, Hodson and Marvin 2010, Smith and Stirling 2010). Evidently, there is a need for integrated governance and management systems that promote stakeholder participation and the ability of these to serve as arenas for learning and improving adaptive and transformative capacities (Andersson *et al.* 2007, Barthel *et al.* 2010, Tidball and Krasny 2007, Krasny and Tidball 2012, Kudryavtsev *et al.* 2012).

3.4 Conclusions

As emphasized in the introduction, urban sustainability and associated practices and policies for a global system of cities must, to a greater extent, consider urban teleconnections (Seto *et al.* 2012b) and dependence on distal populations and ecosystems. To build resilience, urban regions must take increased responsibility for motivating and implementing solutions that take into account their profound connections with and impacts on the rest of the planet. Collaboration across a global system of cities could and should provide a new component of a framework to manage resource chains not only for sustainability but also for resilience. The geographical and cultural diversity within a system of cities can provide powerful support for collective action (Ernstson *et al.* 2010, Olsson and Galaz 2012). Furthermore, the potential for cities to be better connected with nature could not only increase their capacity to effect change and foster stewardship at the planetary scale but also increase their resource security.

Without these considerations, urban resilience may fail to find meaning in rapidly urbanizing areas, or, worse, oversimplified goals of building resilience may have negative effects. Key contributions from research will include a greater understanding of what constitutes generic adaptive and transformative capacity and, finally, how governance might trigger and direct urban transformations. These are far from easy tasks that lie ahead, but as the scale of the global challenge associated with rapid urbanization and climate change grows, traditional conceptualizations of sustainability need to be extended through engagement with resilience.

Acknowledgements

We thank Brian Walker and Oosnie Biggs for valuable comments on the chapter, and Formas for providing a grant as part of the URBES project, which have made this chapter possible.

References

Alberti, M., and J. M. Marzluff. 2004. Ecological resilience in urban ecosystems: Linking urban patterns to human and ecological functions. *Urban Ecosystems* 7: 241–265.

Alberti, M., J. M. Marzluff, E. Shulenberger, G. Bradley, C. Ryan, and C. Zumbrunnen. 2003. Integrating humans into ecology: Opportunities and challenges for studying urban ecosystems. *BioScience* 53: 1169–1179.

Andersson, E. 2006. Urban landscapes and sustainable cities. *Ecology and Society* 11(1): 34.

Andersson, E., S. Barthel, and K. Ahrné. 2007. Measuring social-ecological dynamic behind the generation of ecosystem services. *Ecological Applications* 17(5): 1267–1278.

Bai, X. 2003. The process and mechanism of urban environmental change: An evolutionary view. *International Journal of Environment and Pollution* 19(5): 528–541.

Barthel, S., J. Colding, C. Folke, and T. Elmqvist. 2005. History and local management of a biodiversity rich urban cultural landscape. *Ecology and Society* 10(2): 10. URL: http://www.ecologyandsociety.org/vol10/iss2/art10/.

Barthel, S., C. Folke, and J. Colding. 2010. Social-ecological memory in urban gardens: Retaining the capacity for management of ecosystem services. *Global Environmental Change* 20(2): 255–265.

Batty, M. 2008. The size, scale and shape of cities. *Science* 319: 769–771.

Batty, M., J. Barros, and S. Alves Junior. 2004. *Cities: continuity, transformation, and emergence.* CASA Working Paper Series Number 72, Centre for Advanced Spatial Analysis (CASA), University College London.

Biggs, R., M. Schlüter, D. Biggs, E. L. Bohensky, S. Burnsilver, G. Cundill, V. Dakos, T. Daw, L. Evans, K. Kotschy, A. Leitch, C. Meek, A. Quinlan, C. Raudsepp-Hearne, M. Robards, M. L. Schoon, L. Schultz, and P. C. West. 2012. Towards principles for enhancing the resilience of ecosystem services. *Annual Review of Environment and Resources* 37: 421–448.

Brand, F. S. and K. Jax. 2007. Focusing the meaning(s) of resilience: Resilience as a descriptive concept and a boundary object. *Ecology and Society* 12(1): 23. URL: http://www.ecologyandsociety.org/vol12/iss1/art23/.

Carpenter, S., B. Walker, J. M. Anderies, and N. Abel. 2001. From metaphor to measurement: Resilience of what to what? *Ecosystems* 4(8): 765–781.

Chelleri, L. and M. Olazabal. 2012. *Multidisciplinary perspectives on urban resilience.* BC3, Basque Centre for Climate Change, Bilbao.

Cifdaloz, O., A. Regmi, J. M. Anderies, and A. A. Rodriguez. 2010. Robustness, vulnerability, and adaptive capacity in small-scale social–ecological systems: The Pumpa Irrigation system in Nepal. *Ecology and Society* 15(3): 39. URL: http:// www.ecologyandsociety.org/vol15/iss3/art39/.

Cutter, S. L., L. Barnes, M. Berry, C. Burton, E. Evans, E. Tate, and J. Webb. 2008. A place-based model for understanding community resilience to natural disasters. *Global Environmental Change* 18(4): 598–606.

Decker, E. H., S. Elliott, F. A. Smith, D. R. Blake, and F. S. Rowland. 2000. Energy and material flow through the urban ecosystem. *Annual Review of Energy and Environment* 25: 685–740.

Elmqvist, T., C. Folke, M. Nystrom, G. Peterson, J. Bengston, B. Walker, and J. Norberg. 2003. Response diversity, ecosystem change and resilience. *Frontiers in Ecology and Environment* 1: 488–494.

Elmqvist, T., M. Fragkias, J. Goodness, B. Güneralp, P. Marcotullio, R.I. McDonald, S. Parnell, M. Sendstad, M. Schewenius, K. C. Seto, and C. Wilkinson (eds). 2013. *Global urbanization, biodiversity and ecosystem services – challenges and opportunities: A global assessment.* Springer, Dordrecht.

Ernstson, H., S. E. van der Leeuw, C. L. Redman, D. J. Meffert, G. Davis, C. Alfsen, and T. Elmqvist. 2010. Urban transitions: On urban resilience and human-dominated ecosystems. *Ambio: A Journal of the Human Environment* 39(8): 531–545.

Fabricius, C., C. Folke, G. Cundill, and L. Schultz. 2007. Powerless spectators, coping actors, and adaptive co-managers: A synthesis of the role of communities in ecosystem management. *Ecology and Society* 12: 29. URL: http://www.ecologyandsociety.org/vol12/iss1/art29/.

Felson, A. J. and S. T. A. Pickett. 2005. Designed experiments: New approaches to studying urban ecosystems. *Frontiers in Ecology and the Environment* 3: 549–556.

Folke, C., S. Carpenter, T. Elmqvist, L. Gunderson, C. S. Holling, and B. Walker. 2002. Resilience and sustainable development: Building adaptive capacity in a world of transformations. *Ambio: A Journal of the Human Environment* 31(5): 437–440.

Folke, C., S. R. Carpenter, B. Walker, M. Scheffer, T. Chapin, and J. Rockström. 2010. Resilience thinking: Integrating resilience, adaptability and transformability. *Ecology and Society* 15(4): 20.

Folke, C., A. Jansson, J. Larsson, and R. Costanza. 1997. Ecosystem appropriation by cities. *Ambio: A Journal of the Human Environment* 26: 167–172.

Geels, F. 2004. Sectoral systems of innovation to socio-technical systems: Insights about dynamics and change from sociology and institutional theory. *Research Policy* 33: 897–920.

Gomez-Baggethun, E., A. Gren, E. Andersson, D.N. Barton, T. McPhearson, Z. Hamstead, P. Kremer, P. Langemeyer, and P. O'Farrell. 2013. Urban ecosystem services. In T. Elmqvist *et al.* (eds), *Global urbanization, biodiversity and ecosystem services.* Springer, Dordrecht.

Grimm, N. B., S. H. Faeth, N. E. Golubiewski, C. L. Redman, J. Wu, X. Bai, and J. M. Briggs. 2008. Global change and the ecology of cities. *Science* 319: 756–760.

Hodson, M. and S. Marvin. 2010. Can cities shape socio-technical transitions and how would we know if they were? *Research Policy* 39(4): 477–485.

Holling, C. S. 2001. Understanding the complexity of economic, ecological, and social systems. *Ecosystems* 4(5): 390–405.

IPCC. 2007. Managing the risks of extreme events and disasters to advance climate change adaptation: A special report of Working Groups I and II of the Intergovernmental Panel on Climate Change. IPCC, Cambridge and New York.

Janssen, M. A., O. Bodin, J. M. Anderies, T. Elmqvist, H. Ernstson, R. R. J. McAllister, P. Olsson, and P. Ryan. 2006. Toward a network perspective of the study of resilience in social-ecological systems. *Ecology and Society* 11(1): 15. URL: http://www.ecologyandsociety.org/vol11/iss1/art15/.

Kasperson, R. E., K. Dow, E. R. M. Archer, D.Ca'ceres, T. E. Downing, T. Elmqvist, S.Eriksen, C. Folke, G. Han, K. Iyengar, C. Vogel, K. A. Wilson, and G. Ziervogel. 2005. *Vulnerable peoples and places*, Vol. 6: *Ecosystems and human well-being: Current state and trends*, pp. 143–164. Island Press, Washington, DC. URL: http://www.maweb.org.

Kates, R. W., W. R. Travis, and T. J. Wilbanks. 2012. Transformational adaptation when incremental adaptations to climate change are insufficient. *Proceedings of the National Academy of Sciences of the United States of America* 109(19): 7156–7161.

Krasny, M. E. and K. G. Tidball. 2012. Civic ecology: A pathway for earth stewardship in cities. *Frontiers in Ecology and the Environment* 10: 267–273. URL: http://dx.doi.org/10.1890/110230.

Kudryavtsev, A., M. E. Krasny, and R. C. Stedman. 2012. The impact of environmental education on sense of place among urban youth. *Ecosphere* 3(4): 29. URL: http://dx.doi.org/10.1890/ES11-00318.1.

Leichenko, R. 2011. Climate change and urban resilience. *Current Opinion in Environmental Sustainability* 3(3): 164–168.

Olsson, P. and V. Galaz. 2012. Social-ecological innovation and transformation. In A. Nicholls and A. Murdoch (eds) *Social innovation: Blurring sector boundaries and challenging institutional arrangements*. Palgrave Macmillan, London.

Opperman, J.J., G.E. Galloway, J. Fargione, J.F. Mount, B.D. Richter, and S. Secchi. 2009. Sustainable floodplains through large-scale reconnection to rivers. *Science* 326: 1487–1488.

Parry, M. L., O. F. Canziani, J. P. Palutikof, P. J. van der Linden, and C.E. Hanson (eds). 2007. *Climate change 2007: Impacts, adaptation and vulnerability*. Cambridge University Press, Cambridge.

Pataki, D. *et al.* 2011. Coupling biogeochemical cycles in urban environments: Ecosystem services, green solutions, and misconceptions. *Frontiers Ecology and Environment* 9(1): 27–36.

Pickett, S. T. A., W. R. Burch, S. E. Dalton, T. W. Foresman, J. M. Grove, and R. Rowntree. 1997. A conceptual framework for the study of human ecosystems in urban areas. *Urban Ecosystems* 1: 185–199.

Pickett, S. T. A., M. L. Cadenasso, and J. M. Grove. 2004. Resilient cities: Meaning, models, and metaphor for integrating the ecological, socio-economic, and planning realms. *Landscape and Urban Planning* 69(4): 369–384.

Redman, C. L. 1999. *Human impact on ancient environments*. University of Arizona Press, Tucson.

Rees, W. and M. Wackernagel. 1996. Urban ecological footprints: Why cities cannot be sustainable – and why they are a key to sustainability. *Environmental Impact Assessment Review* 16: 223–248.

Seitzinger, S. *et al.* 2012. Planetary stewardship in an urbanizing world: Beyond city limits. *Ambio: A Journal of the Human Environment* 41: 787–794.

Seto, K., B. Güneralp and L. R. Hutyra. 2012a. Global forecasts of urban expansion to 2030 and direct impacts on biodiversity and carbon pools. *Proceedings of the National Academy of Sciences of the United States of America*, 17 September. URL: http://www.pnas.org/content/early/2012/09/11/1211658109.

Seto, K. C., A. Reenberg, C. G. Boone, M. Fragkias, D. Haase, T. Langanke, P. Marcotullio, D. K. Munroe, *et al.* 2012b. Urban land teleconnections and sustainability. *Proceedings of the National Academy of Sciences of the United States of America* 109: 7687–7692.

Smith, A. and A. Stirling. 2010. The politics of social-ecological resilience and sustainable socio-technical transitions. *Ecology and Society* 15(1): 11.

TEEB. 2011. TEEB manual for cities: Ecosystem services in urban management. UNEP and TEEB – The Economics of Ecosystems and Biodiversity Initiative, Nairobi.

Tidball, K. G. and M. E. Krasny. 2007. From risk to resilience: What role for community greening and civic ecology in cities? In A. Wals (ed.) *Social Learning towards a More Sustainable World*. Wagengingen Academic Press, The Netherlands.

Tuvendal, M. and T. Elmqvist. 2012. Response strategy assessment: A tool for evaluating resilience for the management of social–ecological systems. In T. Plieninger and C. Bieling (eds) *Resilience and the cultural landscape*. Cambridge University Press, Cambridge.

Vale, L. J. and T. J. Campanella. 2005. *The resilient city: How modern cities recover from disaster.* Oxford University Press, Oxford.

Walker, B., C. S. Holling, S. R. Carpenter, and A. Kinzig. 2004. Resilience, adaptability and transformability in social–ecological systems. *Ecology and Society* 9(2): 5.

Walker, B. and D. Salt. 2006. *Resilience thinking*. Island Press, Washington, DC.

Wallace, D. and R. Wallace. 2008. Urban systems during disasters: Factors for resilience. *Ecology and Society* 13(1): 18.

Wilbanks, T. J., P. Leiby, R. Perlack, J. T. Ensminger, and S. B. Wright. 2007. Toward an integrated analysis of mitigation and adaptation: Some preliminary findings. *Mitigation and Adaptation Strategies for Global Change* 12: 713–725.

Wilkinson, C. 2012a. Social-ecological resilience and planning: An interdisciplinary exploration. Ph.D. thesis, Stockholm University.

Wilkinson, C. 2012b. Social-ecological resilience insights and issues for planning theory. *Planning Theory* 11(2): 148–169.

Wilkinson, C., L. Porter, and J. Colding. 2010. Metropolitan planning and resilience thinking: A practitioner's perspective. *Critical Planning* 17: 24–45.

PART TWO

PATHWAYS TO DELIVER RESILIENT,
SUSTAINABLE CITIES

CHAPTER 4

Pathways to a sustainable and resilient urban future

Economic paradigm shifts and policy priorities

John Wiseman, Taegen Edwards and Kate Luckins

> Ultimately, sustainability is a question of imagination.
>
> (WBGU, 2011, p. 25)

4.1 Introduction

This chapter aims to highlight a number of the most important and urgent economic paradigm shifts and policy priorities needed to drive a rapid transition to a sustainable and resilient urban future. The chapter begins by clarifying the potential for city-level economic policy innovation to play a major role in meeting global sustainability and resilience challenges. We identify and explain four major focus areas, highlighting case study examples. The first focus area is the need for economic policies and decision-making to be directed at improving human and ecological wellbeing as opposed to unconstrained growth in consumption and resource use. The second area of focus is on visions for sustainable and resilient cities, along with detailed plans and indicators to achieve them. The third describes the role for social and technological innovation in urban settings. The final focus area addresses the question of costs and considers policy mechanisms capable of ensuring swift implementation of urban transitions to sustainable and resilient futures.

Two key arguments are built throughout the chapter. Firstly, the most urgent threat to urban sustainability and resilience is the accelerating risk of runaway climate change. Rapid, just and sustainable decarbonization is therefore the most urgent of all urban economic policy priorities. Secondly, a 'business as usual' or incremental approach to economic policy priorities and governance will be inadequate. The scale and urgency of climate change and sustainability challenges facing global cities – and the broader global community – call for a fundamental reframing of economic policy paradigms – from unconstrained growth in consumption to a far stronger emphasis on sustaining the long-term wellbeing, resilience and diversity of social and ecological systems.

4.2 The role of cities in meeting global sustainability and resilience challenges

Major global environmental challenges such as climate change clearly require concerted economic policy responses from all communities. Cities are increasingly crucial sites for the achievement of global sustainability and resilience and are worthy of particular attention for three primary reasons.

Firstly, the ecological and carbon footprints of cities continue to accelerate in line with trends in urbanization, population growth and industrialization. More than half of the world's population already lives in cities, and United Nations projections suggest that by 2020 there will be 527 cities with a population of more than one million. The average size of the world's 100 largest cities will be 8.5 million people (Romero-Lankao and Dodman, 2011, p. 114). The global urbanization trend is especially significant because it is the major driving force behind increasing global demand for energy and resources. The expansion of urban areas will create new, long-lived infrastructure today that will impact on and lock in future energy and resource demands and systems (WBGU, 2011).

Secondly, the concentration of people and infrastructure in cities has focused attention on the heightened vulnerability of many urban populations to ecological and climate change impacts. Concerns vary depending on the location of the city, the ecological factors of greatest relevance (e.g. air pollution, food security, sea level rise and storm surge, drought) and the capacity to take effective protective measures – particularly in urban areas which are poorer and more densely populated and have weak governance systems (UN-Habitat, 2011).

Finally, the significance of city-level sustainability and resilience initiatives and leadership has been further heightened by the failure of international governance regimes to effectively coordinate a global response to ecological and climate risks and threats (Anguelovski and Carmin, 2011; Bulkeley, 2010). Cities have the potential to play a crucial role in filling this gap by driving and demonstrating innovative solutions to ecological challenges from the bottom up. The C40 Cities Climate Leadership Group provides a promising example of the ways some of the world's largest cities are demonstrating a commitment to taking joint action to reduce emissions and address climate risks (C40 Cities, n.d.).

4.3 Key characteristics of sustainable and resilient cities

A *sustainable* city can be defined as one in which the needs and priorities of current generations are met in ways which do not significantly compromise the wellbeing of future generations (Brundtland, 1987). A *resilient* city is an urban community which has the capacity to 'bounce back' from external shocks *and* to transform itself proactively in order to reduce the impacts of forthcoming shocks (Maguire and Cartwright, 2008). Both concepts point to the need for cities to take a long-term, future-oriented approach in regard to current policy decisions. Given that, it is likely that strengthening the sustainability and resilience of modern cities will require strong political leadership and the establishment of political, economic and governance institutions capable of successfully driving rapid social and economic change while maintaining democratic accountability and social inclusiveness.

The evidence is now overwhelming that safe climate boundaries have already been crossed (Rockström *et al.*, 2009, pp. 472–473) and that this poses a significant threat to cities around the world and the populations that inhabit them, now and in the future. Responding to the imperative for rapid, just and sustainable decarbonization is arguably therefore the most urgent priority for urban economic policy.

But, what would this decarbonization look like? There is a growing consensus that a swift and equitable decrease in urban ecological footprints and greenhouse gas consumption will require the following overarching requirements (Wiseman and Edwards, 2012):

- A significant and rapid increase in energy efficiency, particularly through improvements in the design and operations of urban infrastructure, buildings, transport, food and water systems.
- A significant and rapid decrease in the consumption of energy and resources at household, neighbourhood and city levels.
- A rapid transition from reliance on fossil fuels to renewable energy.
- A strong emphasis on distributed, localized energy, water and food production and distribution systems.
- The implementation of urban design, housing, food, energy and transport policies needed to strengthen social networks, create sustainable employment opportunities and ensure equitable and timely adaptation to ecological and climatic changes.

Alongside these steps for decarbonization, an extensive body of research (e.g. Canadian Centre for Community Renewal, 2008; Norris et al. 2008) has identified the following general features of resilient communities. Firstly, in relation to local economies, sustainable and resilient cities are likely to exhibit diverse and robust sources of economic prosperity, high-quality economic infrastructure, secure livelihoods and employment opportunities, and an equitable distribution of income and assets.

Secondly, there are several features of a sustainable and resilient city which relate to social connectedness. These include the existence of broad and deep social networks within and beyond the community, experienced and widely resp-ected community leadership, and a strong sense of community pride and optimism. High levels of citizen engagement and access to accurate, up-to-date inform-ation and responsive, reliable communication infrastructure are also indicators of resilience.

Finally, a sustainable and resilient community needs to be both innovative and adaptable. This will require a tradition of self-reliance combined with the capacity to secure external resources. The capacity to collaborate effectively in identifying and achieving shared visions for the future is also important. In addition, cities would benefit from well-resourced, well-linked community organizations and governance systems that enable rapid, flexible responses, alongside well-resourced and innovative education, training and research institutions and networks.

Strengthening these characteristics of resilience, while addressing key decarboni-zation requirements, is the crucial challenge facing designers, planners, leaders and citizens in cities today. The remainder of this chapter is concerned with four focus areas for responding to this challenge, along with illustrative examples of promising initiatives that are already under way.

4.4 Toward sustainable and resilient cities: four key focus areas

Shifting the economic paradigm

Many authors have pointed to the fundamental unsustainability of the current dominant economic paradigm based on the assumption of unconstrained consumption of resources and energy on a finite planet (Meadows *et al.* 1972; Schumacher, 1973; Daly, 1973; Hamilton, 2003; Farley, 2010; Jackson, 2009). It is also increasingly clear that a significant reduction in consumption of energy and resources will be an essential precondition for the rapid transition to a zero emissions global economy required to prevent runaway climate change. As Anderson and Bows (2011, p. 41) note, 'extremely dangerous climate change can only be avoided if economic growth is exchanged at least temporarily for a period of planned austerity within developed countries and a rapid transition from fossil fuelled development within developing nations'. As noted above, the dominant role which cities play in driving growth in energy and resource consumption means that the debate about the nature and extent of future economic growth is of particular relevance to city-level planners and decision-makers.

The economic growth debate is, however, best framed not in terms of 'growth' versus 'de-growth' but in a shift in priorities from limitless growth in the consumption of energy and resources to 'growth' and improvement in important social and ecological priorities. In his 2009 book *Prosperity without growth: Economics for a finite planet*, Tim Jackson argues convincingly that our ability to 'decouple' conventional economic growth from ecological destruction is highly questionable and that our focus must be on a redefinition of prosperity – a vision 'in which it is possible for human beings to flourish, to achieve greater social cohesion, to find higher levels of wellbeing and yet still to reduce their material impact on the environment' (Jackson, 2009, p. 35). This redefinition would include focusing attention on community connectedness; time with family and friends; satisfaction from honest work well done; cooperative and productive working relationships; the health of human and ecological systems; happiness; creativity; and the beauty of built and natural environments (Heinberg, 2011). All of these priorities have significant implications for the social cohesion, resilience and sustainability of urban communities.

Shifting the economic paradigm to allow for greater resilience also means paying closer attention to localized and decentralized modes of economic activity and resource allocation in and around cities. There is increasing evidence of the positive contribution that can be made by more localized production and distribution systems and networks to improving physical resilience, social and institutional flexibility and reduced environmental impact (Biggs *et al.*, 2010). Following this, the implications for urban resource allocation and design include the reduction of distances between home and work and between where essential goods such as energy, food and water are produced and used. As recent experiments in sustainability planning in Rotterdam have demonstrated, more localized approaches to urban sustainability planning and design also have the potential to encourage citizens to take a more active role in the functioning of systems which provide their daily needs, such as creating energy locally, growing food in urban spaces, capturing water where it falls, and using active forms of transport like cycling and walking (Tillie *et al.*, 2012).

The diverse benefits of localized strategies have been well illustrated in the implementation of the Transition Towns initiative, a framework initially designed to re-skill rural and regional communities to strengthen localized production and distribution networks in order to reduce dependence on fossil fuels in food, energy and transport systems (Hopkins, 2008). These approaches are increasingly being applied in urban community settings, and Transition Towns are now present in thirty-four countries (Hopkins, 2008).

There has also been a resurgence of support for local, community-based enterprises, financial institutions, food and energy systems in cities across the United States. Networks and alliances have been established to support the development of revitalized local economies, encouraging the expansion of small, community-controlled banks (see, for example, the Institute for Local Self Reliance (ILSR, n.d.) and the Business Alliance for Local Living Economies, which is committed to a vision of: 'a global system of human-scale, interconnected local living economies that function in harmony with local ecosystems, meet the basic needs of all people, support just and democratic societies, and foster joyful community life' (BALLE, n.d.)). In Ohio, the Oberlin Project provides an impressive example of the potential for collaborative action between the city council, local tertiary college and local businesses to drive an integrated strategy designed to 'revitalize the local economy, eliminate carbon emissions, restore local agriculture, food supply and forestry and create a new sustainable base for economic and community development' (Oberlin Project, n.d.). This integrated approach to building the resilience of communities is proving to be successful through improvements in local economic, social and ecological wellbeing.

Creating imaginative, integrated visions, plans and indicators

The design and implementation of the economic policies required to create sustainable and resilient cities need to be driven by visions with the capacity to galvanize broad support and provide a clear basis for determining resource allocation priorities. The most effective sustainable and resilient city plans will be those informed by the most insightful sources of urban planning expertise and experience as well as input from the widest possible range of citizens and stakeholders.

Recent examples of innovative and influential urban sustainability plans include the City of Portland's Climate Action Plan, Vancouver's 100 Year Sustainability Vision, Barcelona 2159, and Sustainable Sydney 2030 (Parés-Ramos and Dupas, 2010). The sustainability plan for the Swedish city of Växjö outlines a future for a city free of fossil fuels, without significant sacrifice in individual lifestyles and comfort (Williams, 2007). Växjö is now halfway towards achieving this goal and the Växjö visioning process is being replicated across Sweden, creating a network of climate-resilient and sustainable municipalities. In Denmark, partners from across civil society and business have collaborated to create 'Sustainia' – a platform for inspiring and informing public debate about sustainable urban futures (Sustainia, 2012b). Sustainia's *Guide to Copenhagen 2025* describes an integrated sustainability vision for the city encompassing buildings, urban design, transport, energy, food and water, economic, recreational and cultural infrastructure, systems and activities (Sustainia, 2012a).

It is essential that sustainable city plans are informed by a clear understanding of the scale and speed of reductions in ecological and carbon footprints required to prevent runaway climate change and address other urgent ecological challenges. This will require moving beyond the logic of 'win–win' urban sustainability policies which run the risk of obscuring the critical elements required for a sufficiently swift transition to a sustainable post-carbon economy (Alber and Kern, 2008, cited in Bulkeley, 2010). Writing about the future of transport, Gilbert and Perl (2010) high-light the difference between planning for step-changes or 'transport revolutions' and more incremental adjustments to oil-based transport systems. The latter approach, they argue, is likely to entrench a vicious cycle of economic instability driven by oil depletion and price fluctuations. As they note, 'the key to success in communicating the benefits of transport revolutions will be articulating a vision of the future in which the quality of mobility can be seen to improve at the same time that the growth of travel slows down' (Gilbert and Perl, 2010, p. 10).

Effective implementation of long-term sustainability visions and plans needs to be informed and driven by integrated indicator systems which replace monetary and financial metrics with broader measures of social and ecological wellbeing. Sustainability and wellbeing indicator frameworks are increasingly being employed by many cities and communities as tools for debating and setting sustainability pri-orities and for assessing success in achieving these goals. Integrated indicator systems being deployed in a range of jurisdictions include the OECD Better Life Index (OECD, n.d.), the New Economics Foundation's Happy Planet Index (NEF, n.d.), and the Canadian Index of Wellbeing (n.d.). At a regional level, Portland State University, in collaboration with a wide range of local leaders and stakeholders, launched the Greater Portland–Vancouver Indicators framework in 2010 as 'a shared lens to track social, environmental and economic well-being' across several towns and cities in the Portland–Vancouver region (GPVIF, n.d.).

To achieve this goal, it is important that these integrated wellbeing measure-ment frameworks are complemented by the capacity to collect and analyse city- and neighbourhood-level information about trends including renewable energy uptake, energy efficiency measures and emissions (Dodman, 2011; Rosenzweig *et al.*, 2010). In Canada there is a growing 'open data' movement, backed by cities in over twenty municipalities, to access government data on trends in the use of urban space, transport and infrastructure. Aside from increased government trans-parency, this is leading to innovative online applications which allow citizens to report back to policy-makers on progress in improving services and outcomes such as cycling and walking accessibility (Aylett, 2012). By keeping this communication between citizens and local government open, the policies are tailored to the citizens they affect and the benefits can be amplified.

Inspiring technological and social innovation

As noted earlier in this chapter, cities have the potential to be powerful engine rooms for sustainability innovation. This arises in part from the high relative concentration of people and their interactions with each other, leading to a continuous feedback loop of knowledge accumulation and cognitive capacity (Ernstson *et al.*, 2010, pp. 538–539): 'In successful cities, everything is about people who challenge, compete and stimulate each other so that innovation can come about' (Jacobs, 1973, cited in Tillie *et al.*, 2012, p. 6).

The facilitation of creative, blue-sky visioning and cross-disciplinary, cross-sectoral collaboration is one important way in which cities can act to accelerate sustainability and resilience innovation. The Fifth International Architecture Biennale, held in 2012 in Rotterdam, highlighted the ways in which city-level visioning processes could create 'a platform for exploration, for demonstrating new roles and for inhabitants and businesses to illustrate what an attractive, sustainable inner city in Rotterdam would be like . . . to concentrate the city's energy and display a breeding ground for initiatives' (Tillie *et al.*, 2012, p. 2).

While successful, large-scale commercialization of sustainability innovations often requires significant national funding, cities also have a major role to play as demonstration sites for new technologies and service provision systems. In her study of enablers for climate action in three Canadian cities, Burch (2010, citing Geels, 2002) found that social experimentation can play a crucial role in creating innovation 'niches' or protected spaces in which new modes of post-carbon, sustainable living can be explored and tested. The installation of 'living laboratories' – replicable, experimental structures or programmes allowing cities to learn from interactions between people and technology-aided innovation in real-life settings – has become increasingly common. The European Network of Living Labs has been described as the 'birthplace for sustainable cities' (Waltner, 2011). In Stockholm, Sweden, the district of Hammarby Sjostad has become an influential demonstration site for sustainable living (Hammarbysjostad.se, 2010). The Centre for Interactive Research on Sustainability (CIRS), at the University of British Columbia, is another excellent example of a 'living laboratory', where researchers are investigating interactions between the state-of-the-art sustainable building design and the building's inhabitants and users (CIRS, n.d.).

Many cities are already focused on improving urban energy efficiency and waste management policies and systems, and there is vast potential to achieve emissions reductions and cost savings through further scaling up. The Skaftkärr cooperation and experimentation project (2008–2012), which aimed to develop an energy-efficient residential precinct, is one example of the importance of demonstration projects in driving sustainability innovation. This project was established by a partnership between the City of Porvoo, the Finnish Innovation Fund Sitra, the municipal energy company Porvoon Energia Oy Borgå Energi Ab and the regional business development company Posintra Oy. With a focus on integrating efficiency improvements into spatial planning processes, the project aimed to cut consumption of primary energy by 38 per cent and carbon dioxide emissions by 30 per cent (DAC and Cities, 2012).

Driving swift and effective implementation

This final focus area is concerned with identifying key policy instruments that can be utilized in cities to help drive the implementation of the many changes required to move towards more sustainable and resilient futures. This section touches upon pricing, regulation, investment and financing mechanisms that could be, or already are, effectively employed in a variety of jurisdictions.

Price signals continue to provide a crucial tool for driving changes in consumption and behaviour. It is therefore essential that energy and resource prices reflect their full, long-term ecological, social and economic costs. A robust carbon price, set at the level required to drive a rapid shift from fossil fuels to renewable energy, will need to be a central component of any effective suite of urban sustainability and resilience policies. In most instances an effective carbon price regime is likely to require action at national rather than metropolitan levels. There are, however, some interesting city-level exceptions. The Swedish city of Växjö, for example, introduced the world's first carbon tax in 1991. The local government of Växjö followed this up by legislating in 1996 to phase out fossil fuels altogether (Williams, 2007). This in turn led to a range of emissions reduction measures including Växjö's shift to bio-energy and the development of low-emissions transport such as the high-speed electric train between Växjö and Stockholm (Williams, 2007).

A robust carbon price needs to be complemented by other actions required to price resources in ways which reflect full long-term ecological costs and provide incentives for transition to more sustainable resource usage. This may include ending subsidies and tax concessions to fossil fuel and fossil fuel-dependent indus-tries and shifting incentives to encourage deployment of renewable energy and energy efficiency. Feed-in-tariffs, which pay a premium for electricity fed into the grid from renewable energy sources, have been particularly effective in promoting the deployment of solar power. In Germany, the expansion of the feed-in-tariff scheme in 2000 led to dramatic growth in the solar photovoltaic industry, with installed capacity increasing sevenfold to over 1,500 megawatts within five years (Energy Matters, n.d.). However, these policy interventions are typically the domain of national governments. In the context of cities, price signal mechanisms such as the introduction of levies on driving in central London to reduce emissions and traffic congestion (Shove and Walker, 2010) are also being implemented with con-siderable success.

In some cases direct regulation will be the most effective mechanism for driving rapid transitions in investment and consumption (e.g. California's low-emission vehicle regulations, in place since 1990 (California Air Resources Board, n.d.)). In other instances rating systems and procurement policies can provide strong incen-tives encouraging new patterns of household and business investment. Mechanisms such as the Green Star rating system for environmental building design in Australia and ENERGY Star for energy efficient appliances in the United States are widely used, with equivalent versions around the world.

The scale and complexity of the transformational change required to build sustainable and resilient cities will require long-term public sector investment in carefully integrated energy, transport, food, water and communications systems and networks. Many cities have already recognized this and have begun to upgrade or build new infrastructure such as 'smart grids' and sustainable transport connections. In Mannheim, Germany's leading 'smart city', the federally funded E-Energy programme, linking energy-saving technologies with communications systems, has enabled the connection of every household in the city to a smart energy network. The 'smart grid' project in Mannheim allows for a stable electricity supply, incorporating a large amount of decentralized energy production. It also provides households with clearer, timely information about their own energy consumption and expenses, which in turn has the potential to encourage more energy and cost-efficient behaviour at the household level (Shimkus, 2011).

In Californian cities, the goal of rapidly increasing the number of zero-emissions vehicles is supported by the large-scale public and private sector investment required to install an extensive network of electric vehicle charging stations and infrastructure. Charging stations are being installed in key locations around the state, including the major cities of San Francisco, San Diego and Los Angeles (Governor of California, 2012). Looking back to 1994, in Stockholm, a plan for a city-owned information and telecommunications utility was developed and has since been implemented. The company responsible, Stokab, was responsible for rolling out a fibre-optic network across the city, and ultimately creating a 'future-proof infrastructure that's competition neutral and open to all on equal terms' (Smart+Connected Communities Institute, 2012, p. 49). The long-term investment in advanced telecommunications networks provides multiple benefits for the city, supporting innovation, knowledge-intensive jobs, and environmentally friendly choices such as videoconferencing.

Responding to the sustainability challenges faced by cities will necessarily involve shifting priorities away from economic sectors which are polluting or environmentally destructive, and for which clean alternatives are available. Equitable structural adjustment policies are likely to require an integrated mix of investment in, for example, facilitation of the closure of unsustainable industries (e.g. fossil fuel power stations, fossil fuel-based transport systems), and employment and training schemes to enable communities and workers affected to make the transition to new livelihoods. Green economy skills and labour market programmes are also likely to require investment to ensure an adequate supply of skilled labour for emerging industries, such as renewable energy construction and maintenance, energy efficiency and urban agriculture.

In relation to the question of affordability, the German Advisory Council on Global Change has estimated the additional investment required for the transformations required to build truly sustainable post-carbon cities lies somewhere in the region of 2 to 3 per cent of GDP p.a. (WBGU, 2011, p. 6). They also note that these costs are likely to be offset by savings arising from the avoidance of some of the actions required to adapt to or cope with escalating ecological challenges and runaway climate change.

Policy options and mechanisms to facilitate the large-scale reallocation of financial resources needed to finance the transition to sustainable urban futures include the following:

- Carbon price schemes and other 'full-cost' pricing of resources.
- 'Tobin taxes', which are essentially very small fees applied to international financial transactions.

- Redirection and reprioritizing of current taxation revenue and tax incentives (e.g. redirection of subsidies for fossil fuel production and other emissions-intensive activities towards renewable energy alternatives).
- Low-interest loans and loan guarantees to encourage investment in renewable energy enterprises (e.g. UK Enterprise Investment Scheme and US Department of Energy loan guarantees (O'Connor and Chenoweth, 2010)).
- 'Green banks' and 'green bond' schemes (e.g. UK Green Investment Bank, World Bank Green Bonds, US PACE Bonds funding residential energy efficiency retrofits (O'Connor and Chenoweth, 2010)).
- Green pension funds (e.g. AP Pension's Green Power Partners, CalPERS' Green Wave and Climate Change Capital's Carbon Funds (O'Connor and Chenoweth, 2010)).

Aside from a range of public sector financing mechanisms, there is potential for harnessing private finance and community ownership models. Community financing of renewable energy projects has proven very effective in Denmark, for example, where the wind industry is 15 per cent locally and cooperatively owned (O'Connor and Chenoweth, 2010). Hepburn Wind, which has built a 4.1-megawatt wind farm in rural Victoria, has pioneered this community financing and ownership structure in Australia (Hepburn Wind, n.d.).

4.5 Conclusion

Our aim in this chapter has been to strengthen understanding of the necessity, possibility and desirability of a rapid transition to post-carbon, sustainable and resilient cities. While many tough and complex technological and financial challenges remain, it is becoming clear that the key roadblocks to achieving this goal are social and political. The greatest challenges facing sustainable city advocates and policy-makers, therefore, are to inspire the long-term thinking, political mobilization and visionary leadership – at all levels of city governance – required to scale up the increasingly impressive array of innovative ideas and exemplar initiatives swiftly and effectively.

References

Anderson, K. and Bows, A. 2011. Beyond 'dangerous' climate change: Emissions scenarios for a new world. *Philosophical Transactions of the Royal Society*, 369, 20–44.

Anguelovski, I. and Carmin, J. 2011. Something borrowed, everything new: Innovation and institutionalization in urban climate governance. *Current Opinion in Environmental Sustainability*, 3, 169–175.

Aylett, A. 2012. Green cities, open data. Sustainable Cities Canada. Blog post May 29, 2012. Retrieved October 9, 2012 from http://www.sustainablecitiescanada.ca/2012/05/green-cities-green-data/.

BALLE (Business Alliance for Local Living Economies) n.d. About BALLE. Retrieved October 16, 2012 from http://bealocalist.org/about-us.

Biggs, C., Ryan, C. and Wiseman, J. 2010. *Distributed Systems: A Design Model for Sustainable and Resilient Infrastructure*. VEIL Distributed Systems Briefing Paper. Melbourne: University of Melbourne.

Brundtland, G.H. 1987. *Our Common Future*. Oxford: Oxford University Press.

Bulkeley, H. 2010. Cities and the governing of climate change. *Annual Review of Environment and Resources*, 35, 229–253.

Burch, S. 2010. Transforming barriers into enablers of action on climate change: Insights from three municipal case studies in British Columbia, Canada. *Global Environmental Change*, 20, 287–297.

C40 Cities. n.d. About C40. Retrieved October 18, 2012 from http://www.c40cities.org/about.

California Air Resources Board. n.d. Low-emission vehicle program. Retrieved October 22, 2012 from http://www.arb.ca.gov/msprog/levprog/levprog.htm.

Canadian Centre for Community Renewal. 2008. The community resilience manual: A resource for rural recovery and renewal. Retrieved May 3, 2013 from http://communityrenewal.ca/sites/all/files/resource/P200_0.pdf.

Canadian Index of Wellbeing. n.d. Framework. Retrieved November 22, 2012 from https://uwaterloo.ca/canadian-index-wellbeing/our-products/framework.

CIRS. n.d. UBC Centre for Interactive Research on Sustainability (CIRS). University of British Columbia. Retrieved October 12, 2012 from http://cirs.ubc.ca/.

DAC and Cities. 2012. Porvoo: Energy-efficient residential area. Danish Architecture Centre: Sustainable Cities. Retrieved November 29, 2012 from http://www.dac.dk/en/dac-cities/sustainable-cities-2/all-cases/energy/porvoo-energy-efficient-residential-area/?bbredirect=true.

Daly, H. 1973. *Toward a Steady-State Economy*. San Francisco: W. H. Freeman.

Dodman, D. 2011. Forces driving urban greenhouse gas emissions. *Current Opinion in Environmental Sustainability*, 3, 121–125.

Energy Matters. n.d. Feed-in tariff for grid-connected solar power systems. Retrieved October, 22, 2012 from http://www.energymatters.com.au/government-rebates/feedintariff.php#fit-germany.

Ernstson, H., van der Leeuw, S. E., Redman, C. L., Meffert, D. J., Davis, G., Alfsen, C. and Elmqvist, T. 2010. Urban transitions: On urban resilience and human-dominated ecosystems. *Ambio: A Journal of the Human Environment*, 39, 531–545.

Farley, J. 2010. Ecological economics. In Heinberg, R. and Lerch, D. (eds) *The Post Carbon Reader: Managing the 21st Century's Sustainability Crises*. California: Watershed Media and the Post Carbon Institute, pp. 259–278.

Gilbert, R. and Perl, A. 2010. *Transportation in the Post-Carbon World. The Post Carbon Reader Series: Transportation*. Santa Rosa: Post Carbon Institute.

Governor of California. 2012. Governor Brown announces $120 million settlement to fund electric car charging stations across California. March 23, 2012. Retrieved October 12, 2012 from http://gov.ca.gov/news.php?id=17463.

GPVIF (Greater Portland–Vancouver Indicators Framework). n.d. Greater Portland–Vancouver Indicators – overview. Retrieved November 22, 2012 from http://pdx.edu/ims/greater-portland-vancouver-indicators-gpvi-overview.

Hamilton, C. 2003. *Growth Fetish*. Sydney: Allen and Unwin.

Hammarbysjostad.se. 2010. The Hammarby model. Retrieved November 22, 2012 from http://www.hammarbysjostad.se/.

Heinberg, R. 2011. *The End of Growth: Adapting to Our New Economic Reality*. Gabriola Island, British Columbia: New Society.

Hepburn Wind. n.d. About Hepburn Wind. Retrieved October 12, 2012 from http://hepburnwind.com.au/about/.

Hopkins, R. 2008. *The Transition Handbook: From Oil Dependency to Local Resilience*, Foxhole. Dartington, Totnes: Green Books Ltd.

ILSR (Institute for Local Self-Reliance). n.d. About the Institute for Local Self-Reliance. Retrieved October 16, 2012 from http://www.ilsr.org/initiatives/banking/.

Jackson, T. 2009. *Prosperity without growth: Economics for a finite planet.* London: Earthscan.

Maguire, B. and Cartwright, S. 2008. *Assessing a Community's Capacity to Manage Change: A Resilience Approach to Social Assessment.* Canberra: Bureau of Rural Sciences, Australian Government.

Meadows, D.H., Meadows, D.L., Randers, J. and Behrens, W. 1972. *The Limits to Growth.* New York: Universe Books.

NEF (New Economics Foundation). n.d. Happy Planet Index. Retrieved November 22, 2012 from http://www.happyplanetindex.org/.

Norris, F., Stevens, S., Pfefferbaum, B., Wyche, K. and Pfefferbaum, R. 2008. Community resilience as a metaphor, theory, set of capacities, and strategy for disaster readiness. *American Journal of Community Psychology,* 41, 127–150.

Oberlin Project. n.d. About. Retrieved October 18, 2012 from http://www.oberlinproject.org/about.

O'Connor, S. and Chenoweth, J. 2010. Funding the transition to a clean energy economy. Australian Conservation Foundation. Retrieved November 22, 2012 from http://www.acfonline.org.au/sites/default/files/resources/Funding_the_Transition_to_a_Clean_Economy_-_An_ACF_report.pdf.

OECD. n.d. OECD Better Life Index. Retrieved October 12, 2012 from http://www.oecdbetterlifeindex.org/.

Parés-Ramos, I.K. and Dupas, S. 2010. *Governance and Vision: Visions of Cities towards a Low-Energy Future.* Energy Cities, IMAGINE: The Energy Future of Our Cities Initiative. French Ministry for Sustainable Development (MEEDDM), French Environment and Energy Management Agency (ADEME) and Université du Maine.

Rockström, J., Steffen, W., Noone, K., Persson, A., Chapin, F. S. III, Lambin, E.F., Lenton, T.M., Scheffer, M., Folke, C., Schellnhuber, H.J., Nykvist, B., de Wit, C.A., Hughes, T., van der Leeuw, S., Rodhe, H., Sörlin, S., Snyder, P.K., Costanza, R., Svedin, U., Falkenmark, M., Karlberg, L., Corell, R.W., Fabry, V.J., Hansen, J., Walker, B., Liverman, D., Richardson, K., Crutzen, P. and Foley, J.A. 2009. A safe operating space for humanity. *Nature,* 461, 472–475.

Romero-Lankao, P. and Dodman, D. 2011. Cities in transition: Transforming urban centers from hotbeds of GHG emissions and vulnerability to seedbeds of sustainability and resilience: Introduction and editorial overview. *Current Opinion in Environmental Sustainability,* 3, 113–120.

Rosenzweig, C., Solecki, W., Hammer, S.A. and Mehrotra, S. 2010. Cities lead the way in climate-change action. *Nature,* 467, 909–911.

Schumacher, E.F. 1973. *Small is Beautiful: A Study of Economics as if People Mattered.* New York: Harper and Row.

Shimkus, J. 2011. The German model city of Mannheim's smart grid. *Energy Digital.* Blog post June 14, 2011. Retrieved November 12, 2012 from http://www.energydigital.com/green_technology/the-german-model-city-of-mannheims-smart-grid.

Shove, E. and Walker, G. 2010. Governing transitions in the sustainability of everyday life. *Research Policy,* 39, 471–476.

Smart+Connected Communities Institute. 2012. Smart cities exposé: Ten cities in transition. Retrieved October 22, 2012 from http://www.pageturnpro.com/Cisco/41742-Smart-Cities-Expose-10-Cities-in-Transition/index.html#50.

Sustainia. 2012a. *Guide to Copenhagen 2025.* Retrieved October 14, 2012 from http://www.sustainia.me/wp-content/uploads/2012/06/CPH-2025.pdf.

Sustainia. 2012b. The sustainable society of tomorrow. Retrieved October 14, 2012 from http://www.sustainia.me/about-sustainia/.

Tillie, N., Aarts, M., Marijinissen, M., Stenhuijs, L., Borsboom, J., Rietveld, E., Doepel, D., Visschers, J. and Lap, S. 2012. *Rotterdam: People Make the Inner City*. A collaboration between the Municipality of Rotterdam, TNO, Doepel Stijkers, Interreg IVb/Music, LAP Landscape and Urban Design and DRIFT. Rotterdam: Mediacenter Rotterdam.

UN-Habitat. 2011. *Cities and Climate Change: Policy Directions: Global Report on Human Settlements* (abridged edition). London and Washington, DC: United Nations Human Settlements Programme.

Waltner, C. 2011. Living labs guiding sustainable cities innovations in Europe. Smart+Connected Communities Institute. Blog post March 1, 2011. Retrieved October 16, 2012 from http://www.smartconnectedcommunities.org/docs/DOC-1586.

WBGU. 2011. *World in Transition: A Social Contract for Sustainability: Summary for policy-makers*. Berlin: German Advisory Council on Global Change (WBGU). Retrieved May 3, 2013 from http://www.wbgu.de/fileadmin/templates/dateien/veroeffentlichungen/hauptgutachten/jg2011/wbgu_jg2011_kurz_en.pdf.

Williams, L. 2007. Emission possible. *The Age*. June 17, 2007. Retrieved November 9, 2012 from http://www.theage.com.au/news/in-depth/emission-possible/2007/06/17/1182018934799.html?page=fullpage#contentSwap2.

Wiseman, J. and Edwards, T. 2012. *Post Carbon Pathways: Reviewing Post Carbon Economy Transition Strategies*. CPD Occasional Paper 17. Melbourne: Melbourne Sustainable Society Institute and Centre for Policy Development.

CHAPTER 5

Delivering resilient, sustainable cities is *all* about people and place

Gilbert Rochecouste and Leonie J. Pearson

5.1 Introduction

In a time of transition and change, global and planetary challenges, we are called to 'reconnect with place' at a much deeper level; renewing our communities and ecosystems, redefining business and community growth, wellbeing and responsibility. Our chapter focuses on the core ingredients that are necessary for cities to transform from their current state to resilient and sustainable futures. The core ingredients are *people* and *place*. If you start with technology, all you get is technology; if you start with design, all you get is design; but if you start with people and place and with where we are now, then you can deliver real change to real people in their lives.

By holding these two core ingredients as central to our argument we will explore the rationale for why people and place are central – the key characteristics of sustainable and resilient cities and how to achieve these types of characteristics.

A much-maligned fact of current city living is that there is a disjunct between what people want to do and how they live. The new paradigm emerging on city design focuses squarely on aligning these two elements to ensure that future cities are places where living, playing and working occur in ways that support the cultural, social and environmental elements unique to each place. Whilst not a new design concept (Jacobs, 1961), this approach centralizes the person and place in city futures, rather than the built environment or technology. It ensures that the city is understood as a dynamic system that is always changing – there is no desire for cities to 'rebound' to past positions or identities. Cities are analogous to people: as time goes on people get 'older, wiser, and happier', if you believe the studies; they do not go back, rebound to past identities or live in historical imagery.

Therefore, city design needs to enhance and drive this dynamic nature. As an example, the city of Melbourne had a number of laneways and small streets that over time had seen many iterations, but in the 1990s they found themselves as the dark, inhospitable, driveways to internal malls (Context Pty Ltd, 2012). People ventured into them only to deliver goods or quickly dash between 'bright' shops and malls. They were not places to go alone! Change was coming. Melbourne city was growing and using more of its space for large shops, the personable scale was being lost, people felt shuttled and hurtled towards multinational corporate shops and organizations and there were few 'local' attractions and unique attributes that Melbournians could call their own, or that made Melbourne different from every other big city.

Enter place making for Melbourne. Extensive work was done on how to design the city to a scale, pace and shape that was engaging for its people. The laneways were it! The project identified and targeted the development of the laneways to deliver a story of Melbourne that was unique. It had to work with local people, and locals in Melbourne are usually of 'European' heritage. It needed strong leadership to make changes to planning and zoning to close off the laneways to car/delivery traffic and instead turn them into people traffic areas, with tables on the street and wares sold outside in fine weather. The increasing flow of people through the laneways ensured more city commuters stopped for coffee with friends and work colleagues, creating a lively place from early until late for casual meetings and discussions. By increasing the density of businesses in the area, there was an increase in the number of people frequenting the lanes and an increase in the use of them by people throughout the day and night – ensuring they are safe, with many 'eyes on the street'. The productivity of the area increased economic turnover for the city as a whole and provided greater economies of scale for the growing 'affordable restaurant' scene downtown. This enhanced the diversity of the Melbourne city area, making it more attractive for people to *live* and work there, enabling the transformation of under-used office space into apartments. The increasing intensity of enterprises required that 'old ways' of waste and transport were not appropriate for the dense businesses, resulting in the use of 'green' and financially viable alternatives: bike couriers rather than trucks, reducing packaging and stock, sharing delivery quotients, shared outdoor lighting rather than single propriety, reduction of litter and waste. The contrast between the two laneway designs for Melbourne are clear in the before and after photos shown in Figure 5.1.

Figure 5.1 Before (A) and after (B) photos of a laneway in Melbourne
Source: City of Melbourne

This example provides us with some of the critical benefits for why we need to start all city designs with people and place. The benefits are many and varied, including:

- Design for people and place equals happier, healthier communities.
- More places that express their unique cultural and physical assets creating more beautiful, enjoyable and soulful places.
- Better economic outcomes for local communities.
- Greater social, economic and cultural diversity within our communities.
- Sustainable development that respects the earth's resources.

So if these are the benefits of people and place city living, which characteristics are needed in each design to achieve sustainable and resilient cities?

5.2 Essence of sustainable and resilient cities

Whilst designing a city must start with people and place, it is not enough to say that is all it must have. To be honest, the idea of city planning is moving from designing an end-point to setting up elements or attributes that have longevity and are as relevant now as in one hundred years' time. We don't want a single large shopping mall, we want a space people want to use for shopping now and over the next hundred years. Will it change its look, feel and functions over time? Yes! Will it change its identity, shopping? Maybe, maybe not. But a good design will be able to accommodate the change and ensure that the place is still a worthy and useful part of our city fabric for the people and in harmony with the place.

Earlier in this book (Chapter 3) resilience was defined as 'Capacity to change in order to maintain the same identity'. We refine the definition of identity so it is not limited to just physical or economic factors but also must capture the spiritual and cultural dimensions of a city. As such, a resilient city must have the capacity to change in order to maintain its economic, cultural, spiritual and physical identity.

A sustainable city has also been defined earlier, but from a people and place perspective the attributes we think are critical are not only about resource efficiency and minimal use, but relate to safer towns, liveability, clean and green, real meaning to lives (work, love, rituals and celebrations), legacy for future generations, justice and equity for all. This is not an exhaustive list but rather shows that whilst resilience references to the dynamics of the city, the sustainability attributes are the core values that the city is aspiring to achieve.

Based on years of work and insights, we think that all resilient, sustainable cities should possess five essences:

- *People*: Involving the community in decision-making, ongoing management and activation of a place is critical to its success. Creating authentic, transparent and collaborative relationships across all sectors and with all stakeholders is essential to creating a great place with strong community ownership and pride. This is number one!

- *Place*: In its most simple form, place describes the physical aspects of a space. At its most complex it reveals and encourages a relationship between people and their environment, both built and natural. This is where we explore the hard infrastructure. It informs the way we see ourselves and the world. At its best it unleashes the creative capacity of our community, and provides a unique and nourishing sense of home.
- *Programme*: This is where we explore the marketing, events, management and activity occurring in a place. Great places have fantastic activation and marketing programmes. Great programming expresses what is unique and attractive about our place for locals and visitors alike. This can be achieved through place branding and marketing strategies, events, public art and other formal and informal activities. It is essential that the community is involved wherever possible to enliven and animate the public realm.
- *Product*: This is more than simply what is offered for sale. Great places are made up of more than a single identity experience, such as retail: they include civic, cultural, office and residential components, the provision of community services and basic facilities such as bathrooms and children's play areas with access for all, because everyone needs something to do and see in a great place, and to feel welcome.
- *Planet*: This is the relationship between the environment, its climate, bioregional assets, flora and fauna, and the local community. It is the grounding concept that reminds us of our interconnected relationship with the earth that sustains us. Everything around us, from the built form to the food that nourishes our bodies, comes from nature, and now more than ever respecting this relationship is key to building resilient communities that can respond to global environmental challenges.

These five essences are essential for any resilient and sustainable city now and in the future. The challenge is how to activate them.

5.3 Activation for resilient, sustainable cities

Whilst agreeing that our current cities are starting to show some of the essences of resilient and sustainable cities, as a whole they have a long way to go. We need to change the way we do things. We think it's time for a new story. Some people have called this the transition decade, the time when we move how, why and what we do from traditional ways to resilient and sustainable ways of city design. Albert Einstein put it nicely: 'Insanity: doing the same thing over and over again and expecting different results.'

It is essential to remember that when places make change, they do it at the pace, amount and direction that are appropriate and right for them. Picking up on earlier thoughts, some might cope, others adapt (small changes) and still more transform to strive for resilient and sustainable futures. So the question becomes how can we activate the five essences of a city: people, place, programme, product and planet? Four elements are needed to activate city change.

Desire to change

This is a somewhat underrated element that must be in place for change to occur. The desire to change is when the people want their city to change. It seems simple, but no change has successfully been undertaken when the desire to change is not around. Desires can be externally generated, such as floods, droughts or global financial crises, or internally generated through politics, culture, spiritual developments (meaning making) or economics. Some refer to this desire as a 'tipping point' – that is, without desire nothing will happen.

A good example of this is the use of 'brownfield sites' in cities. These under-utilized sities in cities usually sit dormant for many years until a catalyst generates a sudden significant and large change, which turns an undervalued place in the city into a vibrant, highly utilized area. For example, in Newcastle, Australia, this place transformation occurred with the closing down and refocusing of work from large employment-generating shipbuilding companies in the area. The resulting decommissioning of the Newcastle docks (something similar happened in New-castle in the UK) followed many years later with a private–public company estab-lished to redevelop the area. Decades passed before the land was transformed into a lively residential/restaurant area with activities, events and an 'outdoor home' for many Newcastle people (see Dunn *et al.* (1995) for further discussion).

Power of story

It is the story that captures the hearts and minds of the community, the narrative that creates meaning, hope and a spiritual sense of belonging and desire that is essential for our cities to deliver resilience and sustainability into the future. This story can be the 'roadmap' of how and what a resilient and sustainable city will look like; it needs to include the clear engagement of the people and be about head, heart and hands. That is, it has to be 'owned' by the people (heart), provide overall strategic guidance on what needs to be done (head) and explain how it can be achieved, clearly articulating the roles for everyone (hands). Lastly, it must articulate a 'call for action' that overlaps with our desire for change. By including this in the story we start to see the reasons and rationale for what needs to be done and why. It can include loss of place, sense of place, core values and principles.

Chicago is a good example of a city council that has devolved the role and ideas of story down to the local people to ensure that each neighbourhood has its own story to tell and that each includes the hearts, head and hands of the local people involved (Project for Public Spaces and Metropolitan Planning Council, 2008). From Bloomington Trail to Elmhurst City Centre, each place in Chicago has a unique story that once articulated will help unify vision, engender engagement and galvanize action.

Enlightened leadership and engagement

Leadership catalyses and enacts the story. It is a well-accepted and necessary ingredient in making changes in place and people, as will be discussed in further detail in Chapter 24 of this book (see Svara (1990) for further insights). However, we clarify our requirement for leadership as being not only enlightened but also engaged with the community it is leading. Enlightened and engaged leadership is clearly beneficial for communities, as is seen clearly in the successful and happy places that have undergone change and those that have been 'pulled kicking and screaming' through the change process. By 'enlighten' we mean that the essence of resilient and sustainable cities is shared by the leaders, rather than the short-term gains sometimes envisaged (e.g. long-term thinking versus short-term profits). Whilst 'engaged' requires that the leaders adopt collaborative arrangements to share responsibility and success with the people – ensuring a working partnership that requires input from people, rather than the traditional 'lone wolf' approach to leadership that was once often the norm.

We see that leadership can and should come from all sectors of our cities – mayors, private developers, community – and they must all have a clear and supported 'story' of what needs to be done. The support should come from early, transparent and honest engagement with the community. Going back to our people and place core ingredients, these provide the leadership with direction, but there is also a need for strong and enlightened leadership to deliver the desired future.

Brunswick, a suburb of Melbourne, shows how community leadership need not be totally coordinated or organized, but can be subtle and persuasive. This suburb is undergoing gentrification, with the upgrading of older residential houses and the infill of light industrial spaces with new housing or business establishments. Whilst the suburb has a few organized groups, most of the change is occurring through private development and investors. However, the 'identity' of the suburb is so strong that even through the dynamic nature of change the character of the area is surviving. This is supported by current policy which allows for the continuing use of land for light industrial purposes, whilst neighbouring suburbs have become almost purely residential areas. These policies are coupled with continuing community engagement to ensure new development proposals meet 'local style and design' elements. These 'local' elements enable state government to trial new sustainable housing models and densities as they are in keeping with the suburbs' identity of eclecticism and innovation.

Community governance

The last area for putting cities on a pathway to a resilient and sustainable future is the need for community governance. This has been a growing area of interest and research for urban designers and academics since its initiation in US cities during the 1960s and has seen further refinement over the following half century (see Cochrane, 2007). In a practical sense we include in 'community' all the people needed to make and deliver decisions; these may be local people living in the area, those developing the change or leading the change, those owning the land and those spiritually and culturally connected to the place. All of these are essential in the city's governance.

So what is community governance in city design? It is a commitment to coordination; a belief that communities should assume responsibility for their own wellbeing; a conviction that existing public service structures are bureaucratic and self-serving; and a belief that current (local) electoral structures are unrepresentative and exclusionary. As such, we are talking about the institutions, power and responsibility that communities hold in determining and shaping their future. The overall reason for adopting a community governance (rather than the typical centralized governance) approach is that, because it is 'local', its enhanced responsiveness to local issues should deliver greater wellbeing to the community. It will result in more locally relevant and appropriate services, green spaces, and spaces tailored to the needs and priorities of the community (see Hamilton, 2000).

An example of community governance making a difference is Santa Monica, California, through its Sustainable City Plan (SCP; see http://www.stainablesm.org/scpr). Santa Monica is a city that helps its citizens reach for sustainable results. The city government uses its SCP to 'enhance our resources, prevent harm to the natural environment and human health, and benefit the social and economic wellbeing of the community for the sake of current and future generations'. It was adopted in 1994 and updated in 2003 and 2006. The 2003 update was the culmination of a policy that began in July 2001 to engage people with a wide range of interests and resulted in the programme shifting from a primary focus on environmental sustainability within the city government to a 'three-legged stool' model that balances environmental, economic and social sustainability throughout the entire community.

5.4 Conclusion

This short chapter has endeavoured to lay out a practical and socially focused pathway for how our cities can achieve a resilient and sustainable future. It has done this by drawing on practical experiences that are supported by leading-edge thinking. Overall the chapter has highlighted that there are many benefits in moving our design thinking away from traditional goal-focused approaches to those that are more dynamic, inclusive and reflexive by focusing on the essence of cities.

The five urban essences that we believe each city both possesses and needs to enhance can be summarized as: people, place, programme, product and planet. However, these essences need to be activated to achieve a resilient, sustainable future. Activation occurs through four common elements: desire to change, power of story, enlightened leadership and engagement, and community governance. No matter how a city as a whole or a suburb/neighbourhood chooses to pursue its future – through coping, adapting or transforming – all four of these activation strategies are necessary.

Resilient, sustainable cities are a better future for all of us. But to get there, we need to start with people and place.

References

Cochrane, A. 2007. *Understanding Urban Policy: A Critical Approach*. Oxford: Oxford University Press.
Context Pty Ltd. 2012. *Thematic History: A History of the City of Melbourne's Urban Environment*. Melbourne: City of Melbourne.

Dunn, K., McGuirk, P. and Winchester, H.P.M. 1995. Place making: The social construction of Newcastle. *Australian Geographical Research*, 33(2): 149–166.

Hamilton, D.K. 2000. Organizing structure and governance functions in metropolitan areas in response to growth and change: A critical overview. *Journal of Urban Affairs*, 22(1): 65–84.

Jacobs, J. 1961. *The Death and Life of Great American Cities*. New York: Random House.

Project for Public Spaces and Metropolitan Planning Council. 2008. *A Guide to Neighborhood Placemaking in Chicago*. Retrieved December 2011 from http://www.placemakingchicago.com/downloads/.

Svara, J. 1990. *Official Leadership in the City: Patterns of Conflict and Cooperation*. New York: Oxford University Press.

CHAPTER 6

Building urban resilience through green infrastructure pathways

Allen Kearns, Rhiannon Saward, Alex Houlston,
John Rayner and Harry Viraswamy

6.1 Introduction

A resilient urban system has the capacity to absorb disturbances such as natural disasters and rapid urbanisation and reorganise so as to retain essentially the same function, structure, identity and feedbacks. This view of a resilient city, derived from the emerging body of organised knowledge known as resilience theory, is based on the interaction of people, their buildings and infrastructure and the natural environment as a complex adaptive social-ecological system (see Walker and Salt, 2006; Walker *et al.*, 2004).

Green infrastructure can be thought of as the natural part of this urban complex adaptive social-ecological system, as distinct from the bricks, mortar, glass, steel, pipes, pumps, rails and power lines of the built infrastructure. The green mosaic of our cities includes existing ecosystems and remnant habitats that surround and inter-sect our cities, including waterways and ridge tops, parklands and gardens, back-yards and market gardens, street trees and public places, rooftops and vertical walls.

The Australian Institute of Landscape Architects (AILA, 2011) describes 'green infrastructure' as:

> the network of natural landscape assets which underpin the economic, socio-cultural and environmental functionality of our cities and towns – i.e. the green spaces and water systems which intersperse, connect and provide vital life support for humans and other species within our urban environments.

We recognise that there are other operational definitions and bodies of practice for green infrastructure centred on the greening of the built environment. For example, the Australian Green Infrastructure Council (AGIC) is committed to being the catalyst for advancing sustainability in the design, construction and operation of Australian infrastructure. There are also recent examples of green infrastructure development emerging in the UK (Forest Research, 2010) and in the USA (USEPA, 2010).

This chapter looks closely at how we can best protect, enhance and transform the multiscaled vegetation mosaic of our cities by designing and developing green infrastructure pathways in much the same way as we plan, design, invest, construct and maintain other existing urban infrastructures.

Our vision – connected opportunities within a healthy connected network of green spaces

Our vision as urban designers and environmental scientists is to assemble and build the evidence base for better planning, design, construction and maintenance of green infrastructure in our cities and urban regions. Better knowledge will help build resilience into our cities through establishing sound investment cases and improved landscape practices that will enhance the value of green infrastructure as an alternative and regenerative urban development pathway.

Green infrastructure connects all scales from a local place with a few trees and chairs, along tree-lined streets to neighbourhood parks and narrow walkways that lead on to iconic landscaped gardens and riverside and coastal parklands. Our cities connect with forests, nature reserves and national parks as well as bays, estuaries and oceans. Our bioregion holds our sense of place and identity, our biodiversity, our urban fresh food farmlands and forested watersheds as well as our places of recreation and leisure (Thayer, 2003). These same urban and bioregional landscapes also provide currently unpriced ecosystem goods and services like clean water, air purification, urban cooling and pollination that contribute to our social and economic wellbeing. Beyond our own urban consumption landscapes and bioregions are the production landscapes and ecosystems in other people's regions from where we derive what we can't find locally – namely, most of our energy, water, construction materials, food and manufactured goods.

This is a connected world where an individual in a household or an organisation is linked, directly or indirectly, to other people and places by global information exchange, markets, finance systems, political issues, migration, diseases, long-term climate change, extreme events and disasters. Global and local shocks to a connected world ripple through the green, built, cultural, social and economic infrastructures of our cities. The damage to the health and wellbeing of people caused by these shocks depends on the scale of the hazardous event, the exposure of vulnerable people, the quality of planning, design and construction of urban environments, the resilience of urban infrastructure and ecosystems and the adaptive capacity of the community to respond to a shock as well as recover from any damage.

Our view of urban resilience is one where healthy connected networks of spaces across our cities and regions will house multiple ecosystem services and help raise the adaptive capacity of individuals and communities. Green infrastructure can provide an essential systematic organising framework for enhancing well-planned and designed places that produce these ecosystem services and connect people through safe and healthy mobility options.

6.2 Drivers of urban environmental change and transformation

There are many drivers for change in our cities. As highlighted in Chapter 2, key drivers include rapid urbanisation and industrialisation. One of the major environmental outcomes of rapid urbanisation and industrialisation has been rising resource use per person, ecosystem pollution and global climate change. In terms of human history, these rapid changes affect ecosystem responses at local, regional and global scales (Grimm *et al.*, 2008).

A few snapshots of how these urban environmental changes and transformations are dynamically linked in complex adaptive social-ecological systems are outlined below.

- Climate change: From an ecosystems perspective, enhanced or human-induced climate change resulting from human population increase, rapid urbanisation and fossil-fuel-based industrialisation is both a consequence as well as a driver of further ecosystem responses and urban environmental change. While changes are occurring at the global political and economic level on how to deal with these changes, the way we use resources and live in our current cities show little sign of real-world transformation towards low-carbon city development or better housing conditions for vulnerable people in low-lying coastal areas (Kearns, 2011).
- Food security: Rapid urbanisation and climate change are also producing significant urban resource problems for future societies in terms of food security from the loss of food-producing peri-urban landscapes. The loss of rural lands to urbanisation means a loss of fresh food production that is displaced to areas more distant from the city, resulting in higher carbon footprints for food because of the increased distance to market.
- Water security: Rising urban populations and increased use of coal-fired power generation create higher demands for urban water infrastructure in sprawling cities as well as more demand for reliable water to cool remote coal-fired power stations and other manufacturing resources. This diverts resources away from traditional water users of cities, irrigation farming and the local and regional environment.
- Energy security: Threats to energy security are likely to develop not from a short-age of coal or resources for energy production in the short term, but from challenges to the adaptive capacity of the fixed infrastructure (e.g. grid) and current suppliers. For example, how will centralised suppliers of energy infrastructure with long and inefficient transmission systems respond to increasing environmental changes like extreme weather events and institutional changes like carbon pricing and innovative new sources of decentralised energy systems within cities?

6.3 Developing an urban resilience approach to green infrastructure

Green infrastructure is emerging as an integrative approach to urban planning, design and performance assessment for the transformation of cities to meet multiple purposes such as low-carbon development, climate adaptive built environments, safe and affordable food production and buildings that incorporate green infrastructure assets. The knowledge required to develop green infrastructure crosses many disciplinary boundaries as well as having a deep dependence on many other forms of knowledge held by local people, traditional owners of landscapes, urban managers and design practitioners.

The transformation of urban landscapes to retain, maintain and expand green infrastructure will ultimately require harmonising many separate urban planning, design and management programmes. The success of green infrastructure as an alternative urban development pathway will also be based on the effectiveness of sound urban and regional policy implementation and the quality of urban design decisions. How can we better understand the complexity of how cities function and how they will need to change to become resilient and sustainable?

One promising framework for generating insights about how urban landscapes change, adapt and transform is found in the emerging theory of ecological resilience (Walker and Salt, 2006). In this approach, natural systems, human settlements and managed production systems are viewed as complex, adaptive, social-ecological systems. For urban resilience this would imply the ever-changing interactive places where we live, work, build and play in mosaics of ecological, social and built infrastructures. The practical application of resilience theory that would be of interest to urban planners, designers and landscape architects will be in designing and building green infrastructure that raises the adaptive capacity of people, ecosystems and built environments to prepare for and recover from all sorts of surprises and shocks, climate-driven or otherwise. The key concepts in resilience theory as we could apply it to green infrastructure pathways are centred around *resilience*, *triggers*, *thresholds*, *trajectories* and *transformability.*

Resilience is defined by Walker and Salt (2006, p. 164) as 'the amount of change a system can undergo (its capacity to absorb disturbance) and remain within the same regime – essentially retaining the same function, structure and feedbacks'. *Triggers* could be thought of as any action that brings about a set of social or ecological responses and development consequences in the urban landscape. These actions could be triggered by natural systems and occur over multiple scales of time and geographic extent: for example, from extreme weather events such as hail storms or bushfires affecting local areas in coastal Sydney through to large-scale flooding of southeast Queensland. Actions could be triggered by actors within social systems in governments at national, state, regional and local scales responding to climate change by developing new policies and funding mechanisms for green infrastructure.

Implicit in thinking about the resilience of complex, adaptive, social-ecological systems is the notion of *thresholds of change*. Walker and Salt (2006, p. 165) define *thresholds* as 'levels in underlying controlling variables of a system in which feedbacks to the rest of the system change'. In other words, a threshold is some form of tipping point or regime shift where the social-ecological system crosses into an alternate regime of that system, and may not be able to return to a previous alternate state without significant change – and the crossing of another threshold to overcome the resilience of the present state.

Thresholds have been easier for researchers to identify in natural and managed ecosystems such as rangelands, coral reefs, lakes, fisheries, forests and farms (Walker and Meyers, 2004). These natural and managed ecosystems were where resilience theory was first developed and there has been a noticeable lag in developing resilience theory for complex urban landscapes. Of course, 'urban resilience' is a term used widely by social scientists, including psychologists and planners, to explain the resilience of people in cities. However, this use of 'urban resilience' is not attempting to address the fundamental theory of social-ecological systems that is of interest for the development of green infrastructure pathways.

A clear example of a social-ecological threshold for human settlements is provided by Barnett and Adger (2003) when discussing climate change and impacts to societies on atolls in the Pacific. These societies are delicately settled on freshwater lenses for their water supplies and rely on the protection of reefs, sand and coral debris forming the low-lying atoll. A projection of a one-metre sea level rise this century for atoll settlements that are only about two metres above high-tide levels is clearly an example of an ecological threshold with strong triggers for social responses. The coral atoll example has a strong parallel with the coastal lagoons and estuaries of southeastern Australia. Coastal settlements have been found to be vulnerable to sea level rise and are also experiencing incremental damage to built infrastructure, houses and coastal ecosystems from storms and king tides (Department of Climate Change, 2009).

We can identify other urban thresholds that are familiar to urban planners, designers, managers and researchers in terms of impervious surface-cover ratios in urban catchments triggering exponential increases in downstream flooding (Schueler, 1994). Another urban threshold is the number of heatwave days above 35°C (Wang and McAllister, 2011). Each of these thresholds will have green infrastructure responses that could provide temporary or more permanent adaptation options.

The development of any form of urban infrastructure, be it a coal-fired power station, a desalination plant, a cross-city tunnel or freeway, a wave of new building types or new green infrastructure, locks in *trajectories of urban development*. These are forms of technology and materials and patterns of human behaviour that last for decades and cross multiple generations. These *infrastructure trajectories* are often referred to as path dependencies and are well recognised for having unintended consequences or maladaptation outcomes in the long term that were unidentified and avoided during the planning and design process (Barnett and O'Neill, 2010). Trajectories also imply some form of technological lock-in and institutional commitment to maintain the services that flow from these decisions.

Transformation of urban landscapes is emerging as a desirable urban development goal through multiple converging pathways, including green infrastructure. Many organisations are already promoting Healthy Cities, Environmentally Sustainable Cities, Sustainable Communities, and the newly emerging integrative narrative from Japan around Low-Carbon City Development, to name but a few. Water-sensitive urban design is an example of integrated urban policy and design practice that triggers responses resulting in improvements to water use efficiency in cities and the co-benefits of climate adaptation, such as cooling urban environments. Reducing heat stress through enhancing evapotranspiration from the green infrastructure of street trees, green roofs, waterscapes and high reflectance, low heat-absorbing road, roof and wall surfaces based on knowledge summarised by

Rosenfeld *et al.* (1995) and Bowler *et al.* (2010) is an emerging area of green infrastructure development that has the co-benefit of climate adaptation.

In theory, in order to bring about urban transformation, there would need to be a wide range of systematic and system-based changes that address the triggers, thresholds and trajectories of urban social-ecological systems. In resilience theory, this process is referred to as *transformability*. It is defined by Walker and Salt (2006, p. 165) as: 'the capacity to create a fundamentally new system (including new state variables, excluding one or more existing state variables, and usually operating at different scales) when ecological, economic, and/or social conditions make the existing system untenable'.

In practice, we can identify many practical challenges to the development of green infrastructure in cities, including:

- How planners and designers can bring insightful theory and research ideas together with the many forms of sometimes competing local, traditional, cultural and disciplinary knowledge.
- How to connect urban policy and effective investment for implementing new cost-effective designs for green infrastructure that compete with standard practice .
- How to stimulate urban regime shifts towards transformative urban practice that will help overcome significant institutional blockers and barriers to change.
- How to encourage and support visionary city leaders as enablers of transformational development of green infrastructure pathways.

In a cautionary note, Pataki *et al.* (2011, p. 27) 'propose a framework for integrating biogeochemical processes into designing, implementing and evaluating the net effectiveness of green infrastructure'. Based on an extensive review of available literature and evidence, they provide examples of where they consider there is a strong evidence-based case for the role of green infrastructure in greenhouse gas (GHG) mitigation, stormwater runoff mitigation, and improvements in air quality and human health. Pataki *et al.* (2011, p. 27) contend from their review that 'many commonly cited environmental benefits of urban green space are still poorly supported by empirical evidence, adding to the difficulties in designing and implementing green infrastructure programs'. Importantly, their framework recognises not just ecosystem services but potential ecosystem disservices and their unintended costs and consequences on urban maintenance and aspects of human health.

Far from pessimistic, this is a recognition that many of the ecosystem services and benefits cited for urban green space rely on the regulating services of fundamental biogeochemical processes such as carbon and nutrient cycling (nitrogen, phosphorus) as well as the regulation of water and other materials in urban environments. As such, these regulating services and ecosystem disservices can be respectively designed into and out of green infrastructure projects and accounted for in terms of net effectiveness. These regulating services apply from the intensely local scale of green roofs and walls through to parks, street plantings, riparian corridors, urban agriculture and the retention of natural ecosystems. Fundamentally, Pataki *et al.* (2011, p. 27) are stating that 'studies of urban biogeochemistry are greatly needed to improve green space design and monitor its effectiveness in meeting local environmental goals in different regions and urban settings'. In other words, there is a need to provide sound evidence as well as well-intended goals and aspirations for design and implementation of green infrastructure.

Health and wellbeing benefits of green infrastructure

Green infrastructure plays an important part in our psychological and physiological wellbeing through the provision of cultural and physical benefits. The physical benefits are easy to recognise: clean air allows us to breathe freely, shade protects us from the sun's harmful rays, and physical activity creates healthier bodies, which help prevent a range of medical problems. There is strong, consistent epidemiological evidence linking a wide range of important health and social benefits to participation in regular moderate-intensity physical activity (Australian Government Department of Health and Ageing, 2010). We qualitatively know that natural landscapes and urban vegetation are good for our mental and physical health, too. Pataki *et al.* (2011) refer to a growing number of quantitative studies that have shown, for example, shorter hospital stays for patients with views of trees; the presence of trees in public-housing complexes can reduce crime rates, increase safety and security and improve alertness in children with attention deficit disorder.

When connected through nature, planning and design, green infrastructure provides a network of various types of natural and built landscapes. River and creek systems thread their ways through our suburbs, connecting places along their linear paths. The movement of water from the hills surrounding our suburbs, to the wetlands, bays and estuaries and finally to the ocean, integrates our catchments and their land uses. The quality of this runoff water reflects the quality of the planning, design and management of our urban and rural land uses. These linear threads running through our suburbs are connected to a patchwork of parks, squares, reserves and bushlands. Where accessible, all of these different types of local green places can become important to the health and wellbeing and cultural and recreational activities in the everyday lives of people in our communities. We need variety, connectivity and the ability to relate to places to feel happy and healthy, and the changing seasonal patterns of flowering vegetation and birds in urban green spaces can provide this sense of variety through the experience of biodiversity.

Informal opportunities to build social capital, such as recreational pursuits, also contribute to our mental health and general wellbeing. More poetically, the health value of regular walking has been expressed in other ways:

> 'Above all, do not lose your desire to walk. Every day I walk myself into a state of well-being and walk away from every illness. I have walked myself into my best thoughts, and I know of no thought so burdensome that one cannot walk away from it'.
>
> Søren Aabye Kierkegaard: Danish philosopher 1813–1855.
> (Quoted in Gehl, 2010, p. v)

Connecting people to place through green infrastructure

Individuals have differing connections to place and to community. Connections to place rely on physical characteristics of a location, whereas connections to community may transcend locations as they rely on common activities and cultural connections between people. The careful and inclusive planning and design of green spaces can complement and enhance the linkages between people, nature and their built environments on many levels.

On the macro scale, green infrastructure provides a setting for organised groups, informal gatherings and individuals to be amongst others. It is a large web or mosaic of urban patterns that connects many people and places. As part of this mosaic, the smaller spaces are important, too. Local parks, reserves, bushlands and paths are often visited by a smaller catchment of the community. These spaces characterise our neighbourhoods – we have a sense of ownership over them and they in turn provide us with a sense of identity and belonging.

Seddon (1997, p. 113) asserts that it is critical to celebrate uniqueness, for reasons ecological, aesthetic and psychological. He states that the sense of local is threatened by 'international technology and easy communications hav[ing] an homogenising effect . . . that works to reduce regional diversity in urban form, architecture, food, dress and even vegetation'. For example, Melbourne has embraced its local and national identity. This is certainly evident in iconic public landscapes such as its City Square, Federation Square and Birrarung Marr. Melbourne's City Square was redeveloped during the 1990s and early 2000s. Eucalyptus trees and decomposed granite gravel became the dominant landscape features, a deliberate choice to bring Australian vegetation into the city's urban fabric and civic centre. Federation Square, which somewhat replaces the importance of the City Square, is made of striking Australian stone that references the country's cultural heartland – the outback. The stone is sourced from the Kimberley region of Western Australia, some 3,500km away from Melbourne. Birrarung Marr, Melbourne's newest park, established in 2002, is designed with eucalyptus and gravel pathways as the main landscape treatments, but also makes an important interface with the European tree-lined banks of the Yarra River.

Our connection to local place has continued to evolve in the private realm, too. Melbournians are especially aware of the fine balance of the city's need to capture, use and recycle water. The nightly news beams the percentage of water captured in our dams each month into our living rooms via television. This knowledge, which has affected our daily lives through water restrictions, has shaped and strengthened our Australian gardens. We now look for native and indigenous plants, and design water-efficient gardens.

More poignantly, this cultural connection to place – local, private and public – helps to shape our outlook on the broader landscape and forges bonds between people. In Melbourne, a common question or statement that affirms what place you come from and what community you belong to is: 'Which side of the Yarra are you from?' The Yarra River is both a boundary separating north and south in the eastern and north-eastern suburbs, and a link from the Upper Yarra catchment to Port Phillip Bay.

Growing up in Australia before the 1990s involved children being outside in the backyard, down at the creek, under the sprinkler, climbing a tree and playing on local sporting fields. Today, Australian children are participating in afterschool and play activities from their lounge chairs. There are many and varied reasons why our children are now growing up indoors. The common reasons include stranger danger (mass media), risk aversion (helicopter parenting), smaller or no backyards, dangerous streets (cars and people), time-poor parents and a massive shift in our relationship with gaming technology and social media.

This trend has led to an emerging condition known as 'nature deficit disorder' which describes an absence of direct experience with the natural world in children's everyday lives (Charles, 2009). In addition to direct measurements, there is a variety of ways to consider children's nature deficit and its extent. Numerous studies offer both quantitative and qualitative indicators of changes in childhood, including: perception of growing demands on children's time, resulting in less free and unstructured outdoor playtime in nature than experienced by previous generations; reduced mobility and less range for exploration, including reduction in walking or riding a bike to school; growing fear of strangers, traffic and nature itself; and a dramatic rise in obesity and severe overweight, as well as vitamin D deficiency and other health issues that may in part be related to low levels of outdoor activity and a sedentary lifestyle. A lack of knowledge of species may also be an indicator of lack of access to or lack of engagement in nature in an increasingly urbanised world (Charles, 2009).

Nature is important to children's development in every major way – intellectually, emotionally, socially, spiritually and physically. 'Play in nature, particularly during the critical period of middle childhood, appears to be an especially important time for developing the capacities for creativity, problem-solving, and emotional and intellectual development' (Kellert, 2005, p. 83).

Paul Selman, in *Sustainable Landscape Planning* (2012, p. 21), argues that landscape resilience is compromised by 'progressive disconnection and disruption' of people with the landscape. Our daily lives are becoming further removed from open spaces and ecosystem services.

Green infrastructure is ultimately a system of places for connecting with nature.

6.4 Scales of green infrastructure: an approach to transformation

Resilience and transformation are daunting concepts. Where to begin, who takes charge and how can we be part of positive change?

Transformation of our city to be resilient and adaptive relies on the concepts of connectivity and multiplicity. Just as a healthy ecosystem requires multiple organisms and scales – from large trees right down to invisible bacteria – to be healthy, so too does our understanding of diversity in transformation.

Figure 6.1 shows landmass and ownership or management control – excluding farming. Citizens, or the community, control small parcels such as backyards, whilst local government – a first-tier authority – controls a large portion of public open

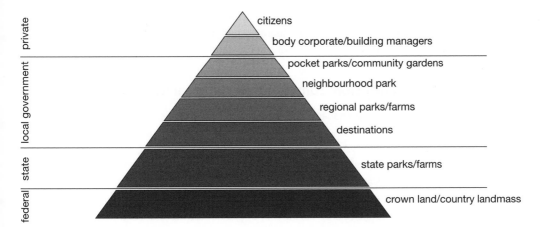

Figure 6.1 Landmass and ownership or management control

space that is fragmented. However, if we include streets as a public realm that contains or could be open space, then we can consider an open mesh of green infrastructure.

Whilst citizens have the smallest land parcels, collectively they control the contiguity of open space. We can now understand the importance of the citizen as a land manager and begin to see the pattern and structure of the mosaic.

The state often controls parcels of land, or linear corridors that have high biodiversity and ecosystem service value. These areas are critical in maintaining and structuring the cities' green infrastructure. Connectivity is assumed by Selman (2012) to increase future multi-functionality, sustainability and resilience.

Multiplicity in this mosaic is the diversity of land managers' objectives and actions. We can consider the 4 million-plus people who live in Melbourne to have differing ideas on how to maintain and enhance their personal space. But, collectively, these backyards and streets create a network of open spaces for ecosystem services to function. Bees and fruit bats, for example, will travel from space to space to search out their daily means of survival.

Fragmentation and leftover spaces, although not necessarily within a contiguous network, can host many vulnerable species that contribute to biodiversity and the functioning of green infrastructure. An example is the presence of bryophytes in nature strips – an indicator of climate (Gibson, 2012) – or weed species that sustain endangered animals.

Local governments manage most of our public realm, acting on behalf of the community. The challenge for transformation is in the collective minds of the community. If we can find a way to understand the mosaic and find beauty in this, then we can work towards a shared vision of an ecological aesthetic (Carlson, 2007). The innovation is in the reframing of public space from traditional gardens and streets to a mosaic of self-evolving urban ecologies: a new landscape that is different and cherished.

This evolving social capital will then generate political will – a translation of values into policy (Layzer, 2012). Governance structures will need to evolve in order to respond to changes and unforeseen situations (Selman, 2012).

This new mosaic – green infrastructure that is connected through opportunity – will work only when truly integrated design and consideration is prepared. Landscape is a dynamic system, not a static stage.

6.5 Conclusion: communities, culture and change

Resilience, sustainability and liveability are ultimately determined by the way we choose to live. At a global scale, we are all connected and our actions impact on one another. As Australians, we have the capacity to choose to act, and live with the daily responsibility of long-term sustainability in our hands.

In Australia, we have experienced the many effects of severe drought, the recurring threat of flooding and fire and the vulnerability of living off some of the least fertile soils on earth. We need to tread with care – and we know it. We can see a growing trend to live sustainably in the private and commercial sectors of our communities. Many Australians have changed or are changing their behaviour in how we use resources like water, energy and food. Some of us install home-made mini-wind turbines; others heat water in black pipes in the sun; people across our cities collect warm-up water in our showers and irrigate our backyard gardens and veggie patches. The more committed, wealthy or well-organised install solar panels and feed excess power back into the grid to provide renewable energy offsets.

Community actions in public spaces that are enhancing green infrastructure are emerging. Local governments across Melbourne are responding to their residents' request for community gardens, farmers' markets and urban agriculture.

Transition Towns is an emerging movement that began in the UK and focuses on local permaculture. There are Transition Towns all over Australia now, supporting citizen action towards reducing oil dependence and building local community resilience and ecological sustainability (http://www.geelongsustainability.org.au/Default. aspx?pageId=174571; http://transitionvictoria.ning.com/).

Yarra City Council in Melbourne is currently promoting an urban agriculture programme that enables community gardens in public spaces, including streets and parks. They have also produced guidelines for neighbourhood gardening, including fruit trees in streets. Other community initiatives include planting out nature strips with produce or native plants and creating free exchanges. These local actions, together with the awareness of water shortage as a common topic in everyday conversations, shows that ordinary Australians are changing the way they live and think about their urban environments. Now our political leaders need to run to catch up.

In any place, especially in Australia with its fragile soils, intermittent rain and rare plants and animals, it is crucial that we first explore what natural systems sustain the place. What are the unique features that make this place different? What makes this place special? In understanding the uniqueness of a place and developing its character and attributes, we enrich the mosaic of the green infrastructure network, so that it is about identity, belonging, place creation and community as well as its ecosystem services.

Places take on values that are impossible to measure, and are then protected by the community for these values. Over the past five years, Knox City Council in

Melbourne has attempted to sell pieces of land that look meaningless and valueless to the outsider. But these pieces of land are of high value to the community because the community has some kind of ownership and connection with the land that is invisible to the eye, a connection that is cultural: a collective and individual memory.

In connections to places, there is an opportunity to activate community use, enrich local biodiversity, sustainability and social capital by fostering people's connections to the landscape. 'The first step in design is recognition, the ability to see what there is. Only then can we ask whether a given structure is appropriate to its setting, or whether a proposed land-use is appropriate in a given environment' (Seddon, 1997, p. 112).

In summary, the true human measure of urban resilience and sustainability is not just how much water and energy we use in our cities. More so, it's how much we have improved the health, wellbeing and liveability of people in their built environments. Individuals and communities are the drivers to achieving this goal. Inspirationally, we need to own the change, fight for access and provision of green infrastructure intermingled in our suburbs and create a future that is based on local food and energy production, local treatment of water and recycling and walkable communities. These are the basic elements of a green infrastructure that builds social capital and celebrates, protects and enhances indigenous plants, animals and dynamic cultural transformations.

Acknowledgements

The authors gratefully acknowledge the contributions of twenty other participants in Workshop 3 ('What is a green infrastructure pathway?') at the Sustainable Urbanization: A Resilient Future Sir Mark Oliphant Conference, held in Melbourne in February 2011. We trust that our elaboration reflects the valuable insights generated during the workshop session.

References

Ahern, J. 2007. Green infrastructure for cities: The spatial dimension. In Vladimir Novotny and Paul Brown (eds) *Cities of the Future: Towards Integrated Sustainable Water and Landscape Management*. London: IWA Publishing.

AILA. 2011. Adapting to climate change: Green infrastructure. http://www.aila.org.au/greeninfrastructure/ (accessed 24/08/11).

Akbari, H., M. Pomeranz, and H. Taha. 2001. Cool surfaces and shade trees to reduce energy use and improve air quality in urban areas. *Solar Energy* 70: 295–310.

Arboriculture Australia. 2013. i-Tree Australia: Summary to date. http://arboriculture.org.au/i-Tree-Australia (accessed 19/02/13).

Australian Bureau of Statistics. 2011. Australian social trends. http://www.abs.gov.au/AUSSTATS/abs@.nsf/Lookup/4102.0Main+Features30Jun+2011#end3 (accessed 15/08/11).

Australian Government Department of Health and Ageing. 2010. Nutrition and physical activity. http://www.health.gov.au/internet/main/publishing.nsf/Content/health-pubhlth-strateg-active-evidence.htm (accessed 15/08/11).

Australian Government Department of Health and Ageing. 2011. Physical activity. http://www.abs.gov.au/AUSSTATS/abs@.nsf/Lookup/4102.0Main+Features30Jun+2011#end3 (accessed 15/08/11).

Barnett, J. and Adger, W.N. 2003. Climate dangers and atoll countries. *Climatic Change* 61: 321–337.

Barnett, J. and O'Neill, S. 2010. Maladaptation. *Global Environmental Change* 20: 211–213.

Birch, E.L. and Wachter, S.M. (eds). 2008. *Growing Greener Cities: Urban Sustainability in the Twenty-first Century*. Philadelphia: University of Pennsylvania Press.

Bowler, D.E., Buyung-Ali, L., Knight, T.M. and Pullin, A.S. 2010. Urban greening to cool towns and cities: A systematic review of the empirical evidence. *Landscape and Urban Planning* 97: 147–155.

Carlson, A. 2007. *The Aesthetics of Human Environments*. Plymouth: Broadview Press.

Charles, C.P. 2009. Children's nature deficit: What we know – and don't know. http://www.childrenandnature.org/ (accessed 15/08/11).

City of Melbourne. 2012. *Future Melbourne (Eco-City) Committee Report*. Melbourne: City of Melbourne Urban Forest Strategy.

City of Port Phillip. 2010. *Greening Port Phillip: An Urban Forest Approach*. Port Phillip: City of Port Phillip.

Cleugh, H.A., Bui, E.N., Simon, D.A.P., Mitchell, V.G. and Xu, J. 2005. The impact of suburban design on water use and microclimate. *MODSIM*, 12–15 December.

Department of Climate Change. 2009. *Climate Change Risks to Australia's Coasts: A First Pass Assessment*. Canberra: Commonwealth of Australia.

European Communities. 2008. *The European Union's Biodiversity Action Plan: 'Halting the Loss of Biodiversity by 2010 – and beyond'*. Luxembourg: Office for Official Publications of the European Communities.

Forest Research. 2010. *Benefits of Green Infrastructure*. Farnham: Forest Research.

Geelong Sustainability Group Inc – Transition Town Bell. 2012. Climate action, local and global: What is a Transition Town? http://www.geelongsustainability.org.au/Default.aspx?pageId=174571 (accessed 20/02/13).

Gehl, J. 2010. *Cities for People*. Washington, DC: Island Press.

Gibson, M. 2012. Our disappearing bryophytes. Address to the Planning for Biodiversity Seminar, Royal Society of Victoria, Melbourne,18 October.

Gill, S.E., Handley, J.F., Ennos, A.R. and Pauleit, S. 2007. Adapting cities for climate change: The role of the green infrastructure. *Built Environment* 33(1): 115–133.

Grimm, N.B., Foster, D., Groffman, P., Grove, J.M., Hopkinson, C.S., Nadelhoffer, K.J., Pataki, D.E. and Peters, D. 2008. The changing landscape: Ecosystem responses to urbanization and pollution across climatic and societal gradients. *Frontiers in Ecology and the Environment* 6(5): 264–272.

Hoban, A. and Wong, T.H.F. 2006. WSUD resilience to Climate Change. Address to the 1st International Hydropolis Conference, Perth, WA.

i-tree. 2012. What is i-tree? http://www.itreetools.org/index.php (accessed 19/02/13).

Jensen, M. 2011. *The Urban Cook: Cooking and Eating for a Sustainable Future*. Sydney: Murdoch.

Kearns, A. 2011. Climate adaptation engineering: A new direction for environmental science, engineering and technology in urban environments. *International Journal for Sustainable Development and World Ecology* 18(3): 201–209.

Kellert, S.R. 2005. *Building for Life: Designing and Understanding the Human–Nature Connection*. Washington, DC: Island Press.

Kilbane, S. 2010. *Green Infrastructure: Continental Planning in the National Interest.* South Melbourne: Landscape Australia.

Layzer, J.A. 2012. *The Environmental Case: Translating Values into Policy.* 3rd ed. Washington, DC: CQ Press.

Mitchell, V.G., Cleugh, H.A., Grimmond, C.B and Xu, J. 2008. Linking urban water balance and energy balance models to analyse urban design options. *Hydrological Processes* 22: 2891–2900.

Ozge, Y.E. and Kaplan, A. 2012. *Green and Ecological Technologies for Urban Planning: Creating Smart Cities.* Hershey, PA : Information Science.

Pataki, D.E., Carreiro, M.M., Cherrier, J., Grulke, N.E., Jennings, V., Pincetl, S., Pouyat, R.V., Whitlow, T.H. and Zipperer, W.C. 2011. Coupling biogeochemical cycles in urban environments: Ecosystem services, green solutions, and misconceptions. *Frontiers in Ecology and the Environment* 9(1): 27–36.

Rosenfeld, A.H., Akbari, H., Bretz, S., Fishman, B.L., Kurn, D.M., Sailor, D. and Taha, H. 1995. Mitigation of urban heat islands: Materials, utility programs, updates. *Energy and Buildings* 22(3): 255–265.

Sanderman, J.F. 2010. *Soil Carbon Sequestration Potential: A Review for Australian Agriculture.* Clayton: CSIRO.

Schandl, H. and West, J. 2010. Resource use and resource efficiency in the Asia–Pacific region. *Global Environmental Change* 20(40): 636–647.

Schueler, T. 1994. The importance of imperviousness. *Watershed Protection Techniques* 1: 100–111.

Seddon, G. 1997. *Landprints: Reflections on Place and Landscape.* Cambridge: Cambridge University Press.

Selman, P.H. 2012. *Sustainable Landscape Planning: The Reconnection Agenda.* Abingdon and New York: Routledge.

Thayer, R. 2003. *LifePlace: Bioregional Thought and Practice.* Berkeley: University of California Press.

United Nations Population Fund. 2007. Linking population, poverty and development. http://www.unfpa.org/pds/urbanization.htm (accessed 17/08/11).

USEPA. 2010. *Green Infrastructure Case Studies: Municipal Policies for Managing Stormwater with Green Infrastructure.* New York: USEPA Office of Wetlands, Oceans and Watersheds.

Walker, B., Holling, C.S., Carpenter, S.R. and Kinzig, A. 2004. Resilience, adaptability and transormability in social-ecological systems. *Ecology and Society* 9(2): 5. http://profesores.usfq.edu.ec/fdelgado/Ecologia%20Humana/articulosdigitales/Walker.pdf (accessed 24/05/13).

Walker, B. and Meyers, J.A. 2004. Thresholds in ecological and social-ecological systems. *Ecology and Society* 9(2): 3. http://www.ecologyandsociety.org/vol9/iss2/art3/ (accessed 24/05/13).

Walker, B. and Salt, D. 2006. *Resilience Thinking: Sustaining Ecosystems and People in a Changing World.* Washington, DC: Island Press.

Walsh, C., Fletcher, T. and Ladson, A. 2005. Stream restoration in urban catchments through redesigning storm water systems: Looking to the catchment to save the stream. *Journal of North American Benthological Society* 24(3): 690–705.

Wang, X. and McAllister, R.J. 2011. Adapting to heatwaves and coastal flooding. In H. Cleugh, M. Stafford Smith, M. Battaglia and P. Graham (eds) *Climate Change: Science and Solutions for Australia.* Melbourne: CSIRO Publishing.

Williams, N., Rayner, J. and Raynor, K. 2010, Green roofs for a wide brown land: Opportunities and barriers for rooftop greening in Australia. *Urban Forestry and Urban Greening* 9: 245–251.

CHAPTER 7

Systems design and social change for resilient, sustainable cities

Janis Birkeland

7.1 Introduction

Cities play a central role in life quality, but also in global problems like pollution, disparities of wealth and reductions in the natural life support system. In fact, the design of the built environment, or physical development generally, underlies most so-called environmental problems, apart from militarism, political corruption and illegal trades. The design of cities has exacerbated the causes and risks of climate change and locked society into structures and lifestyles that are neither sustainable nor resilient, as yet. Cities are also a source of sustainability solutions (Girardet, 1992), but these are still largely unexplored. This chapter examines why, despite fifty years of awareness-raising activities, sustainability issues are still often met with denial and displacement activity. It suggests that this is partly because sustainability requires both social and systems change, and each must precede the other. This complex chicken-and-egg relationship can cause dualistic positions that create ideological impasses.

In sustainable development workshops, debates and discussions, this social-system dualism causes people to talk past each other. Differing viewpoints can be useful and amicable but, often, organizations can get bogged down in polar problem descriptions, strategies and/or action plans. Of course, systems and social change is not an either–or issue. From the time the sustainability movement hit the world stage over thirty years ago (IUCN/UNEP/WWF, 1980 and 1991), it recognized that behavior and personal values were interrelated with institutions and systems. Challenging either can stimulate mutual transformation or inertia. On a deeper level lurks a societal resistance to change *itself* – even to positive change as advocated by sustainability activists. Many professional and academic bodies that were established to improve built environment design have, in effect, become protectionist and apologist. This is ironic, as negative changes are accelerating on a global scale. Perhaps design thinking – imagining and designing positive urban environments – can overcome the fear of change.

When people play intellectual tug-of-war, it is difficult to be open to lateral design solutions. Hence, the new wave of resilient urbanism should take care to avoid the social-system dualisms that we will discuss here (e.g. personal versus political change, bottom up versus change at the top, working inside versus outside systems). Design offers a hybrid strategy to break the tension caused by bipolar positions. It can transcend dualisms by finding syntheses, symbioses and synergies that make everyone better off (Birkeland, 2002b, pp. 26–30). This chapter therefore focuses on false dualisms as barriers to change, and design processes and innovations as a means to overcome them. Some dualisms that impede positive change toward more resilient and sustainable cities in (a) decision-making, (b) design, (c) communication, and (d) action are outlined. This discussion leads to a practical mechanism for improving urban development control and design. First, let us look at how design can achieve sustainability.

Positive Development

Due to their ongoing environmental impacts and vulnerability to climate change, sustainability will not be achieved until cities are retrofitted. Further, to correct the escalating social, ecological and security *deficits*, and improve the life quality of the world population, a substantial increase in social and natural resources is also necessary. Since design can reduce overall material flows as well as meet diverse goals in multi-functional creative, synergistic ways, it is possible to go 'beyond zero' (Birkeland, 2003). This means resilient and sustainable cities must not only regenerate the environment and revitalize the community (Lyle, 1994) but must increase the ecological base beyond that which existed prior to industrial development (Birkeland, 2007). (Chapter 15 describes some ways that simple design interventions in cities can provide positive onsite and/or offsite gains.)

The unique potential of built environment design to address sustainability issues at net economic gains is limited only by our negative design, decision, and development systems. This means a completely different and eco-positive form of urban planning and design is required. The necessary paradigm shift in institutional, physical, and intellectual frameworks from negative to positive is called net Positive Development (or PD). Instead of reducing the relative damage of new buildings, PD would increase universal access to the means of survival, ecological carrying capacity, equity, and future social options through multi-functional urban structures and spaces (see Birkeland, 2008). The prerequisites of 'sustainability' as defined here must include: actively increasing *total* ecological carrying capacity and natural resources, as well as making everyone (current and future) better off and more secure – in perpetuity.

7.2 Sustainability dualisms

We begin by exploring where the opposition to an eco-positive design framework comes from. The barriers to eco-positive design are deeply rooted in the dominant paradigm or 'DP' (PD reverses the DP). One of many analyses about the underlying structure of the DP that was explored in the early sustainability literature was its omnipresent *hierarchical dualisms*, such as nature versus humans, hard versus soft, rational versus emotional, as represented in Figure 7.1 (Gaard, 1993; Warren, 1996; Shiva and Mies, 1993).

Rational versus emotional

Sustainability (pre-Brundtland) was virtually a synonym for rationality: making everyone better off. Historically, of course, rationality was equated with narrow

Figure 7.1 Hierarchical
(and false) dualisms

CULTURE/MALE		NATURE/FEMALE
reason (the rational)	vs	emotion (the irrational)
knowledge	vs	ignorance
(accepted wisdom)	vs	(the occult)
higher (up)	vs	lower (down)
good, positive	vs	negative, bad
mind (ideas), mind	vs	body (flesh), womb
spirit	vs	nature (earth)
order	vs	chaos
control	vs	letting be, spontaneity
objective (outside)	vs	subject (inside)
literal truth, fact	vs	poetic truth, metaphor
goals	vs	process
light	vs	darkness
written text, logic	vs	oral tradition, myth
public sphere	vs	private sphere
seeing, detached	vs	listening, attached
secular	vs	holy and sacred
linear	vs	cyclical
permanence, ideal forms	vs	change, fluctuations
independent, individual	vs	dependent, social
isolated	vs	integrated
hard	vs	soft
dualistic	vs	whole

'self-interest', a view later reinforced by neo-classical economics. Yet everyone's self-interest depends on the life support system and world peace, which relies on adequate and shared resources and ecological carrying capacity, which in turn must be *increased* if accelerating ecological damage is to be halted and reversed. Thus sustainability is rational even when defined only as self-interest. In 1987, however, the Brundtland Report reframed sustainability in the economic rationalist and reductionist framework of the DP, and lowered the target to just meeting basic needs (WCED, 1987). Instead of changing to a positive sustainability paradigm, sustainable development was recaptured by the planning mantra of the 1970s: 'mitigating the bad and enhancing the good'. In practice this meant making irreversible trade-offs of the ecological base for temporary economic and social needs, or slowing the end of nature. Hence, planners and designers tended to forget the needs of ecology.

Eco-efficiency versus eco-positive

Early definitions of sustainability had been about 'increasing life quality within the earth's carrying capacity'. That is, it was presumed that increases in universal life quality were feasible, but that increases in the earth's ecological carrying capacity were not. This was perhaps because 2.8 billion years of intelligent evolution cannot be improved upon. Consequently, it seemed human well-being, health, and environmental quality could be achieved only by reducing human space and impacts – not by increasing the life support system. In this context, saving nature seemed to imply more *efficient* (i.e. more vertical and compact) cities. Gradually, as sustainable development became professionalized, sustainability became confused with eco-efficiency (by the uninitiated) because the concept was already well understood. Efficiency, the ratio of inputs to outputs, has been associated with reduction and downsizing, however, which does not leave much room for nature or community. This efficiency framework concealed the idea that urban design and construction could increase the ecological base. In contrast, PD posits that efficiency can *also* be achieved by multi-functional net positive outcomes for people and nature.

Decision systems versus systems design

When the urban-related professions recognized the centrality of cities to sustainability around the turn of this century, there was little reference to the many critiques of the dominant paradigm. The tendency in urban sustainability was simply to reinvent superficial 'sustainable' design guidelines, indicators and participatory processes of the alternative movements of the 1960s and 1970s. When sustainable development was adapted to 'mainstream' academia and the professions, therefore, it retained vestiges of the DP in its methods, tools, and metrics. For example, the predecessor to most environmental management methods is 'environmental impact assessment', introduced in the US National Environmental Protection Act of 1969, to 'inform' development decisions. The belief was that if decision-makers knew what they were doing, their choices would be better. Over forty years later, however, we still do not know what we are doing, because our decision frameworks and processes evolved when ecology was not really considered (Norton, 2005; Birkeland, 1993). Also, since what has been measured is only the degradation that will occur, only means to reduce the negative impacts of development were considered, not means to increase nature and its resources. Thus, despite advances, so-called 'green' communities and buildings still discriminate against future generations by reducing the ecological base, thus reducing future options.

Hard versus soft

In a bipolar value system, design has been associated with being 'soft' and in opposition to 'hard' rational decision-making systems. Reductionist decision analyses (like economics) are deemed 'hard' because they appear measurable. Open systems that include nature, culture, psychology, or design are deemed 'soft' because they are not easily reduced to numbers. But hard analyses are measurable only because they leave out the ecology, humans, and other dimensions of complex systems (Tansey, 2006). Since only negative (or less negative) impacts are measured, reductions of negative impacts are called 'gains', so most people failed to notice that positive impacts were excluded (Birkeland, 2004). While we 'purport' to measure negative (or less negative) impacts, the complex interactions between immune systems and toxins over time cannot be measured. Yet, ironically, many have maintained that the positive benefits of nature or eco-services cannot be measured. Positive impacts *can* be designed-in and measured, however, and surplus benefits that do no harm need not be measured anyway.

Environment versus ecology

Development assessments largely ignore time and space. That is, to enable conversion to numbers, system boundaries are drawn that pretend negative impacts do not bio-accumulate and spread throughout different environmental media over time. This is arguably due to the tacit assumption that the human environment is all that matters. There are many other systemic biases and omissions linked to anthropocentrism in design, assessment, and development control processes. Most of these biases operate by force of habit, mental programming, and self-censorship, not by formal policy or regulation. For example, most 'triple bottom line' approaches put energy savings and worker productivity in the environmental column instead of the *economic* column; and put human health and thermal comfort in the environmental column instead of the *social* column. In other words, improvements to the *human* environment count as ecological gains. Most scientists would also agree that numbers attached to environmental phenomena are themselves a bit rubbery. Such contradictions suggest our environmental analyses are not really that 'hard' or 'ecological'.

Contraction versus expansion

Even in the sustainable development fields, design has been marginalized by the reductionist logic of binary (either–or) decision-making systems. Decision systems exist to make choices or trade-offs between key stakeholders and/or the general public. Because design has been mistaken as a subset of decision-making, and an end instead of a means, its transformative potential has been stifled. Individual development decision-making (choosing among options and making trade-offs) cannot expand future options and benefits. PD can be achieved by design (multiplication), not decision-making (division) alone. Although the design fields have thus far largely excluded ecology, the potential still remains to create wins for the individual stakeholders, the society at large and the ecology. However, leading-edge design is still about restoration and regeneration of ecosystems and communities to leave things 'better than we found them' – rather than the expansion of nature (see *Building Research and Information*, 2012). While regeneration is imperative, it would not compensate for the increasing population, material flows, toxins, and biodiversity losses, let alone the diminishing food chain. Given the tenacity of the DP, however, the difference between restorative and eco-positive design is hard to grasp from the other side of the looking glass.

City versus nature

In a reductionist decision framework, it is counter-intuitive that cities could increase nature, natural systems, and ecological carrying capacity in absolute terms. Thus, designers tended to see nature protection as a separate issue from urban problems (Register, 1990). Cities can, in fact, save nature, but not by downsizing and densification alone. Generating net positive social and ecological impacts over a development's life cycle requires a radically different use of form, structure and space. Sustainable and resilient cities would look completely different from how they do now. Existing vertical urban spaces, surfaces, sidewalks, atriums, alleyways, and edges in cities offer the infrastructure for natural systems to increase both human and ecosystem health and resilience. In fact, increasing ecological carrying capacity can arguably happen only in cities, as we cannot increase the eco-productivity of natural areas without destroying their evolutionary logic. Preservation and restoration of isolated wilderness areas, while crucial, cannot reimburse the costs of population growth or protect natural areas from feral species, genetically modified organisms, toxic dust from mining, or warfare in other parts of the world.

Conclusion

Design can transcend ideological dualisms and help to overcome the endemic biases in our binary decision systems and cerebral dualisms that block positive and whole-systems thinking. Designers – and we are all potentially designers – can leapfrog these barriers and create urban environments that are eco-positive and multifunctional by design. Of course, polarities concerning 'design solutions' also occur, such as: high versus low density development; high versus low technology; and regulatory versus market-based strategies. The answer to these dualisms is 'neither and both' as it all depends on how things are designed.

7.3 Communication dualisms

Communication is fundamental to social and systems change, and is always problematic. Good design is, among other things, a communication and environmental conflict resolution tool. It can find new alternatives that leave all parties better off than they would be if they won their initial positions. What follows are examples of communication barriers or polarities that frequently arise in sustainability discussions and workshops. These are based on decades of first-hand experience. It is suggested that design, the third way, can help to resolve communication polarities at both the problem description and communication strategy stages.

Problem description polarities

Are cities a stage for social interaction or do they shape social relationships? Most appear to feel that what happens among people in the social sphere has more impact than the biophysical (built and natural) environment. That is, place-making activity is seen as more important than the 'stage set' that supports it (Brown, Dixon, and Gillham, 2009). However, wealth stratification occurs through physical development, which, in turn, shapes social relations. Thus far, social impact assessments have traced the distribution of negative health impacts, but not the political ramifications of development, such as cumulative disempowerment and impoverishment. Good design can create environments that foster community engagement, equity and opportunity.

Must development be in conflict with nature or can it be symbiotic? Most people appear subconsciously to assume that trade-offs between society and nature are necessary. Consequently, they tend to prioritize short-term human problems over ecological ones, as it is hard to empathize with nature. Others feel that nature or urban biodiversity is more urgent because, once constructed, urban development locks people into unsustainable lifestyles for decades. By creating multifunctional 'ecological space' that supports appropriate ecosystems and human life quality, good design can avoid negative trade-offs between nature and society.

Who is responsible: the developer, regulator, designer, contractor, or client? The 'circle of blame' often appears in discussions and in practice. Buck-passing and excuses can be reduced by a design process called 'partnering'. This ensures that everyone involved in the development project shares in the risks and benefits of design. After all, mediation usually drives better outcomes than competitive adversarial processes (Ardagh, 1997). Partnering and collaborative design processes have long been advocated, but not often adopted. Meanwhile, everyone can play an educational role in stakeholder groups to show that whole-system benefits are possible through collaborative and eco-positive design.

Is more private space or public space needed? So far, most green homes celebrated on television and in magazines hog embodied energy, materials, and space. Zero-carbon 'houses on steroids' do not represent progress, as we have long known how to reduce domestic operating energy to near zero anyway (Vale and Vale, 1975, 2000). Energy embodied in the construction supply chain can be reduced by garden-like living environments, and good design can reduce conspicuous consumption, hoarding, and defensive expenditure by increasing the conviviality and security of public and private spaces. It is the land and structures that define spaces that embody energy and waste, not space itself.

Communication strategy polarities

Do we 'name and shame' or send out positive messages? Negative messages can be demoralizing, and can also reinforce the false association of sustainability with 'doom and gloom'. If too optimistic, people may mistakenly believe that problems are being addressed. Studies suggest that there can be optimal ratios of positive and negative messages (Harre, 2011, pp. 20–22). Of course, people will ultimately tend to ignore messages or petitioners that appear to threaten their social or personal standing – whether positive or negative in tone. Instead, people can be inspired by positive images through design, which help people visualize positive alternative futures.

Do we wait for bigger 'crises' or are we already in one? Huge environmental crises have not mobilized people, except in wartime (which may owe more to tribal than altruistic impulses). There are, of course, stunningly selfless public responses to immediate and visible crises. Volunteers emerged in their thousands to help after the Brisbane floods of 2011 and the earthquakes in Christchurch of 2012. But this does not mean people will be mobilized to take *preventative* action by threats of future crises. Meanwhile, good design can future-proof cities at no extra cost by design interventions that address multiple sustainability deficits and risks. (See Chapters 10 to 20 for ideas across multiple sectors.)

Is academic theory or professional practice the best vehicle? There is often a predilection for either 'doing' or 'thinking'. Some practitioners tend to think academics and environmentalists do not understand the complexity of things in the real world of industry and politics. However, many developers do not like to be the 'first' to employ new development ideas, so even best practice can be a barrier to design innovation. Some think that those who reject theory 'are prisoners of old theories', yet they also need to relate to old theories for academic credibility. If informed by critique, good design can bypass past theories and practices, because it need not be based on precedent and can work within any aesthetic.

Do we appeal to reason or emotion? Most environment and development decision systems were designed to ignore or conceal emotional issues as these are deemed the opposite of objectivity and reason. The force of reason alone has proven incapable of overcoming social and systems inertia. However, the environment, peace, and sustainability movements are still called emotional, radical, or irrational. Yet it is rational to get emotional about family and planetary survival, and/or the welfare of the bottom third of the world population. Even though design has often reflected society's psycho-social negativity, good design can speak to people's objective and subjective sides.

7.4 Action dualisms

The tendency toward polarization has been reflected in debates over action plans as well. Below, we explore personal/social change versus systems/institutional change; bottom-up change versus change at the top; and change from within the system versus outside. When sustainability organizations deliberate over action strategies, they usually focus on how to influence policy and decision-makers within the *existing* socio-political structure. After all, the prospects of other structures are seen as utopian or soft. However, the existing playing field is tilted and the goalposts shift. This imbalance underpins some fundamental dilemmas in activism.

Social change dilemmas

The social change end of the spectrum leans toward personal, cultural, and behavioral change as the means to overcome impediments to sustainability. The underlying assumption appears to be that when people realize that everything affects everything else, they will spontaneously adopt more rational behaviors *and* systems. However, in a market economy, more sustainable individual and collective choices may not materialize from awareness (Esty and Wilston, 2006). Also, there is no proof that awareness about the social, ethical and ecological consequences of individual and collective choices is keeping pace with the 'dumbing down' of society by the media (Iserbyt, 1999). Sometimes people talk about personal change but only try to change others – 'if others were like me, the world would be perfect' – and some use personal responsibility as an excuse just to 'grow one's own garden'. Nonetheless, most at this end of the spectrum share a penchant for so-called 'bottom-up' action, and top-down systems are often defined as 'the problem'.

Bottom- or top-driven change? Few in power are motivated to change the system that benefits and insulates them. But can power imbalances be changed by individuals from the bottom up? Certainly, paradigm shifts seem to require person-to-person communication. However, people seldom listen to those 'beneath them' in the social hierarchy. Even when 'alternative' ideas are slowly appropriated by the mainstream, those in the 'bottom' are excluded from the conversation. Those at the higher governance, corporate, or managerial levels are notoriously quick to restructure systems to deal with virtually any problem for the managers themselves. Nonetheless, they often seem unable or unwilling to consider restructuring decision frameworks (Miller, 2012). Elevating the culture and character of society from the bottom is undoubtedly a good thing. However, market and regulatory arenas are captured. Money, position, and marketing can always change public opinion. When everything else fails, dissidents can be co-opted. In contrast, community design projects, such as community centers, public parks, and playgrounds, can pull people together in direct design action, while also providing exemplars and setting positive role models.

Systems design dilemmas

The systems change end of the sustainability spectrum believes that deeply entrenched structures, norms, rules, and conventions limit the individual's sphere of influence. They are less confident that the underlying system can be changed incrementally, or that enlightened attitudes will automatically lead to systems change. Currently, non-sustainable development decisions do not have to be justified on sustainability/ethical grounds. Over time, institutions develop biases toward power relationships, so they cannot be transformed by decree or electoral or market choice alone. Instead, they need to be periodically and delibe-rately updated to meet society's (hopefully) evolving ethical standards. To do so, the hidden omissions and biases that are integral to our institutional, intellectual, and physical frameworks need to be explicitly identified, critiqued, and challenged. But those on the top have trouble seeing biases, and systems redesign is a lot to ask of the disempowered. The sustainability-motivated among the upper echelons tend to divide over whether one can be more effective from inside or outside the tribe.

Inside or outside the system? Trying to change the system from either 'the outside' or 'the inside' has the same dilemma as 'bottom-up' or 'top-down' change. Those on the inside must use the methods, tools, and hence the paradigm of those with vested interests in preserving the system. It is almost impossible to challenge a system within its own self-referential language and arithmetic. Likewise, to be heard from the outside, one is also required to petition those in power using the language of the DP. Today, the official language could be called 'numerology'. Yet speaking in numbers or economics is not enough when only 'select' kinds of numbers are accepted by the paradigm and its algorithms. For example, life-cycle assessments purport to take a whole-system view. Yet while they 'count' living things or ecosystems, they represent them with numbers or units of inert substances like carbon emissions. Design can overcome the biases inherent in reduc-ing living things to numbers by providing the infrastructure and ecological space to support life.

Conclusion

Neither ends of the above spectrums of activists are wrong. Efforts to change systems are unconsciously sabotaged by a web of personal and political power relationships, manifested at both the institutional/intellectual systems and social/personal levels. The environmental crisis is a function of disorganized crime (Birkeland, 1995), so it cannot be addressed merely by goodwill, manipulation, or force. However, envisaging and designing secure, safe, and beautiful environments that make everyone better off would go a long way to removing the need for power and privilege. The alternative to pulling on tug ropes is therefore 'direct action' by physical and institutional design (Birkeland, 2002a, pp. 210–214). The design of ethics-based decision systems is not inherently difficult. The authors of the American Constitution wrote a comprehensive decision framework with quill pens and no internet (although, admittedly, the ecology and the feminine were omitted).

7.5 Alternative approach

One way to convince people of the benefits of change is to identify biases due to the sloped playing field and moving goalposts upon which built environment decision and design systems rest. Most biases against sustainability are due to the ideology underlying decision systems and social values. They are seldom, if ever, prescribed by decision principles, policies, or regulations, so they exist in the mind (Box 7.1). A postgraduate student compared the author's list of over a hundred biases to a world-leading green building rating tool, and another compared it to a comprehensive planning scheme for a city. They could find nothing in either schema that would contradict any of these biases. In other words, individual decision-makers could address biases without violating any rules other than tacit conventions. Thus, changes in planning and project review to ethics-based decision-making with more positive outcomes could be made informally, starting now.

Eco-positive Design Report (EDR)

One mechanism to reduce transaction costs and increase design research is an Eco-positive Design Report to frontload design, coupled with a 'post-occupancy evaluation' to test outcomes against net positive design principles. The object is to turn the circle of blame and competition into a circle of education and collaboration. An EDR would document the efforts that the design team has undertaken to ensure the development makes net positive improvements to the urban context, ecological base, public estate, and future adaptability (Birkeland, 1996). It entails a systematic exploration of passive solar design, eco-technologies, and ecosystem services, and therefore drives design education, professional upskilling, and the integration of research, science, and collaboration – even where eco-positive design cannot yet be achieved. The EDR process would aid and be aided by the following:

- *Front-loading:* Currently, developers' consultants prepare expensive impact assessments that predict downstream damage. To do this, the design needs to be largely completed – when it is usually too late for conversion to a sustainable building. Moreover, in the development control fields, sustainability has become synonymous with rating tools, which are almost the opposite of design (see Schendler and Udall, 2005). Front-loading ecological design is important, because most negative impacts and costs are determined at the schematic design stage – which is typically less than 1 per cent of the life-cycle cost of buildings (see Weizsacker, Lovins, and Lovins, 1997; Hawken, Lovins and Lovins, 1999). To be most cost-effective, passive solar cooling, heating and ventilating, air and water treatment, and so on, should be designed into the basic structure itself. This cannot be outsourced to a consultant after the fact. The Living Future Institute is moving in this direction, although it has yet to adopt an ecological sustainability standard (http://living-future.org/).

- *Benchmarking:* The PD Sustainability Standard recognizes that every site is different and every building project has different functions in relation to its context. It compares development against pre-industrial conditions in the region on a floor area (not ground coverage) basis; that is, the ecological footprint instead of the building footprint. This stretch goal is necessary as some people in the industry still tend to argue that what is not currently done is not feasible 'by definition'. An EDR could not simply reject green technologies because their 'payback is too long', as often happens. Instead, any use of fossil fuels would also have to be justified by its ecological and economic payback period (including externalities) – which it does not have.

- *Burden of proof:* EDRs shift the burden of proof from retrospective accounting schemes to design teams who are best placed to design impacts out of the system. Councils need not purchase complex life-cycle assessment or rating tools and/or be responsible for their inaccuracies later. In the EDR process, council staff would need to verify only the outcomes of the tools used by developers. This requires open books. If the design team cannot achieve net positive impacts on site in key areas (e.g. water, soil, biota, energy, air, and human health), the EDR would need to establish that this was not feasible in this particular time and place. This would have to be supported by professional advice from environmental (i.e. not just building) scientists.

- *Public oversight:* Since everyone is a stakeholder in sustainability and social justice, everyone should have some oversight of decision biases concerning the environment and development. To ensure transparency, the EDR would be made public and subject to challenge by planning staff, decision-makers, citizens, and experts. Developers, managers, decision-makers, and analysts should be required by public and peer pressure to justify their development and design decisions on a level and transparent platform. In more significant developments, information would be provided using SMARTmode sustainability analyses (see Birkeland, 2008, pp. 251–273). New multi-dimensional visualization technologies are being developed that would help make collaborative and participatory PD more exciting, engaging, and informative (Jackson and Simpson, 2012).

- *Cost:* By integrating sustainability considerations into the design process from the outset through the EDR process, designers and developers can save time and money compared to current procedures. If the design work is undertaken professionally, no extra work or cost should be necessary: the report merely documents what a responsible professional should be doing anyway. EDRs could avoid (or supplement) rating tools which have high transactions costs, often involves outsourcing to a specialist for a year to fill in forms, and the purchase of a certificate. The building would instead have a public and transparent POE (a well-established process for assessing human comfort and productivity), which measures actual performance.

In cases where eco-positive design solutions are proven infeasible, the default mode would be to restore the health of the environment beyond the site boundaries or to compensate by the eco-positive retrofitting of other structures (http:// living-future. org). The proviso is that net positive impacts would be required, not just offsetting 'additional' negative impacts, as is currently the case with most trading and transfer schemes or ecological restoration programs.

Box 7.1   Questions for eco-logical design reporting

These diagnostic questions about development control are divided between analysts, assessors, and decision-makers for manageability and are not mutually exclusive. All players in urban design and development need to consider such issues. These are arguably addressed by PD methods, models, and metrics such as SmartMode.

EDR: Questions for analysts (report and measurements)

1 Does the life-cycle analysis or other assessment consider net impacts by putting both positive and negative impacts on the same spectrum (e.g. measuring from −1 to 0 to +1)?
2 Are negative impacts deducted, or are relative reductions in negative impacts mislabeled as positive gains (a reduction in negative impacts should not be labeled a gain)?
3 Does the environmental impact or sustainability assessment consider both the economic benefits of a clean environment and the economic costs of a damaged environment?
4 Is mechanical building equipment treated as cost neutral because it is the norm (ignoring regular maintenance, repair, spare parts, and specialist mechanics) and is it expected to pay back its costs?
5 Is the interior and/or exterior space devoted to healthy ecosystems per person or floor area assessed, as opposed to only replacing the original displaced ground area?
6 Does the design count 'embodied' energy, waste, and water as well as reductions in operational uses of energy, water, and waste production (since resource autonomy has already been achieved)?

7 Are reductions of impacts on human health counted as 'ecological', or are environmental gains for people counted as increases in ecosystem health (when they are actually social and economic)?

8 Is the ratio of space to floor area or volume to embodied energy considered, as space can be usefully framed with multi-functional low-impact and low-energy structures?

9 Is embodied energy assessed in relation to thermal mass to avoid unnecessary excavation and waste (since heat and coolness can be stored in low-impact ways)?

10 Are 'fossil' manufacturing and construction processes favored by tacitly or directly counting the 'sunk cost', or past investment, in existing anti-ecological systems?

11 Are the costs of change to more profitable systems considered in a life cycle (cradle-to-cradle) perspective that includes the long-term resource savings that can pay back certain costs?

12 Does the analysis examine how long the *sources* of materials in nature take to recover to at least 'equivalent' ecosystems, or just their production values (i.e. trees versus forest ecosystems)?

13 Are living things converted to units of money, greenhouse, or energy equivalents as surrogates for eco-productivity and eco-services – thereby omitting their ecological value?

14 Is energy consumption linked to the damage caused by the source of power or using a multiplier so that energy figures reflect the full costs (because market prices may never do so)?

EDR: Questions for assessors (development control)

1 Are both new and retrofitting options considered and compared to the Sustainability Standard (pre-industrial conditions in relation to floor area), and are demolition impacts counted?

2 Has an 'eco-positive retrofitting' option been seriously considered as an alternative to a new building or, alternatively, is the equivalent floor area retrofitted elsewhere?

3 Does the report establish and meet the *net* positive impacts that a development needs to provide to compensate the future for past and ongoing losses?

4 Does the design compensate for any unavoidable waste by significant eco-positive actions, or just aim for zero 'waste to landfill' (a small percentage of waste at the end of the pipe)?

5 Does the project consider the use of land in terms of future urban adaptability and resilience functions to ensure options are kept open, so as not to limit the freedoms of future citizens?

6 Does the EDR address social and ecological PD design criteria as well as meet conventional green guidelines (see *Birkeland*, 2008)?

7 Have all SmartMode analyses been considered on a subjective or objective level, suitable to the scale and impact of the development (see *Birkeland*, 2008)?

8 Will a post-occupancy evaluation (POE) be conducted and a performance bond collected, to be returned after the POE is verified and made public, so everyone can learn from any experience and errors?

9 Are the items in the 'triple bottom line' categories balanced, given that irreversible ecological losses cannot be 'balanced' by short-term social and economic gains?

10 Is the analysis benchmarked in relation to the ecological conditions that existed before 'modern' human settlement (Sustainability Standard), or just relative to code requirements or typical buildings?

11 Have trade-offs been made between, say, indoor air quality and energy efficiency – which are not mutually exclusive – and, where offsets are reasonable, is a net gain achieved?

12 Are rating consultants or builders favoring established 'green' technologies just to reduce their perceived risks and to facilitate the application of numbers used in assessment tools?

13 Are analyses limiting thinking to inputs and outputs at site boundaries or building envelopes, instead of adding value across systems boundaries to other potential beneficiaries offsite?

EDR: Questions for decision-makers (governance)

1 Does the EDR meet the burden of proof, rather than requiring the public sector or NGOs to determine the costs and benefits of the proposal relative to PD criteria?

2 Is wealth generation implicitly given a higher value than small and incremental public health impacts in the assessment, although long-term health costs can be greater over time?

3 Are great 'losses' in the expected profits of a developer considered to outweigh the small, widely dispersed losses to individuals from, say, pollution, as is often the case?

4 Are developers allowed to be (unjustly) enriched due to negative environmental or social impacts, or in excess of contributions to the society, simply because no 'unreasonable harm' is done to others?

5 Is the ultimate purpose of the development good for society or are its functions basically antisocial, such as an eco-efficient cigarette factory, which is efficient but proven to be bad for society?

6 Is ecological damage deemed 'amortized' by long-lasting uses, as financial losses can be offset but ecological losses cannot be (i.e. a dam may pay back the embodied energy, but not the ecology)?

7 Does the process consider only the interests of owners, investors and occupiers, or recognize that everyone is a stakeholder in sustainability and has a right to suggest improvements?

8 Do development decisions ensure that the risks of any 'unavoidable' harm that individuals are subjected to are fairly distributed and offset (e.g. polluting industries are usually found in poor areas)?

9 Is the community given adequate notice of controversial developments so they can provide counter-plans for land, given that the site might have better uses in terms of sustainability in the future?

10 Is the 'no development' option seriously considered, taking into account the highest ecological value of the land, benefits of open space, potential for future climate adaptation, etc.?

11 Is a development allowed simply because other similar developments were previously permitted (i.e. precedent) without taking into account the total cumulative impacts in the region?

12 Will a development delay the transition to whole-systems change as, for example, a recycling industry that perpetuates an undesirable system due to a vested interest in waste streams?

13 Does the application of the precautionary principle apply only to new technologies (if used at all), thus reinforcing the bias towards harmful status quo development, such as nuclear power?

7.6 Conclusion

In summary, this chapter has suggested the institutional and cultural barriers to change are complex but largely in the mind. System biases and personal prejudices have been entrenched by dualistic, rather than design, thinking. Resilient and sustainable decisions and design are not actually barred, since decisions and decision frameworks need to conform only to the letter of the law, and the law is an anchor not a rudder. Citizens as well as analysts and decision-makers can transcend personal and system barriers without transgressing any rubrics but a negative institutional and social culture. Changing human behavior and redesigning institutions in the urban domain would be easy if we adopted a positive perspective. Direct design solutions can find win–win solutions to dualistic positions that halt genuine progress. However, paradigms are like mental rubber bands. When stretched, they want to snap back into position. The challenge is to ensure that they do not squeeze the positive models, methods, and metrics back into the dominant negative paradigm.

References

Ardagh, A. 1997. *Administrative Law*, 3rd ed., Sydney: Butterworths.

Birkeland, J.L. 1993. 'Towards a New System of Environmental Governance', *The Environmentalist* 13(1), 19–32.

Birkeland, J.L. 1995. 'Cultures of Institutional Corruption', in Judith Bessant, Kerry Carrington, and Sandy Cook, eds, *Cultures of Crime and Violence: The Australian Experience*, Victoria, Australia: LaTrobe University Press, 199–212.

Birkeland, J.L. 1996. 'Improving the Design Review Process', *CIB Commission Conference Proceedings*, Melbourne, RMIT, 16 February, 150–155.

Birkeland, J.L. 2002a. 'Legislative Environmental Controls', in *Design for Sustainability: A Sourcebook of Eco-logical Solutions*, London: Earthscan, 210–214.

Birkeland, J.L. 2002b. 'Responsible Design', in *Design for Sustainability: A Sourcebook of Integrated Eco-logical Solutions*, London: Earthscan, 26–30.

Birkeland, J.L. 2003. 'Beyond Zero Waste', paper delivered at Societies for a Sustainable Future, Third UKM–UC International Conference, Canberra, 14–15 April.

Birkeland, J.L. 2004. 'Building Assessment Systems: Reversing Environmental Impacts', paper delivered at Nature and Society Forum, ACT. Available at: http://www.naf.org.au/naf-forum/birkeland-2.pdf.

Birkeland, J.L. 2007. 'GEN 4: Positive Development: Design for Eco-Services', in *BEDP Environmental Design Guide*, Canberra: The Royal Australian Institute of Architects. Available at: http://www.environmentdesignguide.com.au/.

Birkeland, J.L. 2008. *Positive Development: From Vicious Circles to Virtuous Cycles through Built Environment Design*, London: Earthscan.

Birkeland, J.L. Forthcoming. 'Positive Development', in J. Byrne, J. Dodson, and N. Sipe, eds, *Australian Environmental Planning: Challenges and Future Prospects*, London: Routledge.

Brown, L.J., Dixon, D., and Gillham, O. 2009. *Urban Design for an Urban Century: Placemaking for People*, Hoboken, NJ: Wiley.

Building Research and Information. 2012. 40(1) [whole edition on regenerative design].

Eisenhower, D.D. 1961. 'Military-Industrial Complex Speech', *Public Papers of the Presidents*, Dwight D. Eisenhower, 1960, 1035–1040.

Esty, D.C. and Wilston, A.S. 2006. *Green to Gold: How Smart Companies Use Environmental Strategy to Innovate, Create Value and Build Competitive Advantage*, New Haven, CT, and London: Yale University Press.

Gaard, G., ed. 1993. *Ecofeminism: Women, Animals, Nature*, Philadelphia, PA: Temple University Press.

Girardet, H. 1992. *The Gaia Atlas of Cities: New Directions for Sustainable Urban Living*, London: Gaia Books Ltd.

Harre, N. 2011. *Psychology for a Better World: Strategies to Inspire Sustainability*. Available at: http://www.psych.auckland.ac.nz/webdav/site/psych/shared/about/our-people/documents/Psychology%20for%20a%20Better%20World.pdf.

Hawken, P., Lovins, A., and Lovins, H. 1999. *Natural Capitalism: Creating the Next Industrial Revolution*, London: Earthscan.

Iserbyt, C.T. 1999. *The Deliberate Dumbing down of America: A Chronological Paper Trail*, Ohio: Conscience Press.

IUCN/UNEP/WWF 1980. 'World Conservation Strategy', republished 1991 as *Caring for the Earth: A Strategy for Sustainable Living*, London: Earthscan.

Jackson, D. and Simpson, R., eds. 2012. *D_City: Digital Earth, Virtual Nations, Data Cities*, Sydney: DCity.

Lyle, J.T. 1994. *Regenerative Design for Sustainable Development*, New York: Wiley.

Miller, C.L. 2012. *Implementing Sustainability: The New Zealand Experience*, Abingdon and New York: Routledge.

Norton, B.G. 2005. *Sustainability: A Philosophy of Adaptive Ecosystem Management*, Chicago, IL: University of Chicago Press.

Register, R. 1990. *The First International Ecological City Conference*, Berkeley, CA: Urban Ecology.

Schendler, A. and Udall, R. 2005. 'LEED is Broken . . . Let's Fix It', Aspen, CO: Community Office for Resource Efficiency. Available at:http://www01.aspensnowmass.com/environment/images/LEEDisBroken.pdf.

Shiva, V. and Mies, M. 1993. *Ecofeminism*, Halifax, Nova Scotia: Fernwood.

Tansey, J. 2006. 'Industrial Ecology and Planning: Assessing and Socially Embedding Green Technological Systems', *Environment and Planning B: Planning and Design* 33, 381–392.

UNEP. 2005. 'Millennium Ecosystem Assessment: Strengthening Capacity to Manage Ecosystems Sustainably for Human Wellbeing'. Available at: http://ma.caudillweb.com/en/about.overview.aspx.

Vale, B. and Vale, R. 1975, 2000. *The Autonomous House: Design and Planning for Self-sufficiency*, London: Thames & Hudson.

Warren, K., ed. 1996. *Ecological Feminist Philosophies*, Bloomington: Indiana University Press.

WCED. 1987. *Our Common Future*, report of the Brundtland Commission, World Commission on Environment and Development, Oxford: Oxford University Press.

Weizsacker, E. van, Lovins, A., and Lovins, H. 1997. *Factor 4: Doubling Wealth – Halving Resource Use*, London: Earthscan.

CHAPTER 8

The priorities for future sustainable cities

Thomas Kvan

8.1 Introduction

The future will look nothing like the past yet we know nothing that we have not seen. We have, in part, arrived at our current conundrum by taking a nineteenth-century vision of a sustainable future, that of rights to fresh air, community and productive healthy lives, and extrapolated the solutions in the propositions of the proponents of the Garden City Movement and other suburban visions. In these, the prospect of an ideal image made manifest drove the pursuit of an elusive future. These are distinct from the City Beautiful Movement in which proponents sought to 'rectify' cities through monumental and landscape aesthetic interventions to raise moral standards.

Early and naive framing takes the approach of framing these attempts as approaches to a utopian idea of a community, ones in which the elements are in apparent balance. Perhaps starting with Plato's R*epublic* (Plato and Sachs, 2007*)*, the image of an ideal community in which its citizens work in harmony with nature and one another has captivated attention and motivated action. Manifestations and experiments can be easily found around the world today, from catastrophic failures such as Jonestown in Guyana to the operationally successful such as Auroville in Tamil Nadu, India.

In many of these utopian communities, we can recognise aspirations that align with our articulation of resilience and sustainability but the outcomes tell us that the strategies are not replicable. The terminal challenge faced by these utopian exercises is reconciling the aspiration of contained balance with the admission of external factors, the unanticipated and chaos. Such ideal communities are envisioned as isolated units within the bounds of which a balanced system can be achieved ecologically, economically, socially, legally and philosophically. The experiments end when such isolation is found to be untenable; as Popper (1966) noted, the rigidity of such closed systems leads them to totalitarian control over the society. The challenge, then, is scalability. Closed systems do not lend themselves to replication and growth; the ideal envisioned is greatly dependent on a narrow band in size and dynamic (Allen and Holling, 2008).

To put the question of scale into context, consider the needs of the two most populous nations at the moment, China and India. Together, they anticipate that their urban populations will grow by over 700 million people in the period from 2010 to 2030. Urban growth in Africa will be on a similar scale. To address this demand with sustainable urban responses, large scale and rapid implementation is needed. For example, Nanjing Hexi, an area of 94 sq. km to the west of Nanjing city proper, is being developed to accommodate a target population of 800,000 people in 60 sq. km of constructed land. The city is intended to encompass residential, business and industrial areas, and to perform as a low-carbon city. Design goals have been established to achieve metrics of sustainability by supporting a low-carbon economy, deliver energy from sustainable sources, create the environment for a resilient community using primarily public transport or bicycles, and be managed appropriately through policies and mechanisms that sustain these goals. To do so, planning has proceeded on the assumption that the ground plane is not the controlling factor; urban activities are placed both below and above the ground plane. The urban system is granular, conceived at different scales from local to municipal, delivering services and support locally within a five-minute walking radius and municipal services, such as hospitals, within a fifteen-minute vehicular transportation radius. Primary schools are located within 500 metres of all homes, secondary schools within 1,000 metres. Waste is retained and reused; waste heat is translated into district heating. At such a scale, closed systems are not feasible.

8.2 Priorities for future cities

Comparatively more open system approaches are the norm, such as the suburban district in which singular ideological alignment is not demanded. Multiple agendas can be accommodated, although historically suburban development had been driven by both progressive and reactionary ideologies (Davison, 2006), often by the desire to exclude other sectors of society.

We recognise, therefore, that urban strategies are not simply choices about technical and physical alternatives – cars versus pedestrians; urban agriculture versus paved surfaces. The choices are about the values of the citizens and systems to support those values. Lewis Mumford observed that suburban aspirations could be phrased as 'a collective effort to live a private life' (Mumford, 1938, p. 412). As we now recognise, such choices carry consequential outcomes. The collective desire to pursue such privacy demands isolated housing units with open spaces around them that increase distances to be circumnavigated by transportation systems based on individual vehicles, leading ultimately to traffic congestion on major axes.

The future, then, is one of choice; we live today in modes flowing from choices made one or two hundred years ago, for it takes that long for urban transformation to occur in established cities. With the pace of urbanisation observed today, however, we are in a situation where we can realise change more rapidly. Thus, we find ourselves at the moment when we need to envision the alternative yet our experience limits our capacities, as Wiseman, Edwards and Luckins suggested in Chapter 4. They summarise the three dimensions of sustainable cities that must be addressed: namely, economic equity, social connectedness and a capacity to adapt. These are much the same that were articulated some one hundred and fifty years ago, a vision that laid the foundation for communities across much of the world as it developed through the twentieth century.

Warned of conceptualising the resilient and sustainable future as a closed ideal system, we turn instead to conceptualising the urban opportunities as complex adaptive systems (Holling, 1973; Karakiewicz, 2010). Thus, the challenge is getting there from here without attempting to isolate the system through isolation from the wider context of the state, the nation or the global environment.

Birkeland, in Chapter 7, suggests we cannot construe the choice of 'system design' versus 'behaviour change' as the way forward. As she notes, incremental and isolated technical changes, informed through environmental impact assessments, do not lead us to positive outcomes. Such reviews are conducted within narrow system boundaries but they also ignore the need for behavioural changes and the modification of individual and collective aspirations. We can reconceptualise urban systems from being resource consumers to places of increased natural systems and ecological carrying capacity, contributing net positive outcomes to natural systems rather than operating as consumption sinks into which resources are imported.

Production is, in itself, not enough. One of the core resources we consume in our cities is surface area. Common to all strategies of sustainable action is the need to reduce our consumption of resources, not only those that are retrieved from beneath the earth's surface but the surface itself, since many of our resources lie on that surface (food, water, etc). Unless we tackle the spread and coverage of urban settlements, we cannot get to the core of the problem. Every city expansion entails construction taking over productive agricultural land. As Kearns *et al.* note in Chapter 6, when we build over productive agricultural land and dramatically change drainage patterns, we create patterns of living that add to undesirable outcomes of lengthy commutes and long links in supply chains. The development of urban agriculture cannot compensate for this loss since production cannot be as expansive, efficient or easily free of pollutants.

It is not easy, however, to shake off the present and envision a future. Kearns *et al.* quote Walker and Salt (2006) as saying: 'the capacity to create a fundamentally new system (including new state variables, excluding one of more existing state variables, and usually operating at different scales) when ecological, economic, and/ or social conditions make the existing system untenable'. This will require us to test ourselves by exploring the uncomfortable, not sticking to that which pleases us through its familiarity. In the short term, it will need us to take small steps to build confidence and trust but the solutions will more likely come from larger steps in which experimentation will challenge broadly held assumptions. We have done this before, when changing from tightly contained (sometimes walled) cities to suburbs, and succeeded – but only by communicating to the communities the value of such change. Living in suburbs required families to change their financial commitments and spend considerably more on transportation than when they lived in cities.

Change takes decisive action; change for a more sustainable future will be achieved through decisive personal action (Gleeson, 2008). We cannot have partial solutions, and the solutions cannot be extrapolations of particular ideologies. It is clear the problems of sustainable cities are systemic in nature, so solutions will need to be systemic in response. Green infrastructures are a key component of the ecological and social factors but while we remain obsessed with the ground plane, we will not progress. These will demand alternative forms of interaction. The gathering of the community around the neighbourhood sports field, for example, is a common activity around the world, from the footy field in the remote town through to the array of cricket matches that take place on the Rajpath in New Delhi, transforming Lutyens's ceremonial axis into the world's most densely packed cricket field. As an alternative, we can observe basketball games being played on the roof of Raimondi College on Robinson Road in Hong Kong, as it is on the rooftops of many schools and community centres in the city. In a city such as Hong Kong, we find that the ground plane is reinterpreted and the city considered as a volume, not an extrusion from the plane (Shelton *et al.*, 2011). Thus, reinterpretation of our opportunities is one approach to framing resilience.

Underlying any successful change towards more resilient and sustainable cities, however, will be changes in aspirations, expectations and behaviours. As Birkeland notes, it is not either/or; the choice must address systems *and* behaviours. Solutions for whatever larger problems we identify can only be executed locally in specific contexts and by means of simple systems.

As you will read in the following chapters, many urban sub-systems present opportunities for innovation. There are opportunities in the ways in which we produce and access essential resources, such as food, energy and water; mirroring this, we must consider the volumes of waste produced and the manner in which they are handled, seeing these again as opportunities for production rather than as problems of disposal. Supporting these will need to be alternative means of moving around and between such cities, achieving through better design reduced demands to move by intrusive transport systems through better precinct design and more extensive use of communications technologies.

So how do we market the ideas we have? As Rochecouste and Pearson note in Chapter 5, we cannot change if we have failed to capture the imaginations, the hearts and the minds of those who will do the hard work of making change. Change of this sort must be undertaken broadly. Having given the opportunities to live in a particular manner that embraces the notion of self-determination and choice, having sold the notion that individual home-ownership is a laudatory goal and that the image to pursue is that of the family frolicking in its own garden dug in the earth itself, we can only take the next steps by engaging this audience to take the steps for us. Thus, the articulation of a convincing alternative and the means to get there is paramount.

This, then, is the narrative that will engage. Chapter 5 frames this simply around the five urban essences: namely, people, place, programme, product and planet. From a sense of the people and their heritage, place is claimed, activities (programme) developed and cities claimed. Such narratives are alive and dynamic and live by retelling, not repeating, and in each retelling the future is edited and explored. As demographics shift, other cultures are engaged. In Rochecouste and Pearson's example, the 1990s narrative of Melbourne was European in flavour; as the decades have passed, that has shifted and will shift further to encompass more Asian regional stories. The city will evolve and Asian uses of urban space will emerge – a more intensive use of spaces and the transfer of collective activity from private to public space (Shelton *et al.*, 2011). Thus, Federation Square is the city's living room where crowds watch television on a jumbo screen, the viewers no longer sitting alone at home.

8.3 Conclusion

The challenge is how to sell the idea of collective wellbeing in the long term against the strident message of the late twentieth century, which was clearly the message of immediate and selfish gratification. Necessary to create the consumer markets that then drove economic demand and ample reward (for some), this individualist focus on gratification is now well ensconced as a social norm. As Wiseman *et al.* note in Chapter 4, it is this which must change, and in Chapter 5 Rochecouste and Pearson have developed this with the understanding that it will not succeed until we articulate a desirable future and communicate it in a manner that is grounded in authenticity. While leadership is needed, it will not come about through visionaries charging ahead; their contribution can only be to take the communities to places where they wish to go.

Central to this future will be the choices we make in servicing and supporting our endeavours; in other words, choices we make about infrastructures and choices we make about consumption. These are the means by which we obtain our daily necessities, such as food, water and power, and then dispose of our waste safely, by sewers and waste collection, through to the facilities that support the additional qualities of life, such as supporting social engagement and shared activities, be they sports, culture or simply enjoying spending time together in parks and streets. These choices are, in particular, based on a narrative we share and can be pursued in a selfish manner by providing each and every one of us with our own slices (as far as our individual wealth permits), or in a narrative that speaks to a collective engagement.

The challenge of scalability remains a critical issue. Many readers will be resident in established models of urban development faced with incremental growth (or contraction, if you are in parts of Europe). Incremental and linear change may suffice in some communities but for many the change will be dramatic, either because they are in places of rapid urban growth (much of Africa, Asia and South America) or because incremental change as pursued recently has led to unsustainable exposure, as experienced in recent climate-inflicted disasters in North America and Australia. The capacity of privileged closed system experiments such as Auroville are significantly limited (Kapoor, 2007) and are not models for the rest of us. Our investments of time and creativity should focus on inclusive open systems that are supportive of divergent and many cultural desires.

As chapters in this book reflect, we should seek an effective incremental change to which we can collectively subscribe and contribute, not awaiting change driven by catastrophes of war or weather patterns. While much of the impetus for substantive urban change in Europe came about through the intervention of brutal wars, this is unlikely to be the driver in the future on the scale in which change is needed. Today, floods and fires are among the imminent drivers. Instead of awaiting passively for their arrival, desirable change is more likely to succeed if we take the initiative in the manner in which societies are now accustomed, led by marketing and developed on narratives to which social groups subscribe. The future is more likely to be realised through selective choice by social groups than by external imposition; to achieve this, though, we need someone to articulate a narrative that captures our attention and then someone to give us the means to realise the narrative through enablers of finance and regulation. Perhaps that someone is you and then us.

References

Allen, C. R. and Holling, C. S. 2008. *Discontinuities in ecosystems and other complex systems*, New York and Chichester: Columbia University Press.

Davison, A. 2006. Stuck in a cul-de-sac? Suburban history and urban sustainability in Australia, *Urban Policy and Research*, 24 (2), 201–216.

Gleeson, B. 2008. Critical commentary: waking from the dream: an Australian perspective on urban resilience, *Urban Studies*, 45 (13), 2653–2668.

Holling, C. S. 1973. Resilience and stability of ecological systems, *Annual Review of Ecology and Systematics*, 4 (1), 1–23.

Kapoor, R. 2007. Auroville: a spiritual–social experiment in human unity and evolution, *Futures*, 39 (5), 632–643.

Karakiewicz, J. 2010. Data driven urban design, *Proceedings of the 14th Congress of the Iberoamerican Society of Digital Graphics, SIGRADI, Bogota*, pp. 372–375.

Mumford, L. 1938. *The culture of cities*, New York: Harcourt.

Plato and Sachs, J. 2007. *Republic*, Newburyport, MA: Focus.

Popper, K. R. S. 1966. *The open society and its enemies*, volume 1: *The spell of Plato*, London: Routledge & Kegan Paul.

Shelton, B., Karakiewicz, J. and Kvan, T. 2011. *The making of Hong Kong: from vertical to volumetric*, Abingdon: Routledge.

PART THREE

INNOVATION FOR RESILIENT, SUSTAINABLE CITIES

CHAPTER 9

City transitions

Infrastructure innovation, green economy and the eco-city

Peter W. Newton

9.1 Introduction

Three radical and interconnected transitions are central to sustainable urban development and city resilience in the twenty-first century: transition to a green economy, to sustainable urban infrastructures and to eco-cities. These are framed against a formidable set of challenges to urban sustainability and resilience now confronting all societies, as identified by Newton and Doherty (Chapter 2, this volume). These include resource constraints, climate change, extreme events exhibiting shorter return periods, population growth, urbanization and built environment intensification, biosecurity, financial uncertainty, failing infrastructures, widening socio-demographic disparities and fragmenting social and human capital.

This chapter briefly explores the essential features of each transition arena, including some of the critical cross-connections (see Figure 9.1). There is an increasing interdependence emerging. Eco-cities will be critical to sustainable urban development in the twenty-first century. With the world's 9 billion population forecast to be 75 per cent urban by 2050, the sustainability challenge will focus more closely on the consumption emanating from cities – their built environments and their populations. A range of physical infrastructures is required to support urban living: transport, energy, water, waste, communications, and buildings. The consensus is that the sustainability performance of each is currently poor, given that they all emerged in an era when there were few resource constraints and climate constraints. Next-generation infrastructures (defined as Horizon 2 and Horizon 3; see below) demonstrate significantly greater eco-efficiency and resilience in their operation than those that they need to replace. The demand for new urban infrastructures and green services represents the trigger for a raft of innovative infrastructure technologies to move more widely into the urban marketplace. Figure 9.1 also indicates that cities constitute a geographic locus for green industry location, given the agglomeration economies they deliver to firms generally as well as the customer base for green products and services.

The barriers to change are considerable, but evidence of progress in each arena is emerging. A common feature for all transition arenas is the set of critical normative goals that they address, *viz.* using resources more efficiently and reducing non-renewable resource consumption, reducing emissions and utilizing wastes as resources, restoring environmental quality, enhancing human wellbeing, and

---

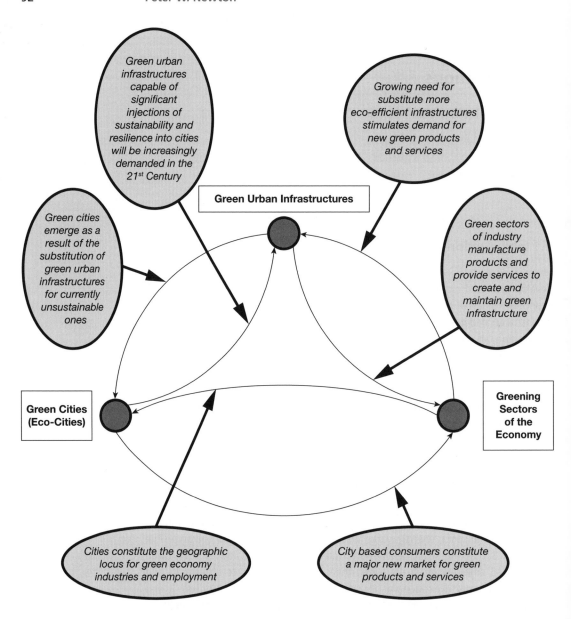

Figure 9.1 Critical connections: green economy, green urban infrastructure and green (eco-)cities

developing human settlements that are liveable, productive, environmentally sustainable, socially inclusive and resilient.

9.2 Green economy transition

A green economy can be defined as one that works with the environment and not against it. It involves a transition from the current model of development that continues to give primacy to economic decisions and assumes that environmental problems and externalities can be solved or accommodated if the economy is sound. It is based on an integration of ecological thinking and innovation into all social and economic planning by government and industry from the beginning – not after the issues have been framed. It involves a recognition that the macro economy is part of a larger natural ecosystem and resource base which has capacity constraints that will be severely tested in the twenty-first century (Daly 1996; Krugman 2010). We are currently at some distance from embracing this paradigm, but some of its central principles and likely features are now being articulated (UNEP 2011; UN DESA, UNEP and UNCTAD 2012). There are both push and pull factors in play.

From a 'pull' perspective, demand for a green economy will come from a need to deal with the mounting pile of global sustainability problems already catalogued. It will necessitate a wholesale restructuring of global societies and economies no less significant than the earlier agricultural, industrial, service and information revolutions. Unlike these earlier transformations, however, there is an *urgency for transition* to a green economy according to the UN DESA (2011), a theme echoed by the OECD (2011), UN Millennium Ecosystem Assessment (2005) and the World Bank (2012).

From a 'push' perspective, a green economy will be driven by what has been advanced as the sixth major wave of socio-technical innovation to emerge since the beginning of the industrial era (see Figure 9.2).

As with prior socio-technical transitions, the green economy will be based on the maturation and diffusion of several *enabling technologies* capable of being supplied into the market. Phillimore (2001) and others view the green economy as revolving primarily around energy and the transition from fossil fuels to renewables. It will rely heavily on the eco-efficiencies of technologies attempting to harness solar, wind,

Figure 9.2 Major techno-economic transitions since the industrial revolution Source: Hargroves and Smith (2005)

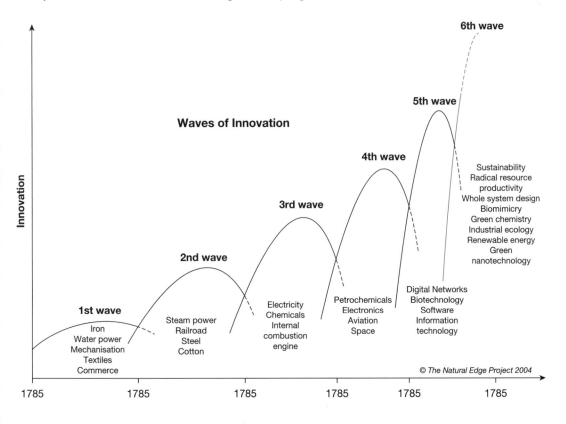

geothermal, bio-energy and hydrogen sources of power (some include nuclear and carbon capture and storage in this cluster, while others exclude them on the grounds of environmental risk).

These 'core green' low-emission energy industries are beginning to emerge, but none represents an easy option. Each nation is developing a roadmap for what could constitute a secure, low-carbon energy future. For example, a comparison of Australian and Korean low-carbon green growth strategies (ATSE and NAEK 2012) indicates that both countries are heavily dependent on fossil fuels and are planning to expand the contributions that renewable technologies can make to the energy mix in combination with the introduction of a price (tax) on carbon emissions. Australia is a net energy exporter while Korea is almost entirely dependent on energy imports. Korea is focused on developing energy technologies for export whereas Australia appears to be focused on development of technologies to address local requirements (e.g. carbon capture and storage).

To stimulate a market for renewable energy in Australia, in 2008 the federal government introduced a target of 20 per cent of the nation's energy supply to be sourced from renewables by 2020, amounting to some 45,000 gigawatt hours (ABARE 2010). Targeted primarily at encouraging the development of large-scale solar thermal on-grid power stations, off-grid solar PV has been more agile in responding to incentives such as state government guaranteed feed-in tariffs for electricity sold by households to the grid. The growth in installed capacity has been rapid (Newton et al. 2012b). It seems likely that distributed (local) energy technologies capable of embedding themselves *within* the built environment will see cities becoming significant producers of energy, whereas historically they have been exclusively consumers (Newton and Newman, 2013).

However, in its broader conceptualization, the green economy extends beyond 'core' industries associated with low- and zero-carbon energy generation (Elder 2009). It can be seen to embrace innovations that enable achievement of green goals relevant to several other major sectors of the economy and the industries within those sectors. Some examples are listed in Table 9.1. A recent UNEP (2011,

Table 9.1 Greening the economy: key sectors and green goals

Industry sectors	Green goals associated with sector
Manufacturing	Cradle-to-cradle; closed-loop production; industrial ecology
Energy utilities	Renewables; distributed (local) generation; green design
Water utilities	Integrated (stormwater, wastewater) systems; water sensitive urban design
Waste	Recycling, reuse; eco-industrial development
Construction	Smart, green building; virtual design and construction; life-cycle analysis
Trade (retail/wholesale)	Zero waste (packaging, food etc.); carbon management
Transport	Hybrid, electric, hydrogen vehicles; land use transport integration
Finance and property	Green accounting; urban retrofitting; building accreditation
Services	Zero waste; reduced consumption, carbon management; e-services
Government	Green procurement; de-coupling policies; sectoral decarbonizing schemes; regulation incentives

Table 9.2 Geography of green economy service jobs in Australia, 2012

	Firms		Population (2011)	
	N	%	N	%
Melbourne Metro	725	75.2%	3,931,430	73.8%
Rest of VIC	239	24.8%	1,396,856	26.2%
Total VIC	964	100.0%	5,328,286	100.0%
Sydney Metro	661	60.6%	4,393,655	63.7%
Rest of NSW	430	39.4%	2,502,010	36.3%
Total NSW	1091	100.0%	6,895,665	100.0%
Brisbane Metro	391	48.9%	2,011,292	46.6%
Rest QLD	408	51.1%	2,301,377	53.4%
Total QLD	799	100.0%	4,312,669	100.0%
Adelaide Metro	231	80.2%	1,173,509	73.8%
Rest of SA	57	19.8%	416,783	26.2%
Total SA	288	100.0%	1,590,292	100.0%
Perth Metro	277	77.8%	1,648,132	74.4%
Rest of WA	79	22.2%	566,615	25.6%
Total WA	356	100.0%	2,214,747	100.0%
Hobart Metro	51	49.5%	192,068	38.9%
Rest of TAS	52	50.5%	301,509	61.1%
Total TAS	103	100.0%	493,577	100.0%
Total All Metro	2351	63.7%	13,436,104	62.8%
Total All Rest of State	1341	36.3%	7,965,331	37.2%
Total Australia	3692	100.0%	21,401,435	100.0%

Source: SENSIS and ABS Census

Note: Data on green economy firms have been derived from an aggregation of entries in SENSIS Business Directory 2012: Active Transport, Green Building, Green Products, Green Services, Green Society, Smart Grid, Smart Home, Solar, Zero Carbon Vehicles

p. 454) report has suggested that green industries are dominated by service industries and tend to be concentrated in the largest consumer markets. A preliminary study of *green service industries* in Australia (see Table 9.2) indicates that at a macro level their distribution is largely reflective of a generally ubiquitous (population-based) demand for these services. More spatially disaggregated analysis, however, is required in order to determine whether there are unique geographies to particular *categories* of green business.

9.3 Urban technology innovation and urban infrastructure transition

Many of the products and services that will characterize a green economy will find their application in the built environment of cities. The most sustainable cities will be

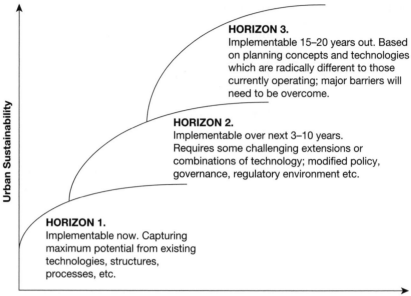

Figure 9.3 The three horizons of urban technology innovation
Source: Newton (2007)

those capable of drawing from a pipeline of innovative technologies, products and processes that can be substituted as existing applications and vintages show signs of failure (Newton 2007). Three horizons of innovation have been identified for such a pipeline, with each making successively superior contributions to sustainable urban development (see Figure 9.3 and Table 9.3).

Horizon 1 (H1) innovations are those where the technology is commercially available and has a demonstrated level of eco-efficiency (cost plus environment) performance that is superior to products or processes currently in the marketplace and which should be rapidly substituted. Examples would include energy rated

Table 9.3 Three horizons of urban technological innovation

Urban infrastructure domain	Level of innovation		
	Horizon 1	Horizon 2	Horizon 3
Energy	Energy efficiencies in housing and industry; dwelling energy rating; appliance rating	Distributed renewable and low emission energy generation systems; methane bridge (substitution of gas for coal)	Renewables-based solar-hydrogen or solar-electric economy
Water	Water-smart appliances; domestic rainwater tanks; desalination	Sewer mining; water sensitive urban design	Integrated urban water systems (recycled stormwater and wastewater)

Urban infrastructure domain	Level of innovation		
	Horizon 1	Horizon 2	Horizon 3
Waste	Product stewardship; waste separation and recycling; domestic composting	Extensive cradle-to-cradle manufacturing based around single enterprises, e.g. motor vehicles, computers, building products	Eco-industrial clusters based on utilization of multiple waste streams
Transport and communications	Road pricing; high-speed rail; telepresence via broadband internet communications	Hybrid and electric vehicles; telecommuting, teleshopping, telebanking etc.	Integrated transport and land use; intelligent transport systems; e-mobility
Buildings	Checkbox system for green building design; tall buildings	Real-time life-cycle sustainability performance assessment during design; building information models; hybrid buildings	Ultra-smart buildings and linked infrastructures; green building materials with embedded sensors

Source: Newton (2012)

housing, energy and water rated appliances, green building products and processes and smart greenfield development, among many others.

Horizon 2 (H2) innovations are those where there are examples in operation but not yet widespread, such as hybrid and electric cars, distributed energy, hybrid buildings or precincts (Newton and Tucker 2010) and water-sensitive urban design (Wong and Brown 2010). These better-performing innovations have a capacity to be applied more broadly, but may require further examination of how they would perform in different regions or markets before becoming more ubiquitous (like H1). Several renewable energy technologies are in this category (Melbourne Energy Institute 2010).

Horizon 3 (H3) innovations are those which reside, for the most part, in research laboratories as prototypes or visionary systems undertaking field trials and awaiting implementation, but whose sustainability impact can be truly transformational. Examples include:

- Integrated urban water systems which enable the creation of a sustainable yield of water in urban regions subject to periods of drought and climate variability, by augmenting diverted water from environmental flows (i.e. dams) with treated greywater and stormwater. The challenge lies in accommodating decentralized integrated water systems with the long-established centralized system networks, as well as addressing current barriers to implementation associated with public health regulations involving water recycling and reuse in domestic settings.

Desalination is an established H2 technology, but suffers from currently being labelled as 'liquid energy'. However, in a context where the high levels of embodied energy used in the treatment of sea water to potable standards can be supplied from renewable forms of energy – enabling a sustainable carbon neutral water supply – the resultant 'integrated energy-water system' would exemplify H3 innovation.

- Eco-industrial clusters can emerge around new industries and products which utilize multiple waste streams and energy streams synergistically, based on industrial ecology principles and advances in green chemistry. Converting waste to resources and products, and creating wealth from waste, represents a major opportunity for shrinking the ecological footprint of cities and creating the basis for new green economy jobs, typically in the employment-poor outer urban regions of cities where eco-industrial parks are likely to be established. Initial involvement of government as a catalyst for the 'integrated' activity is a common feature, given the added complexity of engagement required among multiple firms – unlike the cradle-to-cradle product stewardship involved in closed-loop manufacturing by an individual company.

- A solar-hydrogen/solar-electric economy is one capable of application to both stationary power generation (for buildings and industrial plant) and portable power (e.g. for transportation) and offers the prospect for a totally renewable source of energy which is free of carbon dioxide emissions. There are exemplars of the solar-hydrogen/solar-electric economy penetrating the marketplace seeking to gain a commercial foothold, and all represent technology platforms which are capable of winding back atmospheric concentrations of greenhouse gases – limiting harmful global warming and associated climate change. Variations exist in relation to eco-efficiency performances, and there is the added spatial planning challenge associated with developing urban infrastructures capable of supporting a decarbonization of the housing and transport sectors – innovation which confronts the path dependencies built around each of the still dominant twentieth-century infrastructure regimes. Integration of low- or zero-emission distributed energy generation technologies with a national grid developed for a different (fossil fuel-based) energy generation landscape represents a major challenge at present.

- High-speed wireless digital communications and computing provides a platform for mobile personal connectivity and information processing and exchange – any time, anywhere. This communication infrastructure platform creates an increased menu of flexible location options for both business and workers in determining what activities are undertaken when and where: within cities, nations and globally. The centrifugal forces unleashed by this new platform interplay in a manner not yet well understood with the centripetal forces of agglomeration economies – decentralization *with* centralization (Newton 1995).

- High-speed commuting via high-speed rail converts large towns and provincial cities located up to 200 kilometres from major cities into the equivalent of middle-ring suburbs in those cities, relieving pressure from increasingly unaffordable city housing markets as well as decentralizing jobs (Newton *et al.* 1997). High-speed rail, high-speed telecommunications and intelligent arterial and freeway systems combine to provide the connectivity required for a twenty-first-century mega-metropolitan region. High-speed travel and communications are for the most part H1/H2 urban infrastructures – innovations that will continue to play out in our cities. However, as Table 9.3 suggests, H3 challenges will continue to focus on attempts to achieve more integrated transport and land use *within* cities than has been demonstrable over the last sixty years of urban development. The benefit of more sustainable urban development resulting from integrated land use–transport planning is evident in reductions in carbon footprints of at least 30 per cent with more compact urban forms (Newton *et al.* 1997, 2012b). Opportunities for reducing car dependence and promoting opportunities for e-mobility (environmentally friendly modes of travel such as walking, cycling and public transit) within urban communities then become more achievable.

- Buildings have become the focus for challenging targets relating to environmental performance – carbon neutral, zero carbon or zero energy and zero wastewater; designed for disassembly, reusability and recyclability; and smart, healthy and productive indoor environments. There are many examples of recently constructed buildings that could be classed as meeting these H2 challenges. However, they are but a small percentage of all new buildings and are far removed from the environmental performance of the total existing stock. Radical and accelerated regeneration of housing and associated infrastructure is required in the ageing brownfield and greyfield precincts of cities (Newton 2010; Newton *et al.* 2012b).

- Virtual building and construction is where a convergence of advanced information technologies with knowledge from design science, building sciences, environmental science and engineering is creating a platform for the emergence of the digital city – another major technology contributor to the delivery of sustainable built environments. Building information models and city-information models provide the basis for real-time visualization and automated eco-efficiency performance assessments of virtual designs for buildings, city precincts and urban infrastructure systems, from concept stage to detailed design specification, through construction and into operation and management, providing an ability to evaluate performance prior to and post construction. The order of magnitude of savings in time, capital and life-cycle cost and environmental performance of buildings and urban infrastructures capable of being delivered via technological change is proving to be significant (Newton *et al.* 2009).

In each of the key urban infrastructure domains it is possible to envision a more resilient and sustainable future, based on innovative technology platforms that currently exist across the three horizons of urban technical innovation. Those familiar with attempting to implement technological change will be acutely aware that, to date, the forces opposing technological progress have tended to be stronger than those striving for change. It seems apparent that in each of these domains, institutional change will prove more challenging to achieve than technological change (Geels and Schot 2010; Newton 2012).

9.4 Transition to eco-city

Transition to eco-city is a twenty-first-century challenge. It is a transition yet to be figured out. It involves a more complex and multi-faceted process than the socio-technical transformation of specific urban infrastructures. The performance criteria established for eco-cities extend beyond technological innovation and environmental sustainability to include competitiveness and productivity, liveability, social inclusion and resilience. At yet finer granularity, an eco-city needs to reflect such features as walkability, optimal mix of land uses, small ecological footprint, healthy population and environment, strong local economy with national and global connectivity and so on. There is an extensive set of aspirations for the eco-city (see Figure 9. 4).

Clearly, the multiple processes required for transition to eco-city require a step change in innovation. In listing key processes associated with sustainable urban development, examples are increasingly emerging of instances where a particular jurisdiction or organization has advanced thinking and practice beyond that which could be classed as 'business as usual'. Examples of innovation in key arenas of urban planning and management are summarized in Box 9.1. Taken together, these provide a process for delivering the future eco-city. In an increasingly networked

Figure 9.4 Principal features of an eco-city Source: Ecocity Builders (2012)

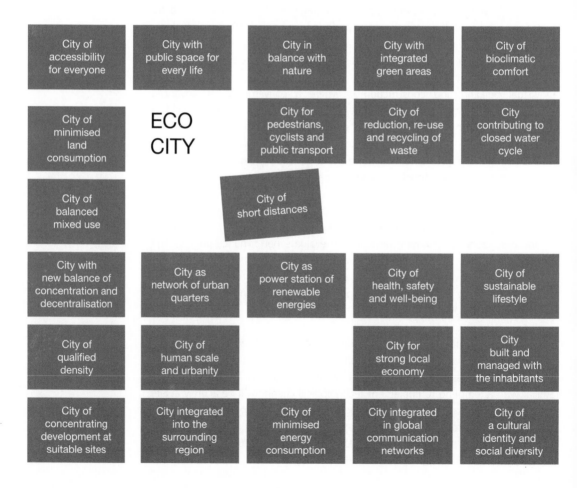

| City of accessibility for everyone | City with public space for every life | City in balance with nature | City with integrated green areas | City of bioclimatic comfort |

ECO CITY

City for pedestrians, cyclists and public transport

City of reduction, re-use and recycling of waste

City contributing to closed water cycle

City of minimised land consumption

City of balanced mixed use

City of short distances

City with new balance of concentration and decentralisation

City as network of urban quarters

City as power station of renewable energies

City of health, safety and well-being

City of sustainable lifestyle

City of qualified density

City of human scale and urbanity

City for strong local economy

City built and managed with the inhabitants

City of concentrating development at suitable sites

City integrated into the surrounding region

City of minimised energy consumption

City integrated in global communication networks

City of a cultural identity and social diversity

world, the identification and 'posting' of such instances of innovation and their rapid communication via the internet as well as face-to-face contacts provide some basis for optimism concerning the emergence of more resilient and sustainable cities in the twenty-first century.

Box 9. 1   Innovation arenas for emerging eco-cities

- *Principles* for sustainable urban development (e.g. *Melbourne Principles for Sustainable Cities*, http://www.iclei.org/fileadmin/user_upload/documents/ANZ/WhatWeDo/TBL/Melbourne_Principles.pdf);
- *Envisioning* what a particular city should become: a realistic image of a not too distant future (e.g. Sustainia's *Guide to Copenhagen 2025* (2012), http://issuu.com/sustainia_me/docs/cph2025?mode=window&backgroundColor=%23222222); narratives of a possible future capable of capturing the imagination and support of a metropolitan population;
- *Leadership* by individuals with a capacity to be change agents (e.g. as represented by the C40 Cities Leadership Group, http://live.c40cities.org/);
- *Urban policy* which conveys an aspirational public statement, usually by the government of the day, concerning long-term objectives for cities (e.g. Council of Australian Governments, http://www.coag.gov.au/coag_meeting_outcomes/2009-12-07/index.cfm#cap_city_strat);
- *Urban governance* operates within a spectrum of political systems ranging from pluralist liberal democracies to one-party states, and across different tiers ranging from national to local. Decision-making arrangements will vary substantially, but 'successful' cities have been found to reflect a common set of themes: high and sustained level of public engagement, consistency of strategic direction, collaboration across different sectors of society, regional cooperation and a political will for cooperation (Kelly 2010);
- *Strategic urban planning* which articulates the spatial form and functioning of a city considered capable of best delivering future competitiveness, liveability, sustainability and social inclusion (e.g. as represented in *Metro Vancouver Regional Growth Strategy*, http://www.metrovancouver.org/planning/development/strategy/Pages/designations.aspx);
- *Twenty-first-century information platform and planning/design tools* enabling visualization and real-time performance assessment during design, construction and management based on digital information platforms (e.g. Esri 2012);
- *Implementation processes*, where most urban planning comes unstuck (Mees 2011); a *traditional* planning process can be represented as: top-down (elites) → impose plan → community resistance (slow or no progress) versus alternative *new* process characterized as: multi-level (multi-actor) → engagement → consensus plan (implementable)

(Roggema 2012); new stakeholder engagement models and tools are needed (Newton *et al.* 2012a);

- *Exemplars* are evidence-based best-practice innovations capable of broad replication (e.g. Ecocities Emerging, http://www.ecocitybuilders.org/ecocity-newsletter/; Living Labs Global, http://www.livinglabs-global.com/; Pecan Street Inc., http://www.pecanstreet.org/; US Institute for Urban Design, http://www.spontaneousinterventions.org); *replicable* exemplars are the holy grail;

- *Measurement and monitoring.* Peter Drucker is credited with the proposition that 'what gets measured improves'. It is critical to assess how cities are performing against eco-city targets established in urban policies or strategic plans (e.g. Sustainable Seattle, http://www.sustainableseattle.org/programs/regional-indicators; State of Australian Cities 2011, http://www.infrastructure.gov.au/infrastructure/mcu/soac_files/00_INFRA1267_MCU_SOAC_2011_FA1.pdf).

9.5 Conclusion

Accelerating the critical connections across the major platforms capable of delivering sustainable and resilient urban development in the twenty-first century – a green economy, green infrastructure and green cities – is an immediate challenge. Kicking hard decisions down the road yet again into the next decade will only serve to confirm that the most recent tranche of warnings from climate scientists and global financial institutions alike (e.g. Global Climate Project 2012; World Bank 2012) of a +4°C world by 2100 are most likely to eventuate. Whether the prospect of consigning future generations to a planet that would be unrecognizable to those reading this book in 2014 is unacceptable remains uncertain in the context of current behaviour in politics, business and society. Sufficient blueprints, roadmaps and pathways exist to guide the necessary transitions. Less clear are the tipping points and catalysts required for decisive action and change.

Acknowledgements

The section of this chapter relating to urban technology innovation has been revised from that published in the *Journal of Urban Technology*, 19(1) (2012), pp. 81–102, with permission from Taylor and Francis.

Funding support for writing this chapter has been provided by Australian Research Council Discovery Project DP110100543: *Green Shoots? Exploring the Genesis and Development of a Green Economy in Australia.*

References

ABARE. 2010. *Energy in Australia 2010*, Department of Resources, Energy and Tourism, Canberra, http://www.abare.gov.au/publications_html/energy/energy_10/energyAUS2010.pdf.

ATSE and NAEK. 2012. *Australia Korea Green Growth: Third International Workshop: Report*, Australian Academy of Technological Sciences and Engineering and National Academy of Engineering of Korea, Seoul.

Brown, R., Keath, N. and Wong, T. 2009. 'Urban water management in cities: Historical, current and future regimes', *Water Science and Technology*, 59(5), pp. 847–855.

Daly, H. 1996. *Beyond Growth: The Economics of Sustainable Development*, Beacon, Boston.

Ecocity Builders. 2012. 'Ecocities emerging: To support humanity's transition into the Ecozoic Era', July, http://archive.constantcontact.com/fs072/1100594362471/archive/1110372977492.html.

Elder, J. 2009. 'Preparing Americans for a green economy', *Sustainability*, 2(4), pp. 240–242.

ESRI. 2012. GeoDesign Summit, Redlands, California, http://video.esri.com/series/66/2012-geodesign-summit.

Fulai, S. 2009. 'What does it take for a transition towards a green economy?', paper presented to the 3rd OECD World Forum on Statistics, Knowledge and Policy: Charting Progress, Building Visions, Improving Life, Busan, Korea, 27–30 October, http://www.oecd.org/dataoecd/39/48/43836043.pdf.

Geels, F. and Schot, J. 2010. 'The dynamics of transitions: A socio-technical perspective', in J. Grin, J. Rotmans and J. Schot (eds), *Transitions to Sustainable Development: New Directions in the Study of Long Term Transformative Change*, Routledge, New York.

Global Climate Project. 2012. *Carbon Budget and Trends 2012*, http://www.globalcarbonproject.org.

Hargroves, K. and Smith, M. H. 2005. *The Natural Advantage of Nations: Business Opportunities, Innovation and Governance in the 21st Century*, Earthscan, London.

Kelly, J.-F. 2010. *Cities: Who Decides?*, Grattan Institute, Melbourne, http://grattan.edu.au/static/files/assets/69a79996/052_cities_who_decides.pdf.

Krugman, P. 2010. 'The finite world', *New York Times*, 26 December.

Major Cities Unit. 2011. *State of Australian Cities 2011*, Major Cities Unit, Department of Infrastructure and Transport, Canberra, http://www.infrastructure.gov.au/infrastructure/mcu/soac_files/00_INFRA1267_MCU_SOAC_2011_FA1.pdf.

Mees, P. 2011. Who killed Melbourne 2030?, *Papers of the State of Australian Cities Conference, Melbourne.*

Melbourne Energy Institute. 2010. *The Future of Renewable Energy in Australia*, University of Melbourne, Melbourne.

Newton, P. W. 1995. 'Changing places? Households, firms and urban hierarchies in the information age', in J. Brotchie, M. Batty, E. Blakeley, P. Hall and P. W. Newton (eds), *Cities in Competition: Productive and Sustainable Cities for the 21st Century*, Longman Cheshire, Melbourne.

Newton, P. W. (ed.). 1997. *Re-Shaping Cities for a More Sustainable Future: Exploring the Link between Urban Form, Air Quality, Energy and Greenhouse Gas Emissions*, Research Monograph No. 6, Australian Housing and Urban Research Institute, Melbourne.

Newton, P. W. 2007. 'Horizon 3 planning: Meshing liveability with sustainability', *Environment and Planning B: Planning and Design*, 34(4), pp. 571–575.

Newton, P. W. (ed.). 2008. *Transitions: Pathways towards Sustainable Urban Development in Australia*, Springer, Dordrecht.

Newton, P. W. 2010. 'Beyond greenfields and brownfields: The challenge of regenerating Australia's greyfield suburbs', *Built Environment*, 36(1), pp. 81–104.

Newton, P. W. (ed.) 2011. *Urban Consumption*, CSIRO Publishing, Melbourne.

Newton, P. W. 2012. 'Liveable *and* sustainable? Socio-technical challenges for 21st century cities', *Journal of Urban Technology*, 19(1), 82–101.

Newton, P. W. and Newman, P. 2013. 'The geography of solar photo voltaics (PU) and a new low carbon urban transition theory', *Sustainability*, 5, pp. 2537–56.

Newton, P. W., Brotchie, J. F. and Gipps, P. G. 1997. *Cities in Transition: Changing Economic and Technological Processes and Australia's Settlement System*, State of the Environment Technical Papers Series (Human Settlements), Department of the Environment, Canberra, http://www.environment.gov.au/soe/1996/publications/technical/pubs/cities.pdfNewton et al. 2009.

Newton, P. W., Hampson, K. and Drogemuller, R. (eds). 2009. *Technology, Design and Process Innovation in the Built Environment*, Taylor and Francis, Abingdon.

Newton, P. W., Newman, P., Glackin, S. and Trubka, R. 2012a. 'Greening the greyfields: Unlocking the redevelopment potential of the middle suburbs in Australian cities', *Proceedings of the International Conference on Urban Planning and Regional Development*, Venice, 14–15 November.

Newton, P. W., Pears, A., Whiteman, J. and Astle, R. 2012b. 'The energy and carbon footprints of housing and transport in Australian urban development: Current trends and future prospects', in R. Tomlinson (ed.), *The Unintended City*, CSIRO Publishing, Melbourne.

Newton, P. W. and Tucker, S. N. 2010. 'Hybrid buildings: Towards zero carbon housing', *Architectural Science Review*, 53(1), pp. 95–106.

OECD. 2011. *Towards Green Growth*, OECD Publishing, Paris.

Phillimore, J. 2001. 'Schumpeter, Schumacher and the greening of technology', *Technology Analysis and Strategic Management*, 13(1), pp. 23–37.

Roggema, R. 2012. *Swarming Landscapes: Advances in Global Climate Change Research*, Springer, Dordrecht.

UN DESA. 2011. *World Economic and Social Survey 2011: The Great Green Technological Transformation*, United Nations Department of Economic and Social Affairs, New York.

UN DESA, UNEP and UNCTAD. 2012. *The Transition to a Green Economy: Benefits, Challenges and Risks from a Sustainable Development Perspective*, United Nations, New York.

UNEP. 2008. *Global Green New Deal: Environmentally Focused Investment Historic Opportunity for 21st Century Prosperity and Job Generation*, United Nations Environment Programme, London and Nairobi, 22 October.

UNEP. 2011. *Towards a Green Economy: Pathways to Sustainable Development and Poverty Eradication*, United Nations Environment Programme, Paris, http://www.unep.org/greeneconomy/greeneconomyreport/tabid/29846/default.aspx.

UN Millennium Ecosystem Assessment. 2005. *Living beyond Our Means: Natural Assets and Human Well-being*, Island Press, Washington, DC.

Wong, T. and Brown, R. 2010. 'Water sensitive urban design', in R. Q. Grafton and K. Hussey (eds), *Water Resources Planning and Management*, Cambridge University Press, Cambridge.

Wood, T. and Edis, T. 2012. *No Easy Choices: Which Way to Australia's Energy Future?*, Grattan Institute, Melbourne, http://grattan.edu.au/static/files/assets/b2ea3306/124_energy_no_easy_choices.pdf.

World Bank. 2012. *4° Turn Down the Heat: Why a 4°C Warmer World Must Be Avoided*, World Bank, Washington, DC.

CHAPTER 10

Planning for biophilic urbanism

The creative strategies cities can take to better integrate nature into urban life

Timothy Beatley

10.1 Introduction

Biophilic cities are cities where nature is abundant, where residents have abundant connections with the natural world, and where there is a curiosity about and caring for the other forms of life that co-inhabit urban environments. Harvard biologist E.O. Wilson is responsible for popularizing the concept of biophilia and argues strongly that we are hard-wired to need contact with nature. As Wilson says, 'the human species has grown up with nature' (quoted in Kellert and Finnegan, 2012; see also Wilson, 1984, and Kellert, Heerwegen, and Mador, 2008). It is not something that is optional, but essential to health, happiness and meaningful lives, it increases our resilience to shocks, stressors and disturbances in the urban system. And the nature we need must be all around us – not something to be visited occasionally on holiday, not a remote and distant nature, but a nearby nature, a nature close to where we live our daily lives. This need for daily connection with the natural world bumps often directly against the processes of urbanization and city building – as the planet becomes ever more urban, a significant challenge exists to find creative ways to integrate that nature into urban form and metropolitan settings.

What constitutes a 'biophilic city' remains an open question. It is a bio-diverse city and a city of abundant nature in close proximity to the urban population. But as Box 10.1 indicates, biophilic urbanism requires more – it holds that urbanites must be actively engaged in that nature; they must care about it, and be knowledgeable about it, and cities must have sufficient resources and institutions to support these nature connections and to foster them actively. More on that later.

The Biophilic Cities Project at the University of Virginia, with funding from the Summit Foundation and George Mitchell Fund, has begun to explore what cities around the world have done, and are doing, to protect and restore nature in urban environments and the different ways in which urban biophilia is being expressed and pursued in these places (though not necessarily using that term; see the Biophilic Cities Project, http://biophiliccities.org/). There are a few important themes and early lessons that emerge from looking at what cities have been doing so far.

Box 10.1   Some important dimensions of biophilic cities (and some possible indicators thereof)

Biophilic conditions and infrastructure

- Percentage of population within a few hundred feet or meters of a park or greenspace.
- Percentage of city land area covered by trees or other vegetation.
- Number of green design features (e.g. green rooftops, green walls, rain gardens).
- Extent of natural images, shapes, forms employed in architecture, and seen in the city.
- Extent of flora and fauna (e.g. species) found within the city.

Biophilic behaviors, patterns, practices, lifestyles

- Average portion of the day spent outside.
- Visitation rates for city parks.
- Percent of trips made by walking.
- Extent of membership and participation in local nature clubs and organizations.

Biophilic attitudes and knowledge

- Percent of residents who express care and concern for nature.
- Percent of residents who can identify common species of flora and fauna.

Biophilic institutions and governance

- Priority given to nature conservation by local government; percent of municipal budget dedicated to biophilic programs.
- Existence of design and planning regulations that promote biophilic conditions (e.g. mandatory green rooftop requirement, bird-friendly building design guidelines).
- Presence and importance of institutions, from aquaria to natural history museums, that promote education and awareness of nature.
- Number/extent of educational programs in local schools aimed at teaching about nature.
- Number of nature organizations and clubs of various sorts in the city, from advocacy to social groups.

Source: Adapted from Beatley (2011)

10.2 There are many ways in which cities can become more biophilic

One of the key goals of the Biophilic Cities Project is to collect the impressive stories of efforts around the US and the globe to restore and grow nature in cities, and to show the variety of ways in which urban environments can be active places of nature. These efforts can and should occur at every geographical scale, from rooftop (or room) to neighborhood, city, region or bioregion.

Here are just a few examples:

- San Francisco has been innovating in the area of turning small spaces in the city into neighborhood parks. Most recently it has created a permit for creation of 'parklets' or very small parks formed from two to three on-street parking spaces. Already more than twenty parklets have been created, creating new places for neighbors to sit and gather. Similar efforts have included its Street Parks and Pavements to Parks initiatives.
- Vitoria-Gasteiz, the capital of the Basque Country in Spain, is notable for its efforts to create a green ring that circles this compact city, providing significant amounts of restored habitat and nature. The city has also protected an extensive system of forests and natural lands outside the city, which connect to the green ring, and most recently envisioned how nature might be brought into the center of the city through an 'interior green ring'.
- Phoenix has a long and impressive history of setting aside large amounts of land for desert parks, and has recently purchased new parklands to the north of downtown. The city of Scottsdale has protected nearly one-third of its city in desert parkland, with a citizen-run conservancy managing these lands.
- Oslo has designated two-thirds of its area protected forestland (what the Norwegians refer to as 'marka'), and the city has an extensive network of urban nature trails. Its latest ambition is to restore and bring back to the surface the city's eight major rivers that flow (currently mostly in pipes underground) from the forests to the fjord.
- Portland, Oregon, has been a leader in many areas of sustainability, especially in piloting new ways to retain stormwater on site, and to integrate these stormwater features into neighborhoods and the built environment through a network of more than 1000 'green streets' that serve to collect rainwater and slow car traffic.
- Milwaukee, a rustbelt city in Wisconsin, has a history of successfully restoring connections to the Milwaukee River, and is now working to restore the Menominee River. A non-profit Urban Ecology Center recently opened its third branch in the city and educates and provides hands-on nature experiences for thousands of residents.
- Singapore aspires to be a 'City in a Garden' and through the work of the Singapore Parks Board (Nparks) has developed an impressive network of urban parks, tied together through nearly 200 kilometers of Park Connectors, many of them in the form of elevated bridges and walking structures that provide unusual experiences of urban nature. Nparks has formed a Skyrise Greening

branch to help advance green walls, green rooftops and other forms of nature in the vertical building realm.

10.3 Making the case for biophilic urbanism? Multiple objectives are key

One initial important lesson from the cities' studies is the value of emphasizing the many and overlapping benefits and value for cities and urbanites from the protecting and restoring of nature and fostering connections. In the Biophilic Cities Project we have emphasized the emotional and psychological values associated with connections to nature – seeing and experiencing the sights and sounds of nature has clear, direct value in enhancing happiness and wellbeing, but there are also important secondary health and community benefits. Greener, more biophilic neighborhoods help propel residents outdoors, help induce walking and physical activity, and therefore help people overcome the otherwise unhealthy, sedentary conditions of modern life.

There are many other important benefits, too. We know, for instance, that preserving urban forests, wetlands and mountain preserves provides important air and water quality benefits, flood retention, among others, and that the economic values of the ecological services are typically quite large. In some cities the need to adapt to climate change represents an opportunity to advance biophilic urbanism. In Rotterdam, for instance, the city has developed an ambitious strategy to make itself 'climate proof' by 2025. Already this city has strongly pushed for the installation of green rooftops (with a goal of 40,000 square meters a year), as well as other urban greening techniques. (And it is pioneering a very interesting idea of 'water plazas', which serve as new public spaces but also periodically retain flood waters.) Of course, installation of green rooftops has intrinsic value, but proponents in Rotterdam have focused largely on their climate-proofing value to gain support.

Multi-sectoral approaches needed in creating biophilic cities

In many of the emerging biophilic cities we have been studying much of the progress is a function of leadership at the top, often a mayor with political clout and a personal commitment to improving city life and to understanding the essential connections between nature and urban livability. Mayoral leadership has been key in many cities. Important examples have included Mayor Bloomberg in New York, (former) Mayor William Daley in Chicago (and now Rahm Emanuel), and Mayor Antonio R. Villaraigosa of Los Angeles, among others. Mayor Villaraigosa, for instance, has championed a program for planting a million trees in LA, creating a series of new parks in underserved neighborhoods, and efforts to restore the LA river, a currently not-very-natural feature that has at least the potential positively to touch virtually every neighborhood in that city. The importance of visionary mayors like Villaraigosa cannot be overstated, but advancing the agenda of biophilic urbanism will require the efforts of a diverse set of groups and interests, governmental and non-governmental alike, working from both the bottom and the top.

In the cities doing the most to promote nature there is an understanding that it must be multi-sectoral – it is local government but also involves local companies from the business sector as well as many non-governmental organizations and non-profits. In San Francisco, for instance, non-profit organizations such as Nature in the City and PlantSF have been key drivers of change, and have played key roles in promoting new urban nature ideas and initiatives. Partnerships are a key way of moving forward in the best examples of biophilic cities.

Biophilic urbanism will also require joint efforts, coordination and cooperation between the line agencies and offices within a city government, and must extend to agencies that may not immediately understand their missions as involving nature. A positive example can be seen in San Francisco, where the city's public works department has been operating a very interesting program called Street Parks, which offers to neighborhoods the median spaces between roads. One or more street 'stewards' must take on the care and management of these small parks and prepare a detailed plan for their use. The results have in many cases been quite dramatic. One example is La Playa Park, a now quite beautiful garden and gathering space, but a mere 550 feet long and 16 feet wide.

Biophilic urbanism suggests the need to involve a variety of urban constituencies. In Singapore, for instance, some of the most dramatic recent examples of bringing nature into the city have happened in primary schools and hospitals (see, e.g., Beatley, 2012). Each of these greening venues involves its own unique group of users and constituents (e.g. parents, teachers and students in the former; patients, doctors and other care-givers in the latter), and its own special opportunities to tap into the power of nature (e.g. for learning and for healing).

Mandates and incentives are both helpful

The experiences of cities advancing biophilic urbanism so far suggests that there is a role for both regulations and mandates, and various ways to encourage or incentivize including nature in urban planning and development. Our research has uncovered impressive examples of both. Many cities, such as Portland, Oregon, for instance, have implemented density bonuses to encourage green features such as the installation of ecological rooftops and permeable paving. Portland's Eco-Roof Bonus provides such a bonus for the installation of green rooftops (a graduated benefit depending on the percentage of the roof covered by greenery). Many other cities, such as Singapore, provide subsidies and grants for urban greening projects, as well as technical assistance. In some cities there are other helpful financial incentives, such as stormwater fees based on the extent of impervious surface (and thus encouraging permeable surfaces and green features that collect and retain stormwater).

Many cities are now modifying their development codes to mandate green elements. Toronto recently became the first major North American city to require the installation of green rooftops for certain types of buildings (see Beatley, 2011). Seattle, as a further example, has created a Green Spaces Factor that requires new commercial and multi-family structures in designated areas of the city to achieve a minimum score, but leaves to designers and developers how the green and natural elements should be included.

Fostering and facilitating connections with urban nature

Biophilic cities can and must think beyond the obvious ways that existing nature can be provided and new nature created. As stated earlier, it is as much about the engagement of residents, providing opportunities for them to be involved in hands-on learning and education, and fostering a culture of curiosity and wonder, as about the actual nature present. Biophilic urbanism requires more and harder work at getting busy urbanites to make the time for nature and to break away, to a certain degree, from the technology and harried lives that make connections with the natural world difficult.

Examples of such efforts at engagement are many and diverse and include programs such as New York City's parks department's summer camping program (providing opportunities for residents to camp in city parks), 'bio-blitzes', and other opportunities to be involved in citizen-science and school-based nature and gardening initiatives. Each city will have its own unique set of programs and opportunities for engaging urbanites with nature. Having rich and abundant opportunities to be personally and intimately involved in experiencing nature – whether through a birdwatching club, a native plants society, or a hands-on stream clean-up or ecological restoration effort – is a key metric of the biophilic city.

Again, biophilic urbanism is an agenda that should – indeed must – be of importance to many individuals and organizations in a city. While local governments play a key role, other social and economic sectors must play important roles, too. In understanding the progress made in advancing urban biophilia, it is critical to assess the capacity of these non-governmental institutions to support biophilic urbanism. Our partner cities and study cities provide some compelling examples. In Milwaukee, for example, the third branch of the City's Urban Ecology Center has just opened, along the Menominee River, providing new opportunities for the nearby neighborhoods and schools to engage with this river and help repair and restore it. The center's two older branches are very actively visited and their programs are enjoyed by many residents in the city. Last year some 80,000 residents visited or took part in the center's programs and likely this number will increase. Each branch is located in a part of the city where it serves as a kind of ecological anchor, hosting nearby schools, partnering with groups in the neighborhood to provide environmental education, and, in the case of the newest branch, taking over a segment of the Menominee River.

Each city will have its own unique set of biophilic assets and institutions that will help foster connections with nature and build awareness of the local and regional natural environment. In Scottsdale, Arizona (adjacent to the city of Phoenix), one of the most impressive stories of citizen-led urban conservation has been unfolding over the last two decades. Local activism has led to the city purchasing one of the largest pieces of desert ecosystem in any city (now more than 17,000 acres in the McDowell Sonoran Preserve, amounting to roughly one-third of the city's total land area). A unique organization, the McDowell Sonoran Conservancy, was formed to manage and care for this (growing) preserve and trail system, with day-to-day management, maintenance and educational functions now assumed by some 400 trained 'stewards'. They are a dedicated group, ranging in age from fifteen to ninety, and are engaged in every aspect of the care of this amazing environment. It is the desert here, but it could be something else in another city, with the chance to find similarly innovative ways to involve and engage residents.

Governance and funding for biophilic cities

A significant challenge in creating greener, more nature-filled cities is how such efforts will be financed and who will manage and care for these spaces. What amount (or percentage) of a city's annual budget goes towards nature, for instance, and is biodiversity conservation and nature protection and restoration of important elements in the city's main governing documents (e.g. the city's comprehensive or general plan)? Are there major cornerstone institutions in the city (say, a natural history museum or an urban ecology center) that provide essential programs and education? Is there a sufficiently clear mission and resources for line agencies to conserve and protect the nature in a city effectively? These are all important biophilic governance questions.

A major issue in partner city San Francisco, for instance, has recently emerged about the tenuous care given to the city's stock of 670,000 trees. Partly motivated by budget-cutting, the city's public works department has been seeking to shift responsibility for care of many of these trees to private property owners. Almost everyone involved appears to appreciate that the current arrangements do not result in what is best for trees, a concern in a city where the tree canopy is already relatively low when compared to other cities. How to pay for the care and maintenance of the urban forest remains a key question there, and a number of options are currently being considered (see Sabatini, 2012). Interestingly, the city's environment department has devised an innovative approach to funding the planting of new fruit trees. It now imposes a 13 per cent climate mitigation charge on city staff travel, which then goes into a carbon fund which is used to pay for planting of the trees.

Part of the governance question clearly goes back to the question of the adequacy of codes and their support for biophilic qualities in a city. Much of the good work in the cities we have been studying is about working to change regulations and codes so as to make it easier to undertake some of the urban greening steps that neighborhoods and non-governmental organizations would like to see. It may then be just as important for cities carefully to examine how existing policies, programs and codes get in the way.

Several good examples can be cited from study cities. San Francisco has recently undertaken a major rewriting of its zoning and development codes to permit urban agriculture, in particular the commercial production of agriculture in the city. Many other North American cities have taken similar steps – for instance, New York City amended its zoning provisions to make bee-keeping permissible, and Toronto now allows the keeping of chickens.

Equally important is the work cities can do to reform and streamline local permitting systems to facilitate community greening initiatives. In San Francisco, largely through the activism of local non-profit PlantSF, the city created a special sidewalk gardens permit that significantly reduces the cost of obtaining such a permit and makes it much easier to undertake such a project.

10.4 Concluding thoughts

As we become an increasingly urbanized planet there are few design and planning issues more challenging (or pressing) than designing urban environments that provide the density and urban qualities we need while also allowing the contact with nature that we need to be healthy and happy. There are a number of emerging positive examples around the world, from San Francisco to Singapore, that show what is possible. Each city will have its own unique natural context and special opportunities, but they are likely to face similar questions and challenges. What form will urban nature take? What kinds and what amounts will be needed? What projects offer the chance to include more nature? What code changes could facilitate biophilic design (and what changes could remove important obstacles)? And what groups and agencies can be enlisted in the growing of a more biophilic urban culture?

References

Beatley, Timothy. 2011. *Biophilic Cities: Integrating Nature into Urban Design and Planning*, Washington, DC: Island Press.

Beatley, Timothy. 2012. 'Singapore: City in a Garden', *Site/Lines, Journal of the Foundation for Landscape Studies*, Fall, pp. 14–17.

Kellert, Stephen and Bill Finnegan. 2012. *Design for Life*, documentary.

Kellert, Stephen, Judith Heerwegen, and Marty Mador, eds. 2008. *Biophilic Design: The Theory, Science and Practice of Bringing Buildings to Life*, New York: Wiley and Sons.

Sabatini, Joshua. 2012. 'Supervisor Wants to Revisit Issue of Tree Maintenance', *San Francisco Examiner*, September 13. Available at: http://www.sfexaminer.com/local/2012/09/supervisor-wants-revisit-issue-tree-maintenance, accessed October 29, 2012.

Wilson, E.O. 1984. *Biophilia*, Cambridge, MA: Harvard University Press.

CHAPTER 11

City food security

Craig Pearson and Robert Dyball

11.1 Introduction

City food security depends on how a city obtains, distributes and consumes its food. The sustainability and resilience of sourcing, distribution and consumption are fundamental to creating (or, in the future, maintaining) sustainable, resilient cities that have adequate and equitable nutrition and wellbeing. In discussing city food security, there are several perspectives that may be applied, as is appropriate for complex, adaptive, social-ecological systems. These include:

1   *Security of origin.* Consideration of food chains and transformations associated with cities leads to consideration of the security of the origin of foods upon which the city depends. Insecurity can arise from trade embargos, harvest failure or cost factors (e.g. fuel prices) that make food unaffordable or unavailable. Globalization and food price spikes over the past decade have, in this context, led to research on self-sufficiency within a city and its surrounding region (what we will henceforth call a 'city-region'). The perspective of supply chains and origins of supply, and concern with energy expenditure (and carbon pollution) along chains, has also given rise to renewed interest in 'food miles' and urban food production. Together these lead some to advocate regional self-sufficiency or 'food sovereignty'.
2   *Chain security.* Globalization of food supply chains and minimization of storage – the corporate philosophy of 'just-in-time' delivery – give rise to consideration of the vulnerability of delivery systems. Security against chain disruption became topical with governments following recognition of bovine spongioform encephalitis (BSE) in 1985, foot and mouth disease in England in 2001, and terrorism in the United States, also in 2001. However, chain vulnerability applies equally to food supplies that may be disrupted by natural or accidental events such as earthquakes, floods, transport accidents or infrastructure (e.g. rail or shipping) failures.
3   *Consumer nutritional security.* Cities are large and heterogeneous, and health specialists have long identified that there are nutritionally poor areas within them. These are areas where, for example, nutritious fresh food is not available, generally unaffordable or so expensive relative to less healthy alternatives that there is a major disincentive to consume it. Lack of retail outlets, the dominance of fast-food outlets and socio-cultural norms of the local community can all compound this problem. The under-consumption of nutritious food contributes to community health issues such as type II diabetes and obesity, usually within communities least likely to take preventative, as distinct from clinical, action.

The purpose of this chapter is to describe each of these city food security perspectives with a focus on city food security in developed Western economies, such as Australia. While we and colleagues have written on some of the approaches to overcome each of the aspects of insecurity, that is not our primary purpose here.

11.2 Security of origin

It is rare for a city – *sensu stricto* – to be self-sufficient in its food supply, and many depend upon the produce of distant landscapes and farmers. Cities in developing economies where transport is poor (e.g. Lagos) or in politically constrained situations (e.g. Havana) come closest to local self-sufficiency. However, with a broader definition of the city which encompasses peri-urban and small-lot food production, many cities approach self-sufficiency for some foodstuffs, most commonly vegetables and perishable fruits that are high value, high yielding per unit of land, and liable to high costs and wastage in transport.

Self-sufficiency or security may be assessed in terms of a city and its hinterland or region. The 'city-region' perspective is gaining currency through such initiatives as: slow food movements, regional product certification and calls for labeling that disclose 'food miles' from origin to point of sale.

Figure 11.1 presents a simple schema showing sources of food for cities. It illustrates the potential importance of regional supply and likelihood of exporting, processing and importing food grown locally. It also draws attention to the potential importance of food production within the city. City food production provides multiple benefits, of which social and health outcomes may be as important as the supply of food (Pearson *et al.*, 2010). Urban food production, or urban agriculture, is traditionally carried out in household plots (backyards, home gardens), community-organized use of otherwise wasteland (allotments), community gardens and along roadways and rights-of-way. A recent innovation has been the utilization

Figure 11. 1 Simple flow diagram of city food security showing inputs, flows and transformations within a city-region, e.g. Australian Capital Region (shaded) and outputs

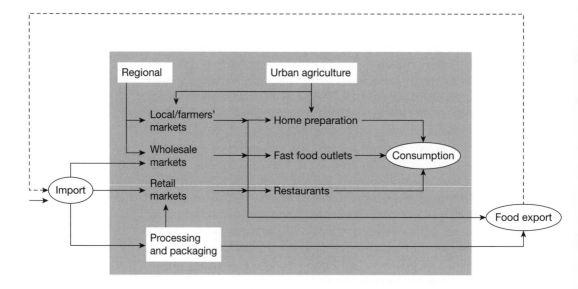

Box 11.1   The Canberra city-region

The Canberra city-region provides an example of the analysis of urban food security. The Australian Capital Region (ACR) comprises the city of Canberra, the 2,400 sq. km jurisdiction of the Australian Capital Territory (ACT) and the surrounding fourteen local government areas of the State of New South Wales. The ACR is a recognized entity for coordinating regional planning and development. It has a total land area of 5.86 million ha, of which 2.4 million ha are grazing lands for sheep and cattle, and a population of 0.55 million, three-quarters of whom reside in Canberra itself or the adjoining NSW city of Queanbeyan. Despite variable and relatively low agricultural productivity – for example, ACR wheat yields are *ca.* 2.0 tonnes per ha – the ACR could be food secure and even export some commodities. However, consumer demand for dietary diversity and processed foods, seasonality of local production, and lack of local storage and processing mean that Canberra relies on well-established, long and relatively insecure food chains: Canberrans' diets comprise largely imported foods, including admixtures of remotely produced and local food that has been exported, processed and then imported. Affluence, relatively high education and short distances to urban food outlets suggest localized nutritional insecurity is likely to be less prevalent in Canberra than in larger cities.

---

of roof gardens, previously developed for vegetation cover (e.g. to mitigate the urban heat island), for food.

In Canberra, Australia's capital, the main staple foods produced in the city-region are sheep meat, beef, cheese, apples and wheat. The population of the ACR could feed itself with these items and generate a considerable surplus (Figure 11.2). This regionally constrained diet would be adequate but monotonous. The inability of

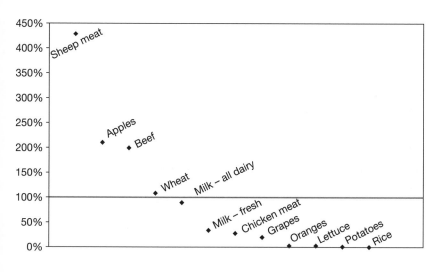

Figure 11.2 Canberra city-region (ACR) percentage of production to consumption in 2005, calculated from whole-weight equivalents: Adapted from Deutsch *et al.* (2009)

the region to produce certain products, such as citrus fruits, could also suggest that there may be health implications of a regionally restricted diet.

More broadly, Australia's five largest cities produce 14 percent of the gross value of their states' agricultural production from just 1.09 percent of the land within and immediately adjacent to them ('peri-urban') and almost 25 percent of total state value from their city-regions (Houston, 2005).

We are unable to obtain data for seasonal flows of food within the ACR or other Australian city-regions, but Figure 11.3 illustrates the seasonality of flows in Kumasi, a large Ghanaian city. Imports vary threefold between seasons. Even during the lean season, almost half the food from the city-region is exported; like Canberra, flows are motivated by markets, storage and processing, not simply by the production and consumption characteristics of the city-region.

In summary, city-region security appears to be a useful concept so long as we recognize that import and export are driven by both biological and socio-economic necessities. Urban food production is gaining publicity, with home-garden and community food-garden groups becoming increasingly popular: in 2012, 53 percent of surveyed Australians indicated that they were growing some of their own food, most commonly fruits and vegetables, with 59 percent of these starting vegetable gardens in the last five years (Australian Food Sovereignty Alliance 2012). Also, rooftop gardens and urban greenhouse production are emerging as new commercial opportunities, and companies are developing businesses based on food production in rooftop greenhouses and direct selling to the public (Figure 11.4). Nonetheless, long and sometimes complex chains are the foreseeable reality. These long chains may be criticized on the basis of the carbon emissions associated with, particularly, truck transport, but the total carbon balance includes the biological productive capacity of the landscape of origin of the food. Against this equation, local land may not be the most suitable for food production. Furthermore, due

Figure 11.3 Flows in and out of Kumasi, showing contributions of imports (from outside the city-region and internationally) and exports, food growth within the region, and within the city (2–14 percent 'urban' agriculture) Adapted from: Cofie *et al.* (2003), citing Gellermann *et al.* (2002)

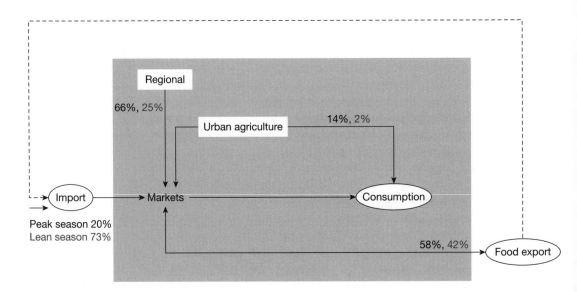

consideration must also be given to consumer behavior. A consumer choosing to drive a 5 km round trip to purchase a single item, such as milk, could result in greater vehicle emissions per food item than the entire transport chain from farm to point of retail.

Figure 11.4 Opportunities for urban food production: community gardens and commercial rooftop greenhouses linked to contractual direct selling to customers Sources: (a) Yue and Khan (2012); (b) Lufa Farms, Montreal (personal communication, 2012)

11.3 Chain security

Food in cities is sold directly from the producer and through retailers (Figure 11.1). Mason and Knowd (2010) provide data for the range of direct marketing for Sydney, Australia, while Chowdhury *et al.* (2005) give an analysis of how traditional chains have simplified and become dominated by supermarkets. Peterson *et al.* (2000) and Bloom and Hinrichs (2011), and many others, provide descriptions of chains and the interrelationships among participants in city food chain logistics.

In Australia, two corporations control 71 percent of full-service supermarket outlets, and although these provide only about 2,285 outlets compared to the 22,110 others in independent stores, convenience stores, delicatessens, butchers, etc. (DAFF, 2012, p. 11), they control the vast bulk of city food availability.

Thus, consideration of the chain logistics for the small number of full-service supermarkets informs chain security of cities. Table 11.1 provides information about the time various items remain in the stores, and within chains. In summary, there is, in Australia, about a month's supply (maybe up to two months) of non-perishable goods in the supply chains, and about fourteen days of perishable goods. Transport operators suggest that about 40 percent of the national road transport fleet moves food, while rail networks move relatively little after the processing stage.

Several consequences arise from these statistics, which might be more exaggerated in Australia – a relatively small, geographically dispersed market in which there is high concentration in two corporate chains – than elsewhere. One is the power of the major food outlets in controlling logistics, and with this comes vulnerability, including potential exposure to corporate pressure over decision-making and prices. Furthermore, industrial disputes, terrorism or natural disasters have potentially greater impact because of this concentration and their 'just in time' supply philosophy that retains relatively little produce within the supply chain. Another is the need to identify critical control points or infrastructures that jeopardize logistical security. For example, floods in Queensland in 2010 showed that Rockhampton, a city of around 75,000, could not be supplied with food from the air when its only road access was cut. The same would apply to larger, but

Table 11.1 Average time food is resident in various stages of the Australian chain

Supply chain stage	Frozen foods combined		Dry foods combined	
	Days per stage	Cumulative days per stage	Days per stage	Cumulative days per stage
Retail distribution center	7 days	7 days	10 days	10 days
	7 days	–14 days	12 days	–22 days
Manufacturer finished foods	5 days	–19 days	29 days	–51 days
Raw materials	27 days	–46 days	29 days	–80 days

Sources: DAFF (2012); Spencer and Kneebone (2012)

equally vulnerable, cities such as Melbourne. Most enterprises and governments recognize the risk but information on logistical security is not used in activities designed to contain that risk (Francis *et al.*, 2008).

A response to the riskiness and lack of resilience in long-distance chains is to recommend internalizing the processing and packaging, undertaking as much production as possible, within a city-region (Figure 11.1). This addresses the risk of reliance on chains, but can raise new risks of its own. For example, if regional and local production fails there may not be reserve markets ready to provide imports to make up the deficit. Expecting that they would begs the question as to how and why such markets and the farmers who supply them would maintain themselves during those periods when their produce was not needed, just to be ready for the occasional periods when it was. Also, as the diagram suggests, warehousing, processing and packaging could move within the region, but any argument for regional infrastructure could lead to duplication of facilities. This could prove expensive and even counterproductive in total material and energy terms. Nevertheless, it is time to debate the benefits, as well as the costs, of regional, appropriate-scale plants that would increase security, reduce greenhouse gas emissions, and more easily treat and recover their own wastes. Urban waste would still occur, but there could be more avenues to recover that waste, such as directly transporting organic material to farms in the region, and harnessing 'free energy' pathways of atmosphere and water to help close nutrient cycles (Pearson, 2007).

11.4 Nutritional security

Nutritional security depends on everyday consumption of a healthy diet. Nutritional insecurity occurs within cities, irrespective of the security of supply and chains. This is because cities are heterogeneous: cultural, economic and social groups aggregate in particular areas, and their attitudes and purchasing power influence the provision of food outlets. In turn, the availability of healthy food at outlets, personal choice and disposable income influence what is purchased – with resulting consequences for nutritional security.

Five to 15 percent of city households in developed countries are food insecure – specifically, short of food – at some time of the year (data from Australia (Booth and Smith, (2001) and USA (Nord *et al.*, 2010) likely reflect differences in definition and survey as much as a real range). In developing economies, insecurity, especially seasonally based inability to access sufficient nutritious food, may be much higher, such as the 47 percent that is cited for Nairobi (Dixon *et al.*, 2007).

Consumption of healthy food is related, not surprisingly, to access to fruit shops and high socio-economic status: access, household income and education are determinants of diet (Burns *et al.*, 2006; Turrell and Kavanagh, 2006). Further, one study has found that people in the poorest socio-economic categories have more than twice the exposure to fast-food outlets than those in the wealthiest category (Reidpath *et al.*, 2002). Proximity to fast-food outlets and advertising are often blamed for poor diets, although research does not always confirm these relationships (Holsten, 2009; Crawford *et al.*, 2010). Programs to encourage local food production in household lots and community gardens and on rooftops may help address 'islands' of food shortage and especially poor nutrition, as well as impacting positively on social cohesion and mental illness (e.g. Pearson *et al.*, 2010).

While shortage of affordable food is the most sensitive symptom of nutritional insecurity, leading to food riots in 2008 and 2010–2011, at the other extreme a growing percentage of populations suffer from obesity and diabetes. The incidence of these diseases is due to poor diet and is more prevalent as a result of choice among richer society in developing countries and in poorer urban classes in developed economies.

11.5 Conclusion

City-regions are typically not food self-sufficient within their jurisdictional boundaries: they rely on networks/chains to be sustainable (i.e. secure) and resilient (i.e. flexible). This short chapter has drawn attention to the desirability of discussion on two issues arising from the concept of city-region food and security. There is a need for consideration of increased regional infrastructure and the costs and benefits of localized processing. This will include debating the desirability of duplication of, for example, supply routes so as to avoid events such as floods and blockades and to build-in redundancy in infrastructure to improve resilience. Such discussion would have to beware being driven by traditional planning approaches, where redundancy is often associated with inefficiency, while also being aware that these are large material, energy and financial investments. The second issue involves a call for greater awareness of vulnerability and identification of weak points in city food chains. Again, discussion on this issue needs to balance the security that localized production may provide with the vulnerability that could arise from a radical disconnect with more extended systems. Such a proposal also raises the ethical issue of its consequences for the farmers who manage these for food export to cities, and the ecological consideration of which landscapes are best suited to being farmed.

In terms of nutritional security, cities are heterogeneous in terms of food availability and affordability, and the quality of the food that is on offer. This increases social diseases and societal costs. Programs to encourage local food production – urban agriculture – and fresh food markets will improve nutritional security, provide social and health co-benefits, and provide resilience in the city food supply chains. In addition to these benefits, there are more intangible outcomes in the form of awareness of, and concern for, the origin of food and the health and wellbeing of the people and landscapes that provide it, wherever on the scale of local to global that might be.

Risks in supply, chain and nutritional security within cities will increase with increasing global population, urbanization and climate change. Australia, for example, has experienced an escalation of city food isolation due to fires and floods in 2011 and 2013. These increase the likelihood of greater fluctuations in consumption of healthy food and thereby challenge the sustainability of urban society. There is a need for debate and action, simplistically to make origins more sustainable, chains more resilient, and nutritional access more equitable. This will particularly involve local governments, emergency service agencies, large logistics and retail companies, and city neighborhoods. As Pearson (2012) pointed out with respect to minimizing food waste, action is most likely to arise from those who have most to gain from change.

References

Australian Food Sovereignty Alliance. 2012. Awareness of food security amongst the Australian adult population. http://www.australianfoodsovereigntyalliance. org/wp-content/uploads/2012/07/20120701-Report-Public-Awareness-of-Food-Security.pdf.

Bloom, C.D., Hinrichs, C.C. 2011. Moving local food through conventional system infrastructure: value chain framework comparisons and insights. *Renewable Agriculture & Food Systems*, 26, 13–24.

Booth, S., Smith, A. 2001. Food security and poverty in Australia: challenges for dieticians. *Australian Journal of Nutrition & Dietetics*, 58, 150–156.

Burns, C., Bentley, R., Thornton, L., Kavanagh, A. 2006. Reduced food access due to lack of money, inability to lift and lack of access to a car for food shopping: a multilevel study in Melbourne, Australia. *Public Health Nutrition*, 9, 375–383.

Chowdhury, S. K., Gulati, A., Gambira-Said, E. 2005. The rise of supermarkets and vertical relationships in the Indonesian food value chain: causes and consequences. *Asian Journal of Agriculture & Development*, 2, 39–48.

Cofie, O.O., Veenhuizen, R. van, Drechsel, P. 2003. Contribution of urban and peri-urban agriculture to food security in sub-Saharan Africa. Africa Session of 3rd WWF, Kyoto.

Crawford, D.A., Timperio, A.F., Salmon, J.A., Baur, L., Giles-Corte, B., Roberts, R.J., Jackson, M.L., Andrianopoulos, N., Ball, K. 2010. Neighborhood fast food outlets and obesity in children and adults: a CLAN study. *Preventive Medicine*, 53, 57–60.

DAFF. 2012. *Resilience in the Australian food supply chain*. Canberra: DAFF.

Deutsch, L., Dumaresq, D., Dyball, R., Matsuda, H., Porter, J., Reenberg, A.,Takeuchi, K. 2009. Global food flows and urban food security: case studies from three IARU cities. *IOP Conference Series: Earth Environmental Science*, 6(51). doi: 10.1088/1755-1307/6/51/512004.

Dixon, J., Omwega, A.M., Friel, S., Curns, C., Donati, K., Carlisle, R. 2007. The health equity dimensions of urban food systems. *Journal of Urban Health*, 84, 118–129.

Donati, K., Taylor, C., Pearson, C.J. 2013. Local food and dietary diversity: farmers' markets and community gardens in Melbourne, Australia, pp. 326–35. In J. Fanzo, D. Hunter, T. Borelli and F. Mattei (eds), *Diversifying Food and Diets*. London: Routledge.

Francis, M., Simons, D., Bourlakis, M. 2008. Value chain analysis in the UK beef foodservice sector. *Supply Chain Management: An International Journal*, 13, 83–91.

Gellermann, J., Cofie, O.O., Drechsel, P., Gyiele, L. 2002. Rural–urban food flows and urban food supply in Ghana. Regional Workshop on Urban Policy Implications of Enhancing Food Security in African Cities, UN HABITAT, FAO, IDRC and SIUPA, Nairobi.

Holsten, J.E. 2009. Obesity and the community food environment: a systematic review. *Public Health Nutrition*, 12, 397–405.

Houston, P. 2005. Re-valuing the fringe: some findings on the value of agricultural production in Australia's peri-urban regions. *Geographical Research*, 43, 209–223.

122 Craig Pearson & Robert Dyball

Mason, D., Knowd, I. 2010. The emergence of urban agriculture: Sydney, Australia. *International Journal of Agricultural Sustainability*, 8, 62–71.

Nord, M., Coleman-Jensen, A., Andrews, M., Carlson, S. 2010. Household food security in the United States, 2009. USDA Economic Research Report No. 108.

Pearson, C.J. 2007. Regenerative, semi-closed systems: a priority for twenty-first-century agriculture. *Bioscience*, 57, 409–418.

Pearson, C.J. 2012. A fresh look at the roots of food insecurity. In: Rayfuse, R., Weisfelt, N. (eds), *The challenge of food security*. Cheltenham: Edward Elgar.

Pearson, L.J., Pearson, L., Pearson, C.J. 2010. Sustainable urban agriculture: stocktake and opportunities. *International Journal of Agricultural Sustainability*, 8, 7–19.

Peterson, J., Cornwell, F., Pearson, C.J. 2000. *Chain stocktake of some Australian agricultural and fishing industries*. Australia: Bureau of Rural Science.

Reidpath, D.D., Burns, C., Garrard, J., Mahoney, M., Townsend, M. 2002. An ecological study of the relationship between social and environmental determinants of obesity. *Health Place*, 8, 141–145.

Ryan, S. 2011. *Buying choices for a more sustainable Canberra: report to the Commissioner for Sustainability & Environment*. Canberra: ACT Government.

Spencer, S., Kneebone, M. 2012. *Foodmap: an analysis of the Australian food supply chain*. Canberra: DAFF.

Turrell, G., Kavanagh, A.M. 2006. Socio-economic pathways to diet: modeling the association between socio-economic position and food purchasing behavior. *Public Health Nutrition*, 9, 375–383.

Yue, A., Khan, R. 2012. Culture. In Pearson, C.J. (ed.), *2020: Vision for a Sustainable Society*. Melbourne: Melbourne Sustainable Society Institute, University of Melbourne.

CHAPTER 12

Resilient and sustainable urban transport

Peter Newman

12.1 Introduction

Transport is the most fundamental infrastructure for a city as it creates the primary form of the city (Newman and Kenworthy, 1999). Resilient cities have a range of characteristics but must include more sustainable transport systems or else they will not work for long. A city's resilience is increased by reducing its use of fossil fuels, as well as through reduced urban sprawl and reduced dependence on expensive and highly vulnerable cars and their associated infrastructure (Newman, Beatley and Boyer, 2009). This is the goal but how do we get there?

Cities, neighbourhoods and regions are increasingly being designed to use energy sparingly by offering walkable, transit-oriented options, more recently supplemented by vehicles powered by renewable energy. The agenda for large cities now is to have more sustainable transport options so as to reduce traffic, as a contribution towards reducing greenhouse gases by 80 per cent by at least 2050, in line with the global agenda set through the International Panel on Climate Change. For many cities, a reduction of car use is not yet on the agenda, though there are signs that all cities in the developed world have peaked in their car use per capita and are already rapidly growing in their sustainable transport (Newman and Kenworthy, 2011a). For example, in Sydney between 2006/7 and 2010/11 there was a decline in per capita car use and total traffic grew by only 1 per cent, yet trains grew 13 per cent, buses 9 per cent, and walking and cycling both 6 per cent.

Developing cities are growing very fast in transit as they build new transit systems (Newman, Glazebrook and Kenworthy, forthcoming). They may also be plateauing in their traffic growth, despite the rapid recent growth in car ownership. However, these cities have much greater density and so much less road space per capita, so they will reach a limit on their car use growth much sooner than low-density cities such as those in Australia and the US (Newman, Glazebrook and Kenworthy, forthcoming).

Resilient and sustainable cities are those that can seriously reduce their ecological footprint whilst enhancing their liveability. In order to do this, it is necessary to manage the growth of cars and trucks and their associated fossil fuel consumption.

Figure 12.1, which shows the variations in private transport fuel use across eighty-four cities, illustrates that there are very large differences in how cities use cars and petroleum fuels (Kenworthy and Laube, 2001). A number of studies have shown that these variations have little to do with climate, culture or politics, and even income is very poorly correlated, but they have a lot to do with the physical

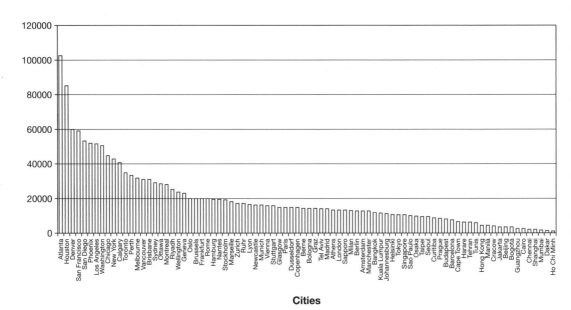

Cities

Figure 12.1 Private passenger transport energy use per person in selected cities, 1995 Source: Kenworthy and Laube (2001)

planning decisions that are made in those cities (Newman and Kenworthy, 1999; Kenworthy *et al.*, 1999). There is debate about the relative importance of urban planning to reduce car use and greenhouse gases, though within the profession there is increasing awareness that sustainable transport will happen only if much greater attention is paid to: urban form and density; infrastructure priorities (especially the relative commitment to public transport compared to cars); and street planning, especially provision for pedestrians and cyclists as part of sustainable mobility management. These issues are addressed further in the remainder of this chapter.

12.2 Urban form and density planning

High-density city centres, like Barcelona (the densest city in Europe) or Hong Kong (one of the densest in Asia), have most destinations within a short walk or they can have highly effective public transport opportunities due to the concentration of people near rail stations. If urban densities are generally lower, but higher along corridors, it is still feasible to have a good transit system, as in most European cities. If, however, low densities are the dominant feature of an entire city, then most activity needs to be based around cars, as they alone can enable people to reach their destinations in a reasonable time. Figure 12.2 shows how cities vary in their fuel use with density.

Public transport in low-density cities like Atlanta and Houston finds it hard to be competitive, as there are just not enough people to justify timely services. Services will always be possible in such areas but the denser the places served, the more viable they become, as density is a multiplier (Newman and Kenworthy, 2006). Most low-density cities are now trying to increase their densities in order to reduce their car dependence (see Newman, Beatley and Boyer, 2009) and the first evidence that

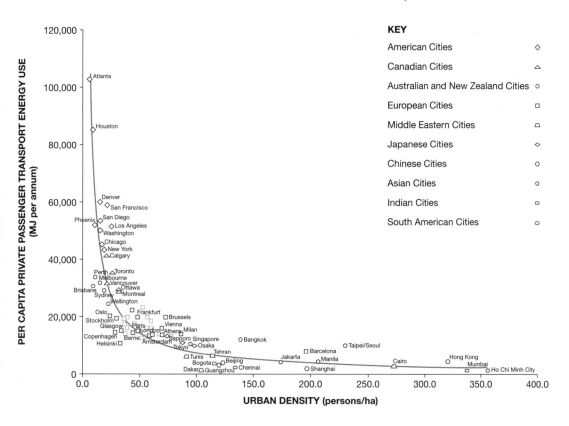

Figure 12.2
Relationship between
energy use and urban
density in the world's
cities
Source: Newman and
Kenworthy (1999)

densities are going up after a century of decline is becoming apparent (Newman and Kenworthy, 2011a). This is being driven by younger people wanting to be in more urban areas; in Sydney, for example, between 2001 and 2011 the inner area grew 15 per cent, the middle suburbs grew 12 per cent and the outer suburbs grew just 7 per cent.

Density is a major tool available to city planners (Newman and Kenworthy, 2006). It is best used where a city has good transit or wants to build transit, as the resulting Transit Oriented Developments (TODs) can reduce car use per capita among its residents by half and save households around 20 per cent of their income, as they have on average one less car, and often none (Cervero, 2008). TODs are thus an affordable housing strategy as well. In the US, according to a study by Ewing *et al.* (2007), shifting 60 per cent of new growth to compact patterns would reduce carbon dioxide emissions by 85 million metric tonnes annually by 2030. TODs reduce ecological footprints of cities and undermine the kind of car-based sprawl that eats into the green agenda. Thus a TOD strategy can enable a city to put in place a clear urban growth boundary and to build a 'green wall' for agriculture, recreation, biodiversity and other natural systems.

If cities are dense, as in many developing countries, but lack adequate public transport and allow too much traffic to develop in their streets, then they can easily develop dysfunctional transport systems. However, their density will always enable them to provide viable public transport solutions if they invest in them, whereas low-density cities are always struggling to provide other options. High density facilitates easier non-car-based access, but it can also mean much greater congestion whenever vehicles are used. If the vehicles in these confined spaces use poorly maintained diesel engines, then serious air pollution can result (Newton and Manins, 1999). Cities need to be very serious about managing the source of such emissions; for example, in most large Indian cities that have switched to CNG in their auto-rickshaw fleets, dramatic air quality improvements have followed (see Salter *et al.*, 2011; Jain, 2004; Rosencranz and Jackson, 2002; UN Habitat, 2009).

12.3 Infrastructure priorities and transit planning

The 'transit to traffic' ratio measures how effective public transport is in competing with the car in terms of speed. The best European and Asian cities for transit have the highest ratio of transit to traffic speeds and have achieved this invariably with fast rail systems (Kenworthy, 2008). Rail systems are faster in every city in the study sample by 10–20 kph over bus systems that, in turn, rarely average over 20 to 25 kph. Busways can be quicker than traffic in car-saturated cities, but in lower-density car-dependent cities, it is important to use the extra speed of rail to establish an advantage over cars in traffic. This is one of the key reasons why railways are being built in over 100 US cities and, in many other cities, modern rail is now seen as the solution for reversing the proliferation of the private car (Newman, Glazebrook and Kenworthy, forthcoming). Rail is also important because it has a density-inducing effect around stations, which can help to provide the focused centres so critical to overcoming car dependence. Rail is also electric, which reduces vulnerability to oil.

Across the world, cities are building modern electric rail systems at vastly increasing rates, as they simultaneously address the challenges of fuel security, decarbonizing the economy in the context of addressing climate change, reducing traffic congestion sustainably, and creating productive city centres. The trend towards fast electric rail in cities is now being called a 'mega trend' (Rubin, 2009). Chinese cities have moved from their road-building phase to building fast, modern rail across the nation. Eighty-two Chinese cities are building metros as well as significant intercity fast rail (Dingding, 2008). Beijing and Shanghai now have the world's biggest metros. Shanghai's now covers 80 per cent of the city and carries 8 million people every day. It was built in just over a decade.

In India fourteen cities are building metros. Delhi and Chenai have begun the first phase of modern electric metro rail systems, which have considerably boosted both cities' pride and belief in the future. The 250 km rail system in Delhi is being built in various stages and will enable 60 per cent of the city to be within fifteen minutes' walking distance of a station (Jain, 2008).

In Perth, Australia, a 172 km modern electric rail system has been built over the past twenty years, with stunning success in terms of patronage. The newest section runs 80 km to the south and attracts 70,000 passengers a day, whereas the bus system carried just 14,000 a day. The difference is that the train has a top speed of

130 kph and averages around 90 kph, so the trip takes just 48 minutes instead of over an hour by car. London, especially with its congestion tax, which is hypothecated into the transit system, and Paris have both shown European leadership in managing the car (see Newman, Beatley and Boyer, 2009). In central London, after a decision was made to prioritize transit and biking over cars, traffic began to fall. It fell by 19 per cent between 2000 and 2009; the number of cars owned in the area peaked in 1990 and has fallen by 37 per cent since 2000. Supporters of 'peak-car' theory see a future in which inner cities like London are given over to pedestrians, cyclists and public transport, and café culture replaces car culture (Pank, 2012).

While greening buildings, developing renewable fuel sources and creating more walkable communities are critical elements of resilient infrastructure in the sustainable transport city, investing in viable, accessible transit systems is the most important component for them to become resilient to waning oil sources and to minimize the contribution of urban areas to climate change. Transit saves oil and helps restructure a city so that it can begin the exponential reduction in oil and car use so necessary for a sustainable future (Newman, Kenworthy and Glazebrook, 2008).

12.4 Street planning and mobility management

If city builders construct freeways, car dependence quickly follows. This is because the extra speed of freeways enables a city to spread outwards quickly into lower-density land uses as the freeway rapidly becomes the preferred option. If, on the other hand, a city does not build freeways but prefers to emphasize transit, it can enable its streets to become an important part of a sustainable transport system. Streets can be designed to favour pedestrians and cyclists, and wherever this is done, cities like London invariably discover that they become much more attractive and business-friendly (Gehl and Gemzoe, 2000; Gehl et al., 2006).

Sustainable mobility management is about 'streets not roads'; the streets are used for a multiplicity of purposes, not just maximizing vehicle flow. The emphasis is on achieving efficiency by maximizing people movement, not car movement, and on achieving a high level of amenity and safety for all street users. This policy also picks up on the concept of using transport facilities as public space. One of the ways that US and European cities are approaching this is through what are called 'complete streets' or, in the UK, 'naked streets'. This new movement aims to create streets where mobility is managed to favour public transport, walking and cycling, as well as lower-speed traffic. The policy often includes removing all large signs for drivers, which means they automatically slow down: in Kensington High Road in London the traffic accident rate has halved because of this.

Building freeways does not help create a resilient city. It will not help a city save fuel, as each lane rapidly fills, leading to similar levels of congestion that existed before the road was built (Nolan and Lem, 2001; Standing Advisory Committee on Trunk Road Assessment, 1994). Indeed, studies have shown that there is little benefit for cities in terms of congestion when they build freeways. There is no overall correlation between delay per driver and the number of lanes of major roads built per head of population for the twenty largest cities in the US (*Urban Transportation Monitor*, 1999).

Thus, for urban planners, the choices for a more sustainable city are quite stark, though politically they are much harder, as the allure of building more road capacity remains very high. Many cities that have confronted the provision of a freeway have been global leaders in the move towards more sustainable transportation. Copenhagen, Zurich, Portland, Vancouver and Toronto all had to face the cathartic experience of a controversial freeway. After a political confrontation, the freeway options were dropped (see Box 12.1 for further insights). They decided instead to provide other, greener options and hence light rail lines, cycleways, traffic calming and associated urban villages began to emerge. All of these cities had citizen groups that pushed visions for a different, less car-oriented city and a political process was created to achieve their innovations. Similar movements are active in Australia (Newman and Kenworthy, 1999).

Cycle-oriented strategies can be combined with the development of greenways that improve the green agenda and lower the ecological footprint. Enough demonstrations now exist to show that pedestrian and bicycle strategies work dramatically to improve city economies and integrate the green and brown agendas. Pedestrian and bicycle strategies in Copenhagen, most Australian cities, London, New York, San Francisco and Bogota, as well as the dramatic changes in Paris with the Velib bicycle scheme and the growing awareness that it works in cities in the developing world too, are all testament to this new approach to cities (Newman and Kenworthy, 2007).

Box 12.1   Removing freeways?

Freeways have blighted the centres of many cities and today there are cities that are trying to remove them. San Francisco removed the Embarcadero Freeway from its waterfront district in the 1990s after the Loma Prieta earthquake. It took three ballots before consensus was reached, but the freeway has been rebuilt as a friendlier, tree-lined boulevard involving pedestrian and cycle spaces. As in all cases where traffic capacity is reduced, the city has not found it difficult to ensure adequate transport, as most of the traffic just disappears. Regeneration of the land uses in the area has followed this change of transportation philosophy (Gordon, 2005).

Seoul has removed a large freeway from its centre that had been built over a major river. The freeway had become controversial because of its blighting impacts on the built environment as well as the river. After a mayoral contest where the vision for a different kind of city was tested politically, the newly elected mayor began a five-year programme that entailed: dismantling the freeway; rehabilitation of the river; restoration of a historical bridge over the river; restoration and rehabilitation of the river foreshores as a public park; restoration of adjacent buildings; and extension of the underground rail system to help replace the traffic. The project has been very symbolic, as the river is a spiritual source of life for the city. Now other car-saturated Asian cities are planning to replace their central city freeways, too (http://www.metro.seoul.kr/kor2000/chungaehome/en/seoul/2sub.htm/).

Figure 12.3 The restoration of the Cheonggyecheon River in Seoul was possible after the freeway over it was removed
Source: Photograph by Peter Newman

These projects have encouraged other cities to 'think of transportation as public space' (Burwell, 2005, p. 3). With this changed approach to city planning, the small-scale systems of pedestrian movement and cycling become much more important. Pedestrian strategies enable each centre in a city to give priority to the most fundamental of human interactions: the walking-based face-to-face contact that gives human life to a city and, in the process, reduces its ecological footprint.

12.5 Conclusion

Sustainable transport strategies are needed that incorporate:

- quality transit down each main transport corridor which is faster than traffic;
- high-density TODs built around each station;
- pedestrian and bicycle strategies for each centre with cycle links across the city;
- cycling and pedestrian infrastructure as part of all street planning; and
- a green wall growth boundary around the city preventing further urban encroachment.

References

Burwell, D. 2005. 'Way to go! Three simple rules to make transportation a positive force in the public realm', *Making Places*, June.
Cervero, R. 2008. *Effects of TOD on Housing, Parking and Travel,* TCRP Report No. 128, Federal Transit Administration, Washington, DC.
Dingding, X. 2008. 'Blueprint of railways development', *China Daily,* 17 November.
Ewing, R.H., Bartholomew, K., Winkelman, S., Walters, J. and Chen, D. 2007.

Growing Cooler: The Evidence on Urban Development and Climate Change, Urban Land Institute, Washington, DC.

Gehl, J. and Gemzoe, L. 2000. *New City Spaces*, Danish Architectural Press, Copenhagen.

Gehl, J., Gemzoe, L., Kirknaes, S. and Sondergaard, B.S. 2006. *New City Life*, Danish Architectural Press, Copenhagen.

Gordon, R. 2005. 'Boulevard of dreams', *SFGate*, 8 September.

Jain, A.K. 2008. *The Delhi Metro*, Delhi Development Authority, Delhi.

Jain, S. 2004. 'Smog city to clean city: How did Delhi do it?', *Mumbai Newsline*, 26 May.

Johnson, C. (ed.). 2008. *Connecting Cities: India*, Metropolis Congress, Sydney.

Kenworthy, J. 2008. 'An international review of the significance of rail in developing more sustainable urban transport systems in higher income cities', *World Transport Policy and Practice* 14(2): 21–37.

Kenworthy, J. and Laube, F. 2001. *The Millennium Cities Database for Sustainable Transport*, UITP, Brussels.

Kenworthy, J., Laube, F., Newman, P., Barter, P., Raad, T., Poboon, C. and Guia, B. 1999. *An International Sourcebook of Automobile Dependence in Cities, 1960–1990*, University Press of Colorado, Boulder.

Kostoff, S. 1991. *The City Shaped*, Thames and Hudson, London.

Lerch, D. 2007. *Post Carbon Cities: Planning for Energy and Climate Uncertainty*, Post Carbon Press, Portland, OR.

Mean, M. and Tims, C. 2005. *People Make Places: Growing the Public Life of Cities*, Demos, London.

Michaelson, J. 2005. 'Lessons from Paris', *Making Places*, June.

Newman, P., Beatley, T. and Boyer, H. 2009. *Resilient Cities: Responding to Peak Oil and Climate Change*, Island Press, Washington, DC.

Newman P., Glazebrook, G. and Kenworthy, J. Forthcoming. 'Peak car and the rise and rise of global rail: Why this is happening and what it means for large and small cities', *Transport Reviews*.

Newman, P. and Kenworthy, J. 1999. *Sustainability and Cities: Overcoming Automobile Dependence*, Island Press, Washington, DC.

Newman, P. and Kenworthy, J.R. 2006. 'Urban design and automobile dependence: How much development will make urban centres viable', *Opolis* 2(1): 35–52.

Newman, P. and Kenworthy, J. 2007. 'Greening urban transport', in *State of the World, 2007*, World Watch Institute, Washington, DC.

Newman, P. and Kenworthy, J. 2011a. 'Peak car use: Understanding the demise of automobile dependence', *World Transport Policy and Practice* 17(2): 32–42.

Newman, P. and Kenworthy, J. 2011b. 'The density multiplier: A response to Mees', *World Transport Policy and Practice* 17(3): 32–44.

Newman, P., Kenworthy, J. and Glazebrook, G. 2008. 'How to create exponential decline in car use in Australian cities', *Australian Planner* 45(3): 17–19.

Newton, P. and Manins, P. 1999. 'Cities and air pollution', in Brotchie, J., Newton, P., Hall, P. and Dickey, J. (eds), *East–West Perspectives on 21st Century Urban Development*, Ashgate, Aldershot.

Nolan, R.B. and Lem, L.L. 2001. *A Review of the Evidence for Induced Travel and Changes in Transportation and Environmental Policy in the United States and the United Kingdom*, Centre for Transport Studies, Imperial College, London.

Pank, P. 2012. 'Welcome to the age of the bike: Cyclists "must be first" as car use passes its peak', *The Times*, 6 November.

Revkin, A. 2008. 'Car-free, solar city in Gulf could set a new standard for green design', *New York Times*, 5 February.

Rosencranz, A. and Jackson, M. 2002. 'Clean Air Initiative for Asian cities: The Delhi pollution case', New Delhi, http://www.indlaw.com.

Rubin, J. 2009. *Why Your World is About to Get a Whole Lot Smaller: Oil and Globalization*, Random House, New York.

SACTRA. 1994. *Trunk Roads and the Generation of Traffic*, UK Department of Transport, London.

Salter, R., Dhar, S. and Newman, P. 2011. *Technologies for Climate Change Mitigation: Transport*, TNA Guidebook Series, UNEP Riso Centre for Energy, Climate and Sustainable Development, Roskilde.

Standing Advisory Committee on Trunk Road Assessment. 1994. *Trunk Roads and the Generation of Traffic*, Department of Transport, London.

Urban Transportation Monitor, 1999. 'Summary information from Texas Transportation Institute Annual Mobility Report', *Urban Transportation Monitor* 13(22), Lawley Publications, Burke, VA.

UN Habitat (2009) *Revisiting Urban Planning: Global Report on Human Settlements*, UN Habitat, Nairobi.

Wiley-Schwartz, A. 2006. 'A revolutionary change in transportation planning: The slow road movement', *New York Times*, 10 July.

CHAPTER 13

Integrated urban water planning

Realising Water Sensitive Cities

Tony Wong and Rebekah Brown

13.1 Introduction

Globally, cities are facing significant water challenges largely driven by changing demographics and climate variability. At the same time, urban water ecosystems can be highly degraded and water infrastructure is often approaching the end of its lifespan, especially in developed cities. The traditional water servicing model of large, centralised, potable supply systems and wastewater disposal systems (some cities have combined wastewater and stormwater drainage systems) is increasingly accepted as not providing communities with the flexibility needed for meeting sustainable development goals, nor the ability to address future conditions.

Understanding the hydro-social contracts underpinning this dominant practice helps explain the current dilemma. These contracts are the implicit agreements (shaped by cultures and value sets) between governments and communities that manifest in institutional arrangements and regulatory frameworks for urban water service delivery expectations. The urban water transitions framework for cities (Figure 13.1) presents a typology of historical and current urban hydro-social contracts at the city scale, characterised as a nested continuum of socio-political drivers and service delivery responses. Future contracts are hypothesised by anticipating the social and institutional factors underpinning the principles of integration and resilience espoused in proposed future management paradigms.

The 'Water Supply', 'Sewered' and 'Drained' city management regimes shown in Figure 13.1 are largely representative of the traditional water management approach underpinned by the (false) beliefs that technocrats can control for environmental variation (such as droughts, floods, heatwaves) and reliably predict changes in patterns of consumption, resource allocation, and population growth and decline (Wong and Brown, 2011).

Research has shown that a number of developed cities are now transitioning towards the 'Waterways' city in practice (rather than policy rhetoric alone) with far more attention on protecting waterway health and addressing urban stormwater quality issues (Roy *et al.*, 2008; Jefferies and Duffy, 2011). Over recent years there has also been a shift in a number of developed cities transitioning towards the 'Water Cycle' city recognising that, along with changing consumption habits and expectations, sustainable development is more likely to be achieved through a diverse suite of alternative supplies, such as recycled wastewater, greywater and stormwater. This strategy, if realised through the adoption of decentralised

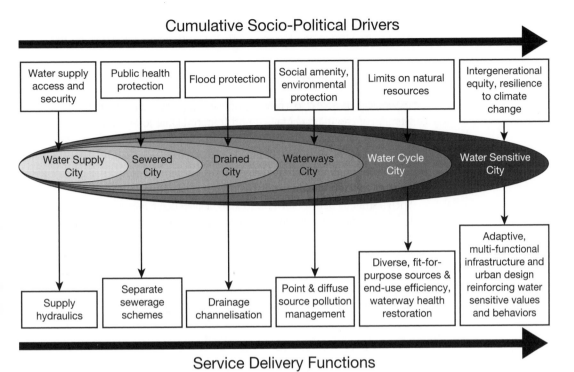

Figure 13.1 Urban water management transitions framework Source: Brown *et al.* (2009), with permission from IWA Publishing

technologies augmenting centralised infrastructure, can often result in protection of urban waterway health from stressors associated with urban stormwater/combined sewer pollution and changed hydrologic conditions. These hybrid systems thus build flexibility into servicing options. This observed shift in focus is largely in terms of policy development, local research investment, and some progressive demonstration projects in practice (Wong and Brown, 2011). But this is yet to be realised as a mainstream, on-the-ground practice.

As cities move towards the 'Water Sensitive City', water management becomes necessarily more complex, but also more resilient to major system 'disturbances' (such as floods, droughts, heatwaves and waterway health degradation), and improves its adaptive capacity to create opportunities from these disturbances for innovation and development or even the pursuit of new trajectories. Conversely, earlier types of management regime are representative of more 'vulnerable' systems, when even small disturbances, such as extended storm events, are likely to cause dramatic social consequences.

13.2 The Water Sensitive City: principles for practice

Realising the idea of the Water Sensitive City is extremely challenging as it will require a major socio-technical overhaul of conventional approaches and their socio-institutional settings amongst cities worldwide. While there is not one example in the world of a Water Sensitive City at present, several cities are taking the lead on distinct and varying attributes of the water sensitive approach that offer insights into the overarching 'principles' (or pillars) that should underpin this new paradigm of practice (see Wong and Brown, 2009, 2011). There are three such pillars.

Cities as water supply catchments

Cities would have access to a diversity of water sources in addition to the established convention of capturing rainfall–run-off from rural and forested catchments. These alternative water sources could include a mix of groundwater, urban stormwater (catchment run-off), rainwater (roof run-off), recycled wastewater and desalinated water. These sources would be delivered through an integrated mix of centralised and decentralised infrastructure.

Such a strategy of diverse water sources delivered at a mix of water infrastructure scales would allow cities the flexibility to access a portfolio of sources at least environmental, social and economic cost. Each of the alternative water sources will have an individual reliability, environmental risk and cost profile. This pillar ensures that cities contain both centralised and decentralised water supply schemes, such as a simple domestic rainwater tank for non-potable use, through to city-scale indirect potable reuse schemes and a pipeline grid linking regional reservoirs.

Cities providing ecosystem services

Cities would comprise low-carbon urban ecosystem services (such as water quality treatment and city cooling) through new forms of green infrastructure integrated into urban landscape design.

Landscapes are the product of varying natural and human-induced forces, interacting within a regional and global ecosystem. Traditionally spaces in the public domain are essential features of urban amenity. However, in Water Sensitive Cities these urban landscapes must be ecologically functional as well as providing spatial amenity. These ecological landscapes are achieved through the integration of urban landscape design with sustainable urban water management technologies and practices to buffer the impact of climate change (in particular increased frequency of extreme storm events) and increasing urban densities on natural aquatic environments in order to preserve and/or re-establish ecosystem services. Our urban landscapes therefore need to be designed and retrofitted to capture the essence of sustainable water management, micro-climate influences, facilitation of carbon sinks and potential use for urban food production.

Cities comprising water sensitive communities and institutions

The social and institutional capital inherent in the city is reflected in:

1 the community living an ecologically sustainability lifestyle and cognisant of the ongoing balance and tension between consumption and conservation of the city-region's natural capital;
2 the capacity of industry and the professions to innovate and adapt as reflective practitioners in city building; and

3   government policies that facilitate the ongoing adaptive evolution of the Water Sensitive City.

The capacity of existing institutions to advance sustainable urban water management is essential. Unless new technologies are embedded into the local institutional and social context, their development in isolation will not be enough to ensure their successful implementation in practice. Therefore, the approach of the Water Sensitive City would be underpinned by a flexible institutional regime and coexisting, diverse infrastructure.

13.3 Cooperative Research Centres for Water Sensitive Cities

The Australian government has identified the creation of liveable, sustainable and productive cities as a national priority (Melbourne City Council, 2009; Brisbane City Council, 2010; Department of Infrastructure and Transport, 2011; Department of Sustainability and Environment, 2011; National Water Commission, 2011). In November 2012, the Australian government announced the establishment of two new Cooperative Research Centres (CRCs) focused on improving the sustainability of the built environment (the CRC for Low Carbon Living and the CRC for Water Sensitive Cities). The national traction of the Water Sensitive City aspiration is reflected by the significant investment in the CRC for Water Sensitive Cities (CRCWSC) comprising A$30 million in Australian government funding, and a further A$89 million of collective support from higher education institutions, government and non-government organisations, water utilities and the private sector.

With a total research budget of approximately A$120 million, the research and industry engagement of the CRCWSC over the next nine years will guide an estimated capital investment of more than A$100 billion by the Australian water sector and more than A$550 billion of private sector investment in urban development over the next fifteen years. This is the first substantial investment by Australian government, industries and research and higher education sectors in a partnership to support dedicated interdisciplinary research and multi-sectoral engagement in research adoption.

The Water Sensitive Cities initiative is responding to a general consensus across multiple sectoral stakeholders (particularly those focused on urban planning and design of future cities) that existing water services and planning processes are poorly equipped to support projected population growth and slow to respond to economic or climatic uncertainty. In essence, this recognises the limitations and the inherent vulnerabilities of the first three city-state conditions (see Figure 13.1) – i.e. cities can no longer try to meet twenty-first-century challenges by reinvesting in nineteenth-century strategies and infrastructures.

To address the complex interdependencies of the many socio-technical factors influencing water management in cities of the future effectively, the CRCWSC will employ an interdisciplinary and multi-sectoral research partnership approach, placing practitioners, policy-makers and regulators in interdisciplinary teams with researchers with expertise from twenty different disciplines, including: water engineering; urban planning; commercial and property law; urban ecology; urban climatology and global climate science; social and institutional science; organisational behaviour; change management; the water economy; risk assessment; social marketing; and community health.

Research activities are grouped into four research programmes:

- *Programme A: Society* – with a focus on understanding and delivering the social transformations needed to support Water Sensitive Cities, including community attitude and behavioural change, governance and economic assessment practices, management systems and technological innovation.
- *Programme B: Water sensitive urbanism* – with a focus on investigating the influence of urban configurations on resource flows across a range of scales. It will apply green infrastructure and climate responsive design principles to water security, flood protection and the ecological health of terrestrial and aquatic landscapes ranging from whole-of-catchment to street level.
- *Programme C: Future technologies* – with a focus on developing integrated and multi-functional urban water systems that manage and/or use multiple water sources at a range of scales. It will deliver innovative technologies for: integrative management of urban water systems; fit-for-purpose production of water; the recovery of energy, nutrients and other valuable materials embedded in urban water; minimising the carbon footprint and ecological impacts of water systems; and maximising the potential multiple beneficial values of urban water services.
- *Programme D: Adoption pathways* – with a focus on delivering a suite of capacity-building projects and socio-technical modelling tools that will provide a focus for participants and stakeholders at national, regional and community levels to interact, experiment and learn from each other. This, in turn, will: improve community engagement; enrich educational and training programmes at the professional and sub-professional levels; and support the development of robust science–policy partnerships.

More details on the centre, its programme and achievements can be accessed through its website: http://www.watersensitivecities.org.au.

13.4 Concluding remarks

Cities and towns have always been the platforms for 'socio-technical experiments' and the intersection of competing and complementary objectives. It is in these 'melting pots' that the practice of urban planning and design integrate the socio-technical strategies and solutions to emerging and expanding urban water management objectives.

Establishing Water Sensitive Cities will require a major socio-technical overhaul of conventional approaches. It requires the transformation of urban water systems from a focus on water supply and wastewater disposal to more complex, flexible systems that: integrate various sources of water; operate through a combination of centralised and decentralised systems; deliver a wider range of services to communities (e.g. ecosystem services, urban heat mitigation); and integrate into urban design practices.

Many developed countries are often encumbered by 'path-dependency' or system-wide 'lock-in' owing to institutional legacy limiting the range of acceptable solutions/interventions to those that would fit into the existing institutional paradigm. Studies have identified numerous factors leading to such lock-in and this is often expressed in attempts to secure improved system resilience and sustainability simply by improving the efficiency of the existing urban water system. A typical lock-in-type argument is reflected by the significant weight given to the 'sunk cost' associated with past infrastructure investments in current decision-making processes.

Developing countries where infrastructure and institutions are not well established are therefore potentially more flexible and conducive to unconventional solutions. It is for this reason that cities in developing countries are better placed to leap-frog from a Water Supply City directly to a Water Sensitive City. This is on the proviso that international aid programmes do not inadvertently impose (through various direct and indirect mechanisms) developed-world conventional thinking, planning and design of water systems on these countries.

Adaptive and integrated management approaches offer an alternative to the traditional urban water regime and present new urban water governance frameworks to support more sustainable and resilient practices. Sustainable urban water management regimes would emphasise a systems approach whereby interconnections between the management of the urban water streams and other related urban water governance functions such as land use planning, urban design, infrastructure delivery and maintenance, project financing, etc., would deliver and protect multiple benefits, and are more resilient to unanticipated outcomes by being prepared for multiple potential future conditions.

Urban planning objectives that strategically place green spaces and corridors throughout the city footprint will provide greater amenity, enhance urban biodiversity, protect water environments from urban stormwater pollution, promote harvesting of stormwater, influence micro-climates and provide safe detention and conveyance of flood waters. These benefits can be realised through retrofitting (substituting) emerging technologies for fit-for-purpose water production, resource recovery (water, energy and nutrients) from our sewerage system and supporting multi-functional hybrid centralised and decentralised water infrastructure.

In summary, future Water Sensitive Cities: efficiently use the diversity of water resources available within cities; enhance and protect the health of urban and natural waterways; and mitigate against flood risk and damage. Public spaces are green infrastructure that harvest, clean and recycle water, increase biodiversity, support carbon sequestration and reduce urban heat island effects.

References

Brisbane City Council. 2010. *WaterSmart Strategy: Supporting the Liveability of Brisbane by Managing Water Sustainably*, Brisbane City Council, Brisbane.

Brown, R., Keath, N. and Wong, T. 2009. 'Urban Water Management in Cities: Historical, Current and Future Regimes', *Water Science and Technology* 59(5), 847–855.

Department of Infrastructure and Transport. 2011. *Our Cities, Our Future: A National Urban Policy for a Productive, Sustainable and Liveable Future*, Department of Infrastructure and Transport, Canberra.

Department of Sustainability and Environment. 2011. *Living Melbourne, Living Victoria Roadmap*, Department of Sustainability and Environment, State Government of Victoria, Melbourne.

Jefferies, C. and Duffy, A. 2011. *The SWITCH Transition Manual*, University of Abertay, Dundee.

Melbourne City Council. 2009. *Total WaterMark: City as a Catchment*, Melbourne City Council, Melbourne.

National Water Commission. 2011. *Urban Water in Australia: Future Directions*, National Water Commission, Canberra.

Roy, A.H., Wenger, S.J., Fletcher, T.D., Walsh, C.J., Ladson, A.R., Shuster, W.D., Thurston, H.W. and Brown, R.R. 2008. 'Impediments and Solutions to Sustainable, Watershed-Scale Urban Stormwater Management: Lessons from Australia and the United States', *Environmental Management* 42, 344–359.

Wong, T.H.F. and Brown, R.R. 2009. 'The Water Sensitive City: Principles for Practice', *Water Science and Technology* 60, 673–682.

Wong, T.H.F and Brown, R.R. 2011. 'Water Sensitive Urban Design', in Grafton, Q. and Hussey, K. (eds), *Water Resources, Planning and Management: Challenges and Solutions*, Cambridge University Press, Cambridge, 483–504.

CHAPTER 14

Urban waste

Closing the loop

María José Zapata Campos and Patrik Zapata

14.1 Introduction

Resilient and sustainable cities need to develop more sustainable modes of organizing urban waste. This challenge requires the embedding of new and robust linkages between the design, production, and consumption of goods and services, and the management of the resultant waste, closing the manufacturing and consumption loop (Zapata Campos and Hall, 2013).

In Europe, the 'Waste Hierarchy' model (EC, 2008) is the framework developed to govern waste management. This model states that waste prevention should have priority over, in descending order, product reuse, recycling, incineration, and, finally – the least desirable option – landfilling. As a result, in countries such as Sweden, a declining fraction of the waste produced is disposed of in landfills. Instead, new waste infrastructures, such as recycling stations, waste-to-energy incinerators, waste-to-biogas plants, and repair and reuse centers, coexist.

This chapter explores the principles of urban waste in resilient and sustainable cities by citing examples of two waste infrastructures with sustainability performance records aligned with Waste Hierarchy priorities in the city of Gothenburg, Sweden. Specifically, the chapter explores the physical, legal, economic, and symbolic transformations enacted by these infrastructures, as viewed through the lens of the *crossing point* concept (Hawkins, 2006, 2009), explained in the next section, and their implications for more sustainable urban transformations.

14.2 Urban waste infrastructures and sustainable crossing points

A number of exchanges and transformations occur along the waste management chain. Hawkins (2006) describes how the sound of breaking glass in a recycling container signals the moment when empty bottles are reborn in the recycling economy. At the instant the bottle's owner throws it into the container, it passes a crossing point in the waste chain. The bottle is not a bottle any more, but glass that is animated, in Bennett's terminology (2001, 2004), and transformed in the recycling economy. The transformation of empty bottles into recyclable glass does not mark the moment when bottles die but the moment when a new use and value is added – 'a beginning, not an ending' (Hawkins, 2006, p. 93).

The transformations enacted within the spectrum of urban waste infrastructures, such as the recycling container, activate the materials and energy existing in waste. However, they can also enact less benign animations, such as pollutants and emissions that are hazardous to the environment and to human health (Gregson, Watkins, and Calestani, 2010). The reused goods, and the recovered materials and energy, can also gain new economic value when they are connected to corresponding new and emerging markets. In this material metamorphosis, these goods and materials gain new meanings and uses associated with their new owners.

In a nutshell, infrastructures associated with waste management emerge as crossing points, places for physical, material, semiotic, etymological, symbolic, social, legal, and organizational transformations. Waste infrastructures are also interfaces between different organizational worlds; for example, the collective actions of citizens and householders and of the local authorities responsible for household waste collection meet at recycling stations.

The transformations enacted at crossing points can have various implications for sustainable urban development, implications that are not always positive. To exemplify, illegal dumps – in streets, roadside ditches, gutters and drains, along riverbanks, and in the form of burn barrels – are *in extremis* uncontrolled crossing points with many costly implications for cities and their inhabitants: higher costs to the authorities collecting waste; damage caused by flooding when riverbanks, gutters, and storm drains are blocked by waste; lost opportunities to recover recyclable material due to ineffective waste handling; pollution of air and soils; and direct public health impacts, such as the proliferation of vermin and the spread of vector-borne diseases. More *controlled* crossing points, such as waste transfer stations, even with their downsides, instead favor more benign transformations.

Sustainable and resilient cities are challenged constantly to create, maintain, control, and renew waste management crossing points, or urban waste infrastructures, leading toward sustainable and 'enchanting' practices, materials, and values, as illustrated in this chapter.

14.3 Crossing points in the EU Waste Hierarchy

Next we present two urban waste infrastructures embedded in different steps of the EU Waste Hierarchy that can be found in the city of Gothenburg, Sweden – i.e. the Sävenäs waste incinerator and the Alelyckan recycling and reuse park – where innovative, resilient, and sustainable urban practices have been reported (C40 Cities and Clinton Climate Initiative, 2010; Swedish Waste Management, 2011b).

Sävenäs is the municipally owned combined heat and power incineration plant in the Gothenburg Metropolitan Area that has existed for more than forty years (see Figure 14.1). Benchmarked against other European incinerators, Sävenäs stands out for generating considerable energy per tonne of waste (3.3 MWh) and reducing landfill to a minimum with relatively low carbon dioxide emissions. The plant separates out pollutants in the waste very effectively and is one of Europe's cleanest waste-to-energy plants, operating well within the margins of all applicable environmental regulations (C40 Cities and Clinton Climate Initiative, 2010).

The plant produces 5 percent of the electricity and 30 percent of the district heating annually consumed in the city of Gothenburg (Renova, 2011, p. 5):

> When biological waste is deposited in landfills and breaks down, methane – which is a particularly damaging greenhouse gas – is formed. At the waste-to-energy plant in Sävenäs, instead we transform that waste into energy. This helps to reduce pollution in our communities as well. By burning the waste and cleaning the emissions to the air and water effectively, we are taking environmentally damaging substances out of circulation in the natural environment. Ensuring that we are closing the waste cycle and creating inputs to new production processes – from waste to clean energy.

Figure 14.1 The Sävenäs combined heat and power incineration Source: © María José Zapata Campos and Patrik Zapata

Consequently, Sävenäs has been singled out as a best-practice case of the successful transformation of waste into clean energy by the Clinton Climate Initiatives Cities Program (C40 Cities and Clinton Climate Initiative, 2010).

In Sävenäs, clean energy is generated from waste in the form of heat and electricity. Incineration plants such as Sävenäs are, when well regulated and carefully developed, among the crossing points in society where 'enchantment' – Bennett's (2001, 2004) term – occurs and pollutants such as dioxins are destroyed.

By constantly investing in research and development, the incineration plant has transformed itself from an agent of potential pollution into a place where climate change is locally contested. Sävenäs has become a 'dioxin sink' where waste physically disappears ('unbecomes') as an environmental problem; instead, it is transformed into non-fossil-fuel energy in the form of 'clean' electricity and district heating. Following Bennett (2001, 2004), the Sävenäs plant as a crossing point has become a place of enchantment where material is metamorphosed, leading toward more sustainable urban transformations.

Notwithstanding this, high-technology and environmentally benign waste incineration plants such as Sävenäs are still relatively rare. Waste incineration continues to threaten human health and the environment in many cities around the world, triggering strong community opposition on environmental grounds (Rootes and Leonard, 2010).

Even in Gothenburg itself, other waste infrastructures will ultimately take over from waste incineration. Waste infrastructures with a sustainable record, such as Sävenäs, may evolve over time into a lock-in, slowing the emergence of still more sustainable urban infrastructures and innovations (Corvellec, Zapata Campos, and Zapata, 2013). Resilient cities are those that are adaptable and open to more sustainable and innovative solutions. In Gothenburg, new urban waste infrastructures such as the Alelyckan recycling and reuse park have recently been created in an effort to move up the Waste Hierarchy.

The innovation of the Alelyckan eco-cycle park is that it provides visitors with the opportunity to donate reusable materials instead of simply recycling them, and to buy donated (sometimes repaired) goods in thrift shops located in the park. Products that are still in good condition are sold for reuse in the shops; the rest are sorted out for material recycling or energy recovery in the Sävenäs incineration plant.

By combining the functions of a *recycling* station and a *reuse* park, this waste infrastructure enacts multiple transformations toward more sustainable lifestyles in the city. The flow of unwanted goods is transformed into secondhand products (changing owners, eventually partially reconstructed or repaired, and reused), recyclable materials, and clean energy. In all cases, the *connection of the flow of waste to the market* underlies the positive transformations.

At Alelyckan, materials and items 'unbecome' waste. Reusing products in the eco-cycle park prevents 360 tonnes of waste every year that otherwise would have been incinerated or recycled, or – in the case of construction materials – gone into landfills (Swedish Waste Management, 2011b). The environmental benefits amount to savings of 1300 tonnes of carbon dioxide equivalents and 5700 MWh of saved primary energy, compared with a regular recycling park. Alelyckan, as a sustainable crossing point, converts waste into secondhand products, recyclable materials, and green energy. As in Sävenäs, waste becomes a solution to environmental problems such as climate change and the depletion of the earth's natural resources.

Positive feelings of doing something right, 'a positive energy that emanates from the place', and happiness, as reported in recycling centers elsewhere (Lisberg-Jensen, 2012), have been observed in this recycling park. Visitors are 'pleasantly surprised' (Alelyckan employee) that people can reuse their discarded objects. Unlike an ordinary recycling center, Alelyckan has a recreation area, a cozy eco-café, and a

Box 14.1   Alelyckan eco-cycle park

Alelyckan is an eco-cycle park in Gothenburg and, according to the municipality, the largest such park in the world, covering more than 30,000 square meters. Opened in 2007, the park is run by the city of Gothenburg in cooperation with local non-governmental organizations. The park has a recycling station, a reuse center for construction material, information offices, a secondhand shop, a return house with a workshop for repairs, an eco-café, an eco store, and a picnic area.

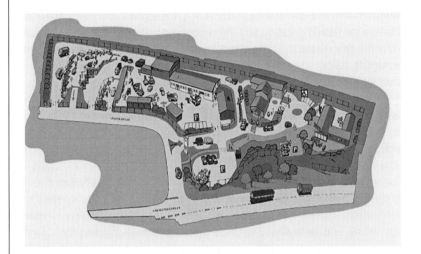

Figure 14.2 Alelyckan eco-cycle park
Source: City of Gothenburg

Figure 14.3 The eco-café at Alelyckan eco-cycle park
Source: © María José Zapata Campos and Patrik Zapata

clean and odorless environment where waste becomes something valuable. It is a fun place that radiates happiness, a deliberately created 'positive environment' (in the words of another Alelyckan employee) where sorting waste becomes a leisure experience. Positive feelings, experiences, and values are mingled with the waste and related infrastructures.

Waste infrastructures are proving to be strong catalysts for mobilizing urban change and resilience (Zapata Campos and Zapata, 2012). The environment and the practices enacted at Alelyckan can also ('magically', as only crossing points can) change visitors' attitudes and behaviors. At Alelyckan, the display of possible new waste-minimizing and -eliminating practices (e.g. the secondhand shops that visitors pass before the recycling station and the depot for donating undesired but reusable goods at the entry to the recycling station) and the information provided by the staff in the sorting tunnel all contribute to new understandings of waste by promoting positive transformations. Crossing points such as Alelyckan have the ability to change the socio-materiality of waste – that is, how we engage with the materiality of waste in the course of our everyday lives (Gregson, 2009; Corvellec and Hultman, 2012; Hultman and Corvellec, 2012) – to foster a new ethics of environmental protection and responsible consumption that leads to the reduction of what might become waste in the future.

Finally, contemplation of the unending waste flows entering Alelyckan does not leave visitors unaffected. The visual and physical contact with the materiality of waste in urban waste infrastructures such as Alelyckan has the ability to change beliefs, values, and behaviors. The place succeeds in reestablishing the cognitive linkages between our consumption behavior and its environmental consequences.

The park, however, is relatively unknown as yet, with only approximately 18 percent of the city's inhabitants frequenting it (Swedish Waste Management, 2011b). As with any new infrastructure, it needs to be anchored in both city management and residents' practices, which takes time.

14. 4. Conclusions

Kevin Lynch (1990, p. 3), through his concept of a 'wasteless cacotopia', conveys a vision of a society in which waste does not exist, noting that 'wasting is a necessary part of living, yet if the processes are not well managed, life itself is threatened'. Urban infrastructures change over time, coexist with other types of infrastructure in the Waste Hierarchy, and are progressively replaced with more innovative and sustainable technologies and organizational solutions. The resilient city implies 'an ongoing recovery process that, for many people, will never quite end' (Vale and Campanella, 2005, p. 14). Resilient cities are those that persistently question the comfortable locking-in power of well-established infrastructures and instead are permeated by new ideas, values, knowledge, solutions, and technologies.

The governance of waste to give rise to more sustainable urban transformations entails the challenge of envisioning, imagining, creating, and anchoring new crossing points. New waste-related urban infrastructures will have to enable a move up the Waste Hierarchy, forming new pathways toward 'wasting less' regimes (Corvellec and Hultman, 2012) and decoupling urban development from waste production.

References

Bennett, J. 2001. *The enchantment of modern life: Attachments, crossings, and ethics*. Princeton, NJ: Princeton University Press.

Bennett, J. 2004. The force of things: Steps toward an ecology of matter. *Political Theory*, 32(3), 347–372.

C40 Cities and Clinton Climate Initiative. 2010. Waste, Gothenburg, Sweden. Retrieved on August 6, 2010: http://www.c40cities.org/bestpractices/waste/gothenburg_system.jsp.

Corvellec, H. and Hultman, J. 2012. From 'less landfilling' to 'wasting less': Societal narratives, socio-materiality, and organizations. *Journal of Organizational Change Management*, 25(2), 297–314.

Corvellec, H., Zapata Campos, M. J., and Zapata, P. 2013. Infrastructures, lock-in, and sustainable urban development: The case of waste incineration in the Gothenburg Metropolitan Area. *Journal of Cleaner Production, 50,* 32–39.

European Commission. 2008. Directive 2008/98/EC of the European Parliament and the Council on Waste and Repealing. *Official Journal of the European Union* L 312/3. Brussels: European Commission.

Gregson, N. 2009. Recycling as policy and assemblage. *Geography*, 94(1), pp. 61–65.

Gregson, N., Watkins, H., and Calestani, M. 2010. Inextinguishable fibres: Demolition and the vital materialisms of asbestos. *Environment and Planning A*, 42(5), 1065–1083.

Hawkins, G. 2006. *The ethics of waste: How we relate to rubbish*. Oxford: Rowman and Littlefield.

Hawkins, G. 2009. The politics of bottled water. *Journal of Cultural Economy*, 2(1), 183–195.

Hultman, J. and Corvellec, H. 2012. The waste hierarchy model: From the socio-materiality of waste to a politics of consumption. *Environment and Planning A*, 44(10), 2413–2427.

Lisberg-Jensen, E. 2012. Observations of recycling staff at recycling stations at Malmö, Sweden. Unpublished report.

Lynch, K. 1990. *Wasting away – an exploration of waste: What it is, how it happens, why we fear it, how to do it well*. San Francisco, CA: Sierra Club Books.

Renova. 2011. *Annual Environmental Report*. Gothenburg: Renova.

Rootes, C. and Leonard, L. (eds). 2010. *Environmental movements and waste infrastructure*. London: Taylor and Francis.

Swedish Waste Management. 2011a. Avfall Sverige/Swedish Waste Management. Accessed on December 3, 2012 at: http://www.avfallsverige.se.

Swedish Waste Management. 2011b. *Good examples of waste prevention in municipalities: A compilation of ideas for more sustainable production and consumption*. Report No. U2011:05. Gothenburg: Swedish Waste Management.

Vale, L. J. and Campanella, T. J. 2005. *The resilient city: How modern cities recover from disaster*. New York: Oxford University Press.

Zapata Campos, M. J. and Hall, M. C. (eds). 2013. *Organizing waste in the city: International perspectives on narratives and practices*. Bristol: Policy Press.

Zapata Campos, M. J. and Zapata, P. 2012. Changing La Chureca: Organising city resilience through action nets. *Journal of Change Management*, 12(3), 323–337.

CHAPTER 15

Resilient and sustainable buildings

Janis Birkeland

15.1 Introduction

Due to accelerating changes in population, disparities of wealth and biodiversity losses, built environments must increase the ecological base and public estate, while improving urban life quality and future proofing cities (Birkeland, 2003). This chapter provides an example of how this can be done: retrofitting urban structures with natural systems to provide eco-services surplus to the needs of the occupants. This is already possible at the building scale. There are already many low-cost eco-solutions that could generate net positive gains with multiple synergistic benefits (see Birkeland, 2009). For example, an eco-positive design proposal was assessed for net greenhouse emissions and it was found that, within the life cycle, integrated interior planting could sequester the building's greenhouse emissions, an important eco-service (Renger, Birkeland and Midmore, 2013). Net positive outcomes at the urban scale are also possible if cities actually support their bioregions, as opposed to acting like 'black holes' (Rees, 2002). For example, since wind entering a forest comes out the other side with less carbon dioxide, this could theoretically happen across cities if they were sufficiently 'greened' (but see Strohbach and Haase, 2012). The frameworks, methods and tools to achieve net positive development have been introduced elsewhere (Birkeland, 2008). Here, two basic strategies for helping to convert cities into drivers of sustainability are discussed:

- 'Eco-positive retrofitting': reducing total resource flows and increasing the ecological base beyond that which existed on site before any development in the region.
- 'Design for eco-services': increasing not only ecosystem goods and services (benefits to humans) but also ecosystem integrity, resilience and diversity (benefits to nature).

Several variations on 'green scaffolding' are used below to illustrate how new and retrofitted buildings could support most ecosystem functions and services, and increase the natural life support system of cities.

State of the art

Competent architects have always at least tried to improve *social* wellbeing, equity, health and vitality by creating urban environments that benefit the general public as well as the building stakeholders. Social capital can be fostered by, for example, public space, equitable living conditions, educational environments and playgardens (see below). But while most architects design buildings with resource efficiency and the health and welfare of building occupants in mind, they have inadvertently forgotten the life support system. Efficiency – using less water, energy, and toxins than typical buildings – does *not* protect or improve the urban or regional ecology.

Moreover, 'mono-efficiency' has contributed to sterile buildings and urban environments that are sub-optimal from social as well as ecological perspectives. Even 'green' buildings often segregate human and natural functions and create dead single-function interior spaces. In fact, the morphologies of cemeteries and cities are remarkably similar. 'Zero carbon' buildings fall well short of a sustainable target, as they do not attempt to increase the life support system. Reductionist forms of efficiency that focus on energy or water create lost opportunities, as design can create multiple synergistic benefits with fewer resources, while increasing functions and/or usable space for people and nature. Let us briefly consider why energy should not be the central issue.

Operating energy: Currently, the energy to operate buildings constitutes a large portion of total waste, energy and greenhouse gas emissions. Even certified 'green' commercial or office buildings can be energy guzzlers and greenhouse gas emitters, due in part to assessment tools that allow trade-offs among different criteria. In fact, many green buildings have curtain glass walls for aesthetic reasons, despite their many sustainability defects (Safamanesh and Byrd, 2012). The increased urban temperatures these cause can erase the operating energy savings gained by other efficiencies. Moreover, the urban heat island effect – known about since 1818 – results in many needless deaths every year (Gartland, 2011). Premature deaths are not socially sustainable. Fortunately, buildings can be retrofitted to produce and/or reduce energy for less cost than doing nothing (Romm, 1999). For example, curtain glass walls could be covered with new transparent films that resist heat gain in summer and heat loss in winter, combined with embedded photovoltaic cells for electricity production or sound insulation. Parts of over-glazed facades could be covered by pollution-absorbing filters and sound-absorbing materials as well, or even planting modules in some cases.

Energy sources: While most green buildings reduce operating energy, there is no shortage of clean energy sources anyway. Clean energy production is not a technical problem. There is enough solar or wind energy available to power all the activities of humans without fossil fuels (Elliston, Diesendorf and MacGill, 2011). In fact, there have been modern 'resource autonomous' homes and even buildings for decades that harvest their own energy, remediate their land, and collect and treat their own water (Vale and Vale, 1975; Mobbs, 1998). Large building roofs or suburban neighbourhoods could be retrofitted with solar discs or vertical shaft wind generators to provide independent and resilient power supplies (Lovegrove, Burgess and Pye, 2011). Cost is no longer an excuse. Renewable energy sources only appear more expensive because market distortions transfer costs onto the general public, and they have not had the subsidies enjoyed by fossil fuels until recently (Scheer, 2004). However, they are less expensive from a whole-system perspective. Operating energy is just a political problem.

Embodied energy: The real issue is 'embodied energy', which is that used in the construction supply chain, such as transport, mining, forestry and building. Embodied energy now roughly equals operating energy overall, but it would far exceed operating energy if buildings used 'passive solar' heating, cooling and ventilating. It should be the only form of net energy usage in buildings, and it could be 'repaid' (in a sense) by building-integrated renewable energy generation. Because it is hard to measure, embodied energy has been largely ignored in building assessment processes. Thus most green buildings still, in effect, waste 'embodied' materials, energy, water and ecosystems. These are seldom even offset by positive impacts in other areas, such as providing the infrastructure for ecological incubators, eco-services or nature corridors.

Leading-edge

A few leading-edge designers have begun to try to design buildings that regenerate the environment, revitalize the community and green the city as well as conserve or generate energy. However, even these buildings usually fail to consider the ecology, except metaphorically. Some projects protect ecosystems onsite or offsite, but the building still replaces *net* land and ecosystems with structures. Even buildings that 'mimic' ecosystems in efficiency (see Benyus, 1997) are little compensation when we have lost a third of the species that make life for humans possible (UNEP, 2005). Since development has exceeded the earth's ecological carrying capacity, sustainability requires far more than ecological remediation or regeneration. Ecosystems cannot be increased without space, so the total space for (interior/exterior) nature must be radically increased. This can occur only in urban areas.

15.2 Eco-positive retrofitting

City councils, developers and designers could achieve eco-positive design now, with or without the new models, methods and metrics foreshadowed in *Positive Development* (Birkeland, 2008). However, net positive impacts are easier to achieve by retrofitting and, due to the ongoing and system-wide impacts of cities, eco-positive retrofitting is a precondition of biophysical sustainability. After all, replacing cities and buildings with new green ones would involve too much time, money, resources and ecological damage – and would not address the problems left behind in old cities. Even if all new buildings were 'green', the reduction of energy usage would still be minuscule, as only about 2 per cent of the building stock is new each year. Moreover, embodied energy usage (currently about 20 per cent of total energy use) would substantially increase.

Conventional renovation

At present, little renovation is undertaken with sustainability or even energy in mind. In some places, renovations account for a third of construction activity, and renovation and demolition waste can account for 90 per cent of (often toxic) construction debris each year. Of the roughly 136 million tons of building-related debris wasted each year in the USA, about a fourth is recycled (Sandler and Swingle, 2006). Only 9 per cent of construction waste is attributed to new construction (BMRA, 2008). Therefore, changing the way we upgrade new or abandoned urban areas is essential to achieving a sustainable, resilient society. So far, however, retrofitting has been focused on operating energy to the exclusion of the life support system.

Energy retrofitting

Mere energy retrofitting can generate a net economic gain for developers, occupants and society as a whole (US EPA, 1998: Heede *et al.*, 1995). It is now established that renovations for resource and energy efficiency *alone* can be cheaper than doing nothing, while simultaneously reducing the public costs of development, like pollution, waste and carbon emissions (Birkeland, 1995, 2000; Miller and Birkeland, 2009). Investments in retrofits compare favourably with stocks and bonds, and one can buy securities in eco-retrofitting without being directly involved in development (Romm, 1999). However, interventions to reduce risks of climate change or impacts of typical buildings are not net positive, as they do not increase sustainability. So why have we not retrofitted in ways that increase *net* sustainability?

Eco-positive retrofitting

Eco-positive retrofitting means (among other things) increasing ecological space beyond indigenous conditions. We can design out negative impacts while retrofitting our cities to become eco-productive, bio-diverse and multi-functional environments (Birkeland, 2005). Many energy service companies are already geared up for energy retrofitting through 'performance contracting', where the owner, contractor and public all profit from the savings. As renovations are constantly occurring anyway, there are opportunities to increase positive benefits in urban environments and buildings in each instance while reducing environmental costs. Where new construction is necessary, developers could retrofit the equivalent floor area in older buildings to offset negative impacts, as this is a secure investment. So why is there resistance to eco-positive retrofitting? One of many reasons for this is how we evaluate green buildings (for other reasons, see Birkeland, 2008, p. 284).

Assessment

We still choose not to measure positive impacts and exclude many negative impacts. Since most tools count only 'less negative' impacts, the idea of increasing the life support system or ecological base is still inconceivable to many designers. Then, there is double counting that often accompanies accounting-based assessment. For example, when a new efficient building has more landscaping than the previous building on the site, or uses less water and energy consumption than the norm, these actions are counted as positive. However, if the development nonetheless increases total resource outflows and inflows that damage the ecology, the net impacts are negative. This is often concealed by putting economic or social benefits (like energy efficiency, clean indoor air, day-lighting or thermal comfort) in the ecological column of the triple bottom line. Then, offsets are often used to allow *additional* environmental impacts, rather than compensate for unavoidable ones.

Some assessments are beginning to encourage restorative or regenerative design, but do not yet assess ecosystem carrying capacity or eco-services, and are benchmarked against non-sustainable buildings. Where applying numbers to nature is impractical to guide design, an alternative approach is the Hierarchy of Eco-innovation (Box 15.1), which looks at public benefits by design to counterbalance the tendency toward reducing negatives or 'downsizing'.

Box 15.1   Hierarchy of Eco-innovation (HE) analysis

This is a short summary of HE analysis as a long version can be found in *Positive Development* (Birkeland, 2008). Most assessment tools look at efficiency or energy, which is not the same as ethics, ecology or the public good. HE analysis assesses the public values of alternative design options. It includes ethical considerations, and considers the net effect on total resource flows and total ecological health. Unlike rating tools, HE analysis allows design ideas to be self-assessed during the design process before there are time or ego investments in a particular design or irreversible decisions are made. Design strategies are assessed according to their potential to influence system-wide ecological and social gains and net public good. The hierarchy ranges from 'ordinary' (1) to 'eco-positive' (6) below:

1 New designs, products or production systems that increase resource flows, but at less negative impact per unit than the norm, only reduce the relative impacts of future actions.
2 Innovations that reduce the impacts of waste from ongoing processes or activities, through reuse, recycling or reassembly, can still involve some waste and a reduction of use value or 'down-cycling'.
3 Innovations that reduce the impacts of past development (toxins or waste already in the environment) add economic value, but 'up-cycling' could involve an increase in conspicuous consumption and resource flows.
4 'No-loop' refers to innovations where waste is 'designed out' of an existing, ongoing or future system entirely. This could still create unnecessary products or have a rebound effect, where the resource savings are spent on harmful activities.
5 Eco-cycling is up-cycling that contributes to human and ecological health (i.e. is net positive) and does not increase total resource flows. However, this may still not increase access to the means of survival and resource security – the public estate.

6   Innovations at the net positive level improve whole systems and increase both the public estate and ecological base. They can be at the building or system level:

    (a)   Net positive development reverses existing impacts and increases the ecological base and public estate beyond pre-development site conditions.

    (b)   Net positive systems innovations create levers for biophysical improvements and social transformation at the 'glocal' scale (e.g. converting cities from fossil to solar).

Benchmarking

Measurement is essential to eco-innovation, but only if we measure the right things in the right ways. Perhaps the biggest problem is the green building benchmark: 'better than average' (green), or even 'better than before construction' (regenerative). Contemporary sustainable development maxims are:

- 'meet basic needs' (the Brundtland Report);
- 'recycle everything' (zero waste);
- 'up-cycle to a higher value' (cradle to cradle);
- 'design with nature' (integrative design);
- 'design like nature' (biomimicry);
- 'revive natural environments' (restorative design); and
- 'leave natural environments better than before' (regenerative design).

These concepts are inspiring, but do not address the existing social and ecological deficits and trajectories, such as overpopulation and species extinctions. Net positive would require increasing total ecological carrying capacity, ecosystems and eco-services relative to the human population and indigenous conditions in the region on a floor-area basis (for an illustration of the new metrics, see Jackson and Simpson, 2012, pp. 24–25). One way to achieve eco-positive retrofitting that can achieve this sustainability standard is design for eco-services.

15.3 Design for eco-services

Rather than using nature as a source and sink, eco-positive cities and buildings could generate their own 'eco-services' (see Beattie and Ehrlich, 2004). Design for eco-services means planning and design strategies that create ecological infrastructure and space within and around structures to support appropriate biodiversity, ecosystem integrity and resilience (Birkeland, 2007). Due to the edges, space and structures in urban areas, cities could create *surplus* eco-services and other net positive impacts to become net positive as a whole. There are design proposals that may achieve this, but they have not yet been fully assessed or built due to lack of funding (see www.sustainability.org.au). A project already in operation, the Omega Institute in New York, uses a living machine to treat catchment water before it enters the Hudson River. While this is perhaps only restorative, it provides positive offsite environmental impacts.

Green scaffolding

Green scaffolding is one example of how design for eco-services can retrofit structures for multiple synergistic functions. This is like a space frame that wraps an ecological envelope partially around existing buildings to increase their life span, functionality, resource security and a full range of climatic control functions and eco-services (Birkeland, 2007). Although ecological design is necessarily site-specific, generic concepts for green scaffolding can be adapted for different conditions, climates and structures. They can be pre-fabricated, low in embodied energy and waste, and adaptable, demountable and portable. Versions of green scaffolding can also be free-standing in parks or over streets or combined with fences. They need not cover whole facades and can be interspersed with decks or greenhouses to provide visual diversity. A list of eco-services that can be integrated with green scaffolding systems is provided in Box 15.2.

Commercial green scaffolding: Green scaffolding would facilitate the eco-retrofitting of urban areas, particularly on or in old brick two- to eight-storey buildings outside the CBD (below strong wind loads). Being connected to the structure, it can prolong the functional and structural life of old buildings and also future-proof against wind, lightning, earthquakes, extreme weather and fires. At the same time it can increase universal access to the means of survival in case of civil emergency (e.g. food and clean water). Planning incentives could allow green scaffolding in legislated building setback areas, or even above sidewalks in the case of CBDs. These extensions can include balconies or bay windows to improve life quality and real estate values to offset costs. One design uses solar fans to duct heat horizontally to Trombe walls for thermal mass, and from there around to the cooler rooms on the shady side of the building. The facade has a combination of new decks and greenhouse windows for individual thermal controls.

Domestic green scaffolding: Many post-war homes are poorly insulated and/or mouldy, causing serious health issues among low-income people. A domestic version of green scaffolding could replace fossil-fuel-based energy with integrated passive solar design. Such modules provide many functions, such as clothes-drying for rainy days, food and soil production, water cleaning and storage, day-lighting with integrated light shelves, biodiversity habitats, sound and thermal insulation, ventilation, and potentially earthquake and cyclone protection (e.g. use of cables). These can complement the aesthetics of the original house, and/or combine with fences, carports or garden structures like gazebos. There are many variations that can be mixed and matched to suit the home and its dimensions. These can be pre-fabricated or put together by a do-it-yourself owner or local builder.

Box 15.2   Services of green scaffolding (GS) to society and nature

Buildings can increase the space for nature yet also contribute to urban social and cultural amenities. The life quality and cultural benefits provided by nature include: sense of place belonging, identity and community; education and sense of wonder; cultural and aesthetic heritage; creative inspiration for the arts; physical recreation, sports, outdoor pursuits or relaxation; psychological therapy and improvement of emotional and physical health. These benefits are things that architecture and planning usually try to support in urban environments, so they are not discussed here. There are other eco-services that are not practical to integrate with the urban environment due to issues of scale or health and safety issues. These include essential minerals, grain crops such as wheat, grazing animals, and materials and fibre for buildings, clothing and furniture.

All the following eco-services could hypothetically be combined in one 'ecological envelope' on one building. Note that many functions below support both humans and nature, often simultaneously. Which functions are to be included depends on the context and its existing deficits.

Providing human habitats (materials, energy, resources, transport)

• *Electricity production:* Distributed energy systems provide resource security in times of crisis but are often not considered efficient from a market-based price perspective. However, urban wind generation can be added to existing signs, and solar cells can be integrated with shading structures.
• *Fuel production (e.g. biomass decomposition or algae):* Transparent tubes of algae can consume carbon while producing biofuels and fertilizer, without competing with land for food. Large-scale vertical composters in urban areas (or in GS) can produce biogas and compost for urban uses.
• *Material salvaging:* GS can replace high-value building facade materials for use elsewhere, while providing multiple new functions. For example, thermal mass and insulation can be combined with GS structures to replace metals (e.g. glass-covered gabion rock walls to store and distribute heat).
• *Urban forests:* While not suitable for building-integrated GS, urban forests of timber, hemp or bamboo can remediate land unsuitable for food production and provide materials for fuels or construction. Plants can be grown in independent vertical GS at the outskirts of cities as buffers.
• *Genetic resources:* Diverse gene stocks can provide a hedge against disease that has plagued monocultures. Seed companies have greatly reduced the gene pool of seed in recent decades, so there are frozen seed banks. GS provides an opportunity to protect indigenous species.

- *Transport reduction:* Food is a significant cause of transport impacts which vertical farms can reduce. Some transport impacts will be alleviated by electric cars, but there are many other impacts, such as the spread of feral seeds by tyres, not to mention the millions of people killed by cars.
- *Building longevity:* GS could reduce the damage to facades from wind loads, storms, rain and earth movement by, for example, providing a reinforcing (exterior or interior) space frame with cables.

Providing comfort and health (heating, noise, pollution, oxygen)

- *Thermal comfort:* Passive solar systems are well established, although under-utilized in modern buildings. GS can include passive solar heating, heat storage and ventilating, and support integrated 'solar stacks' and 'wind scoops' to cool the air, controlled by occupants.
- *Urban acoustics:* Noise can be mitigated by structures and forms that break up sound waves. Over-glazed facades could be covered by materials in the GS that also absorb urban traffic noise and dust. Earth in GS planters is also a good sound absorber that treats pollution.
- *Day-lighting:* Daylight is more beneficial than artificial lighting. Shelves and mirrors can be built into the GS structure to bounce daylight further into the room. While reflected light loses some energy, it can be adjusted mechanically or manually to optimize day-lighting during the day.
- *UV radiation and ozone depletion:* Shade cloth, vines or products like ETFE, supported by the GS, can be used to protect occupants on balconies or decks from the sun, while increasing the facade's multiple functions, such as electricity generation.
- *Indoor air:* Plants produce almost as much oxygen as they absorb carbon. However, few buildings are designed to support interior plants adequately. GS configurations that use reflected light can support interior vegetables and vegetation for air cleaning.
- *Pests, diseases and pathogens:* Mosquito-borne illnesses are moving into urban areas due to climate change. Screens and flytraps, like bottles that attract insect pests, can be included in the structure. Bee hives can be supported in higher levels of GS with the honey harvested from inside.
- *Particulates:* Plants are known for their ability to reduce particulates, which are implicated in many health issues. GS can also include many kinds of toxic urban dust filters to supplement the work of plants as well as reduce noise.

Providing essentials of survival (food, soil and clean air)

- *Food production:* Local urban agriculture and vertical farming are rapidly becoming accepted as necessities. People could grow their own salad bars outside their windows. Boutique vertical farming restaurants could also protect food diversity.

- *Omega 3 production:* Omega 3 is essential for health, but fish stocks are diminishing. Algae tubes, supported by GS, can provide this nutrient in urban areas. Other biochemicals and medicines from plants could conceivably be produced in these frameworks, if accessed from the inside.
- *Generating oxygen:* What is called 'algaetecture' is composed of translucent tubes of algae supported by a building structure. The algae grows very fast and consumes carbon while producing oxygen for office workers, as well as biomass for fuel or fertilizer.
- *Food chain and biodiversity:* To reduce habitat fragmentation, GS can provide vertical green corridors for small animals, insects and birds, especially endangered ones. For example, peregrine falcons have reduced the urban pigeon problem in many cities.
- *Topsoil, soil fertility and natural fertilizers:* Vertical composters are already in operation at numerous scales from units in parks to industrial processors. They use bacteria that do not smell. The composted material can be harvested from the bottom of the GS, accessed by trucks at night.
- *Recycling organic wastes:* Biolytics is an example of using layers of natural substances like peat moss to treat used water and even sewage. Such office-scale systems can be arranged vertically in a GS and include worm farms for scraps from office kitchens.
- *Aquaponics:* Many sizes or scales of aquaponic systems are now available. They grow fish and provide fertilizer for plants in a closed-loop system. They can be supported by GS systems to save land area and provide aquariums for windows of office workers.

Providing essentials of survival (water)

- *Treating toxins and pollutants:* Living machines are a well-established technology with many demonstration centres. The concept could be used vertically or horizontally in a GS of sufficient scale, accessed from the inside or outside. It could be concealed with greenery where preferred.
- *Reducing stormwater run-off:* GS, like a green roof, can collect water and filter it through soil and pebbles to reduce stormwater run-off from the roof. This also reduces soil erosion and sediment loss downstream that can pollute rivers and oceans.
- *Water collection:* Water can be collected, stored and treated in GS for non-potable uses like landscaping and toilets where there is no room on the roof. If managed on a large scale, GS can produce potable water from rainwater collected on roofs (e.g. AguaPura treats water using gravity).
- *Recycling nutrients:* Vertical wetlands, contained in an interior GS, can treat water and grow plants at the same time while providing cool, clean

air and even negative ions. It is theoretically possible to extract chemicals from plants and earthworms that have cleaned the air and water.

- *Insulation:* Stored water can be used as a heat storage medium and/or insulator. Storage tanks can double as walls that absorb and store excess heat collected during the day, and insulators to reduce diurnal temperature swings.
- *Water production:* In humid climates, water can be collected from the air (called dew harvesting), and glass/plastic can clean water by evaporation. Similarly, existing products like evaporative water cones could be integrated with the GS to treat water to a high level.
- *River quality and eutrophication:* GS can also pre-treat the water before it returns to the environment. Also, water quality in rivers and lakes, or in office lobbies, can be improved by floating 'restorers' that also provide habitats for endangered species.

Mitigating risks from natural disasters and climate extremes

- *Sequestering carbon:* Over time, permanent or undisturbed vegetation and soil sequester carbon. There are other materials that absorb carbon and/or other pollutants (e.g. titanium dioxide, ovaline), but such materials may be toxic in the mining or production process.
- *Mitigating the urban climate:* Currently, most urban structures contribute to the urban heat island effect, which causes thousands of premature deaths each year. GS reduces the heat island effect and stimulates the vertical circulation of air to reduce temperature stratification.
- *Droughts, fires, floods:* GS can contain water supplies from stored rainwater to alleviate urban droughts, and even provide sprays to cool the streets or fight fires. Given the economic costs of these events, this could pay for itself in one emergency.
- *Emergency supplies:* Recent disasters have shown that food and water supplies can be seriously impacted in emergencies. Sometimes survivors cannot escape, or even be reached by relief efforts. GS could provide interim supplies for worst-case scenarios.
- *Adaptability and flexibility:* Ecosystems evolve over long periods of time to adjust to new contexts. GS can be converted quickly to respond to threats to biodiversity. Where a GS does not perform well, it can be corrected by replacing internal components or their contents where required.

Interior green scaffolding: In the case of historic buildings, a vertical landscape on the interior could reinforce and renovate the old structure. To improve natural air circulation, natural light and air quality, an interior atrium could be added without affecting the facade, using skylights and light shelves. In one design, light from the atrium skylight bounces off a suspended sculpture of shiny round pipes, or 'green chandelier', which reflects the light to all parts of the atrium and planting wall as needed (although some energy is lost in reflection). The pipes could be controlled electronically to adjust to the changing position of the sun. A catwalk to service the vertical planting wall would also provide usable social space.

Green space walls

The green space wall for *new* construction challenges the nature/society barrier. Ecological spaces in indoor and outdoor areas are part of the building envelope itself (Birkeland, 2007). In other words, green scaffolding becomes the wall, structure and space for ecosystems and eco-services. The contents of the demountable modules would depend on the orientation of the wall as well as functional needs. The modules' micro-climates combine to insulate and circulate heat and coolness, and produce clean energy, air, water and soil. However, the modules also support a range of visual and ecological functions, from micro-gardens to insect-breeding spaces, reptile or frog preserves, and bee hives (maintained by local nature clubs and schools). Space for ecosystems and biodiversity are combined with practical functions of the building skin, such as integrated solar stacks for ventilation, internal gabion walls for heat storage, and/or lightweight wind generators.

Playgardens

Playgardens are a form of green scaffolding for positive child development (social sustainability). They could be seen as botanical 'exploratoriums' that encourage children to develop positive early experiences in nature, even when confined to urban environments (Birkeland, 1994). Low-impact and safe structures designed to facilitate exploratory, imaginative and interactive play are integrated with plants, trees and the natural features of the site. They bring nature back into the human habitat, place child development in the natural environment and provide eco-services for humans and nature. Vegetation is placed strategically to slow children down and reduce collisions, and appropriate plants in thick mulch helps to prevent serious injury (the plants recover). Playgardens integrate with the landscape and do not conflict visually with buildings. They also create a place for different age groups to play together or engage in quite social play, lunch or storytelling.

15.4 Conclusion

Conventional forms of economic growth and physical developments have serious limits that have already been breached, as evidenced by climate change and species extinction. While there are real limits to negative forms of growth, there is no limit to eco-positive forms of growth. PD can decouple economic growth from environmental impacts while increasing the natural life support system, life quality and health. The opportunities to undo past system design errors, make things better, and save the planet through eco-positive environments are boundless.

References

Beattie, A. and Ehrlich, P. 2004. *Wildsolutions* (2nd edn), New Haven, CT: Yale University Press.

Benyus, J. 1997. *Bimimicry: Innovation Inspired by Nature*, New York: William Morrow and Co.

Birkeland, J.L. 1994. 'Ecofeminist Playgardens', *International Play Journal* 2, 49–59.

Birkeland, J.L. 1995. 'Priorities for Environmental Professionals', paper presented at Linking and Prioritising Environmental Criteria, CIB TG-8 Workshop, Ontario.

Birkeland, J.L. 2000. *Eco-Retrofitting: A Proposal for the National Environmental Education Council*, Canberra: Environment Australia.

Birkeland, J.L. 2003. 'Beyond Zero Waste', paper presented at Societies for a Sustainable Future, 3rd UKM–UC International Conference, Canberra.

Birkeland, J.L. 2004. 'Building Assessment Systems: Reversing Environmental Impacts', paper presented at Nature and Society Forum, ACT. Available at: http://www.naf.org.au/naf-forum.

Birkeland, J.L. 2005. 'The Case for Eco-Retrofitting', *Solar Progress* 26(2), 7–9.

Birkeland, J.L. 2007. 'GEN 4: Positive Development: Design for Eco-Services', in *BEDP Environmental Design Guide of the Australian Institute of Architects.* Available at: http://www.environmentdesignguide.com.au/.

Birkeland, J.L. 2008. *Positive Development: From Vicious Circles to Virtuous Cycles through Built Environment Design*, London: Earthscan._

Birkeland, J.L. 2009. 'GEN 77: Design for Eco-Services, Environmental Services' and 'GEN 78: Design for Eco-Services, Building Services', in *BEDP Environmental Design Guide of the Australian Institute of Architects.* Available at: http://www.environmentdesignguide.com.au/.

BMRA. 2008. Building Materials and Reuse Association website. Available at: http://www.bmra.org/.

Elliston, B., Diesendorf, M. and MacGill, I. 2011. 'Simulations of Scenarios with 100% Renewable Electricity in the Australian National Electricity Market', paper presented at Solar 2011 Conference, Australian Solar Energy Society, Sydney. Available at: http://www.ies.unsw.edu.au/docs/Solar2011-100percent.pdf.

Gartland, L. 2011. *Heat Islands: Understanding and Mitigating Heat in Urban Areas*, London: Earthscan.

Harrisville, N., Hongping, Y. and Shen, L. 2011. 'Trend of the Research on Construction and Demolition Waste Management', *Waste Management* 31, 670–679.

Heede, R. *et al.* 1995. *Homemade Money*, New Hampshire: Rocky Mountain Institute with Brick House Publishing.

Jackson, D. and Simpson, R. (eds). 2012. *D_City: Digital Earth, Virtual Nations, Data Cities*, Sydney: DCity.

Lovegrove, K., Burgess, G. and Pye, J. 2011. 'A New 500 m^2 paraboloidal dish solar concentrator', *Solar Energy* 85(4), 620–626. Available at: http://dx.doi.org/10.1016/j.solener.2010.01.009.

Miller, W. and Birkeland, J.L. 2009. 'Green Energy: Sustainable Energy Sources and Alternative Technologies', in T. Yigitcanlar (ed.) *Sustainable Urban and Regional Infrastructure Development: Technologies, Applications and Management*, Hershey, PA: Information Science Reference (IGI Global), 1–16.

Mobbs, M. 1998. *Sustainable House*, Sydney: Choice Books.

Rees, W.E. 2002. 'Eco-footprints and Eco-logical Design', in J. Birkeland (ed.) *Design for Sustainability: A Sourcebook of Integrated Eco-logical Solutions*, London: Earthscan, 73.

Renger, C., Birkeland, J.L. and Midmore, D. 2013. 'Positive Development: Design for Urban Climate Mitigation and Ecological Gains', Stream 5-Pushing the Boundaries: Net Positive Buildings (SB13) CaGBC National Conference and Expo. Vancouver BC, June 4–6, 2013.

Romm, J. 1999. *Cool Companies: How the Best Businesses Boost Profits and Productivity by Cutting Greenhouse-Gas Emissions*, Washington, DC: Island Press.

Safamanesh, B. and Byrd, H. 2012. 'The Two Sides of a Double-skin Facade: Built Intelligent Skin or Brand Image Scam', paper presented at the 46th Architectural Science Association Conference, Griffith University, Gold Coast.

Sandler, K. and Swingle, P. 2006. *OSWER Innovations Pilot: Building Deconstruction and Reuse*. Available at: http://www.epa.gov/oswer/.

Scheer, H. 2004. *The Solar Economy*, London: Earthscan.

Strohbach, M.W., Arnold, E. and Haase, D. 2012. 'The Carbon Footprint of Urban Green Space: A Life Cycle Approach', *Landscape and Urban Planning* 104, 220–229.

UNEP. 2005. *Millennium Ecosystem Assessment: Strengthening Capacity to Manage Ecosystems Sustainably for Human Wellbeing*. Available at: http://ma.caudillweb.com/en/about.overview.aspx.

US EPA. 1998. *Market Values for Home Energy Efficiency*, Washington, DC: Environmental Protection Agency.

Vale, B. and Vale, R. 1975. *The Autonomous House: Design and Planning for Self-sufficiency*, London: Thames and Hudson. (For a summary, see Vale, R. and Vale, B. 2002. 'Autonomous Servicing', in J. Birkeland (ed.) *Design for Sustainability: A Sourcebook of Ecological Solutions*, London: Earthscan, 182–185.)

CHAPTER 16

Money matters

Financing the transition to a resilient and sustainable urban energy system

Nigel Jollands

16.1 Introduction: why the Rolling Stones were 'on the money'

Is there anything the Rolling Stones can't do? Beyond being mega international rock stars it seems they also have some useful insights into achieving resilient urban systems. In 1964 the Rolling Stones released an album featuring a cover of the song 'Money'. The lyrics are profound: 'Money ain't everything it's true / But what it can't buy I can't use.' When it comes to securing a resilient and sustainable energy future for our urban systems, nothing could be closer to the truth: money is not everything, but it is a necessary condition for achieving our goals.

The scale of the need for investments in sustainable and resilient urban energy systems is enormous. The International Energy Agency estimates that over the next decade, nearly US$600 billion annually in additional investments is required globally to avoid catastrophic climate change effects (IEA, 2012). Given that around two-thirds of energy use occurs within urban systems (IEA, 2008), it is clear that the need for investment in cities is critical.

Unfortunately, the scale of investment required seems to far outstrip the level of actual investment. While it is difficult to measure investment flows into sustainable and resilient energy systems, estimates by the IEA (2010) suggest that only around a quarter of the required investment has been realised. If this is the case, why are these investments so low and how can investment levels be increased?

16.2 Why is actual (sustainable/resilient) investment so low relative to what is required?

Stimulating investment in sustainable and resilient urban energy systems should be straightforward – at least in theory. For example, many analyses of marginal cost curves for climate change abatement show that investment in energy efficiency and renewable energy systems can be made at negative costs (see, for example, McKinsey & Company, 2006, and IEA, 2012). Yet, in reality, getting investments happening on the ground is proving to be challenging. The reason for this is that often the benefits of resilient energy systems are 'invisible' (especially in the case of energy efficiency) and difficult to quantify. Furthermore, investment and resilient energy systems are the subject of many pervasive barriers that have received considerable attention in the literature (see, for example, de t'Serclaes and Jollands, 2010, IEA, 2007 and 2010, and Sorrell *et al.*, 2004). These barriers include:

- the lack of information about the benefits of such systems;
- the perceived risks and lack of certainty associated with returns and benefits from resilient energy systems investments;
- the low priority many people give to reducing energy costs through energy efficiency improvements;
- energy prices not fully reflecting externalities; and
- principal–agent problems.

Finally, what the marginal abatement cost curves often do not show are the transaction costs associated with sustainable and resilient energy system investments. Such an energy system encourages distributed generation and distribution as well as energy efficiency improvements across myriad urban energy users. In other words, a resilient energy system involves many tens, and often hundreds or thousands, of actors. As a result, the transaction costs involved in bringing all of these actors together into one bankable deal is considerable – especially when compared to a €500 million power plant investment involving a single client.

16.3 Glimmers of light

Despite the challenges, there are glimmers of light where financing sustainable and resilient energy systems is achieving results. These examples predominantly come from public-sector banks (such as the World Bank, the Asian Development Bank, the Inter-American Development Bank, KfW, and the European Bank for Reconstruction and Development (EBRD)) charged with leadership in this area. The experience of the EBRD is pertinent in this regard, particularly as it has recently passed the €10 billion mark for investments in sustainable energy (see Box 16.1).

Box 16.1   European Bank for Reconstruction and Development (EBRD) Sustainable Energy Initiative

The EBRD is an international financial institution (IFI) working in the region from Central and Eastern Europe to Central Asia and the southern and eastern Mediterranean (see http://www.ebrd.com/pages/country.shtml for more information). The aim of the EBRD is to foster transition towards open and democratic market economies. The finance 'tool box' used to stimulate investments to achieve these aims includes a range of financial instruments from direct investment, structured finance (for use in specialised transactions such as energy performance contracting), intermediated finance (where the EBRD lends to local banks who then on-lend to customers) and use of climate finance funds (such as the Clean Technology Fund, Strategic Climate Fund, Global Environment Facility and the Adaptation Fund). Importantly, the majority of EBRD investments are made at commercial rates: the EBRD applies internal guidelines on using subsidies in a way that minimises distortions and prevents crowding out of private finance.

Applying the bank's investment approach to sustainable energy is considered a critical part of achieving the EBRD's transition goals. In 2006 the EBRD launched the Sustainable Energy Initiative (SEI) in response to the increasing importance of sustainable energy to the region of operations and the call of the G8 for IFIs to scale up their activity to address climate change. Through the SEI, the EBRD has been able to liberate significant sustainable energy finance. From 2006 to November 2012 SEI financing reached €10 billion in 552 projects with a total project value of €55 billion. These investments are expected to deliver an estimated reduction of 50 million tonnes of carbon dioxide per year.

Investments in the bank's 'urban portfolio' (referred to internally as 'municipal and environmental infrastructure') have reached just over €1.3 billion since 2006, delivering an estimated abatement of around 2 million tonnes of carbon dioxide per year.

Investments in urban public transport and district heating dominated the urban portfolio at a cumulative volume of just over €600 million and €372 million, respectively (Figure 16.1). Examples of public transport projects include the Bursa light rail project in Turkey (sustainable energy component accounting for €70 million of the total project of more than €200 million) and the Warsaw metro project (€35.8 million SEI component). The demand for increased investment in public transport is not surprising. It reflects a mounting crisis with urban traffic congestion and emissions in the EBRD region as a result of steady growth in private vehicle ownership over the past decade. Water and wastewater treatment accounted for around 12 per cent of the total sustainable energy investment portfolio, with the remainder of the portfolio covering municipal services and renewable energy investments.

Figure 16.1 EBRD sustainable energy 'urban' investments by sector
Source: EBRD

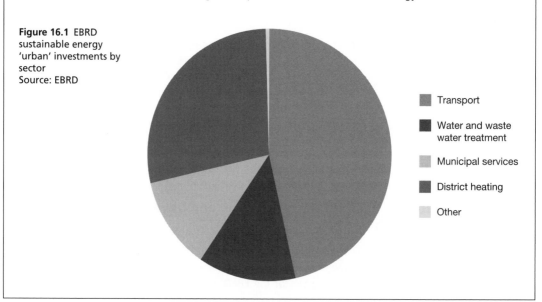

The scale of the urban-related sustainable energy investments shown in Box 16.1 are all the more surprising given the increasingly challenging environment within which the EBRD works. Many sub-sovereign clients (particularly in Central Europe) are facing debt-capacity limits, reducing their ability to invest in much-needed infrastructure improvements. In addition, challenges with budget code requirements in Russia and Ukraine make business for the EBRD difficult in these countries with significant needs in district heating rehabilitation.

It is important to note that many of these investments would not have been possible without two ingredients in addition to the finance: donor-supported technical assistance and policy dialogue. Technical assistance is critical to finding and developing projects. Engineers and technical advisers support project preparation, project implementation and capacity building in order to bring a well-developed project to the bank. For example, donor-funded engineers play a pivotal role in identifying and developing district heating projects to the point they are ready to be put in front of bankers for their appraisal.

Policy dialogue is another critical part of the EBRD approach to increasing investments in urban sustainable energy projects. The EBRD uses policy dialogue to help shape and change the policy environment for sustainable energy in countries. In doing so, it works with governments to remove barriers to energy efficiency and renewable energy. Examples of policy dialogue activities carried out by the EBRD are diverse. For example, the bank works with the government of Ukraine to draft energy efficiency regulations for residential buildings. This work directly relates to preparing the ground for a residential energy efficiency credit line facility for Ukraine. The EBRD is also working directly with authorities in Russia to change legislation relating to energy service companies – a necessary precursor to enabling the bank to provide much-needed capital for renovating municipally owned buildings in Russia. For the period 2009 to 2011, the EBRD mobilised €108 million of donor resources to support the technical assistance and policy dialogue of the SEI.

16.4 Lessons and conclusions

The EBRD's Sustainable Energy Initiative has been very successful – particularly given the challenging context within which it works. The question, then, is what lessons can the EBRD provide for others pursuing sustainable energy investments in the urban context? The answer lies in what could be referred to as the EBRD's 'business and operational models'. In the words of the Sustainable Energy Initiative Phase III document (EBRD, 2011) the 'SEI builds on its alignment with the unique EBRD business model, that is, transition-driven, private sector focused, market-oriented, commercially motivated projects crowding-in the private sector and paving the way for sustainable market-supported financing structures'.

In particular, the SEI is able to deliver results in urban sustainable energy investments because it combines three critical – and inseparable – elements:

- project financing of specific energy efficiency and renewable energy investments with clear estimates of energy savings and carbon dioxide emission reductions;
- technical assistance to support project preparation, project implementation and capacity building; and
- policy dialogue to support the development of an enabling environment for sustainable energy.

So, it seems the Rolling Stones had it right. Money isn't everything, it's true. It is very important, but without the support of technical assistance and transformational policy changes, it will be impossible to answer the call to increase investments in sustainable and resilient energy urban infrastructure significantly and immediately.

References

de t'Serclaes, P. and Jollands, N. 2010. How to Make the Finance Flow. *Environmental Finance*, March, pp. 26–27.

European Bank for Reconstruction and Development (EBRD). 2011. Sustainable Energy Initiative: Phase 3. Unpublished document. Summary available at: http://www.ebrd.com/downloads/research/brochures/sei.pdf.

International Energy Agency. 2007. *Mind the Gap: Quantifying Principal–Agent Problems in Energy Efficiency*. Paris: IEA/OECD.

International Energy Agency. 2008. *World Energy Outlook*. Paris: IEA/OECD.

International Energy Agency. 2010. *Money Matters: Mitigating Risk to Spark Private Investments in Energy Efficiency*. Paris: IEA/OECD. Available at: http://www.iea.org/publications/freepublications/publication/money_matters.pdf.

International Energy Agency. 2012. *Energy Technology Perspectives*. Paris: IEA/OECD.

McKinsey & Company. 2006. *Productivity of Growing Global Energy Demand: A Micro-Economic Perspective*. San Francisco: McKinsey & Company.

Sorrell, S., O'Malley, E., Schleich, J. and Scott, S. 2004. *The Economics of Energy Efficiency: Barriers to Cost-Effective Investment*. Cheltenham: Edward Elgar.

CHAPTER 17

Networked city and society

Federico Casalegno and Pelin Arslan

17.1 Introduction

Rethinking urbanism in a sustainable way promotes social and economic inclusion as well as environmental consciousness with an aim of creating resilient cities. At the core of the idea of sustainable cities is the notion of solving urban problems from a holistic approach, analysing overlapping issues, understanding co-relations and foreseeing long-lasting solution strategies through collaboration with various actors in the urban system.

Sustainable cities are also connected cities, employing ubiquitous, networked intelligence to ensure not only the efficient and responsible use of the scarce resources – particularly energy and water – that are required for a city's operation, together with the effective management of waste products that a city produces, such as carbon emissions to the atmosphere, but also the democratization of individuals' participative ideas through media locative tools. The principal evolutionary eras here are:

- *Skeletons and skins.* The earliest cities consisted of little more than skeleton and skin. They provided walls, floors, and roofs for shelter and protection, in combination with simple structural skeletons to hold them up. The intelligence needed to operate these cities resided in the heads of their inhabitants.
- *Mechanical metabolisms.* In the industrial era, urban networks multiplied, differentiated, and grew in scale. Furthermore, they added mechanical metabolic systems and massive infrastructures to the skeletons and skins that they had traditionally provided. These systems then became major consumers of energy and producers of waste and pollution.
- *Electronic nervous systems.* At the dawn of the electronic era, buildings and cities began to develop primitive nervous systems. Telegraph, telephone, and radio communication systems provided the first artificial nerves. These allowed architectural and urban systems to develop simple reflexes and feedback loops.
- *Internet era.* In this era, the primitive nervous systems rapidly evolved into something approximating the advanced nervous systems of higher organisms. Ubiquitous digital networks supplanted the older analog networks and formed a new kind of urban infrastructure. Distributed systems of networked computers and server farms became the brains of cities. Pervasive sensing connected vast, new streams of data about urban activities to these brains. In future, the flows of resources into cities, the processing and distribution of materials,

energy, and products, the coordination of the actions of individuals and organizations, and the eventual removal or recycling of waste can be increasingly informed, coordinated, and controlled by the new, rapidly growing, digital nervous systems.

Informed, responsible choices

In our digitally networked, information-saturated era, ignorance of the consequences can be no excuse for ill-considered actions. It is increasingly possible to keep close track of our energy, water, and carbon footprints so that we can evaluate the sustainability consequences of our daily choices and actions. We have, at our fingertips, the tools and computation power to enable participation in sophisticated new fields, such as media, learning, and wellbeing. Connected sustainable cities will encourage new forms of personal and group responsibility, and will establish powerful incentives to meet those responsibilities.

Like individuals, government institutions and businesses – be they small or medium enterprises, or large corporations – also have responsible choices to make. The success of a connected sustainable city depends on coordinated policy and action in the development and introduction of information and communication technologies. Governments at every level (federal, regional, municipal) need to adopt policies and regulations that promote such choices. Worldwide organizations also play a crucial role, and are especially important in fostering the development of connected sustainable cities and social sustainability.

17.2 The next generation of ICT tools

New tools and applications are becoming available that make it less expensive, easier, and more effective than ever to coordinate collective action among people who can promote sustainable development and behavior. Often referred to as Web 2.0, these technologies allow easier knowledge and information sharing, both crucial to the development of connected sustainable cities. Boyd (2009) and Shirky (2008) argue that the ease with which we can now connect, communicate, produce, share, replicate, locate, and distribute information has had, and continues to have, a profound impact on our social, cultural, and technological practices. On these emerging collaborative platforms, people can share and capitalize on lessons learned from best practices around the world. These types of tools can advance the rise of new bottom-up cultures of decision-making and promote civic engagement on topics of great importance, encouraging people to get involved and take action locally and on a global level.

As mobile devices with high-quality recording abilities proliferate, production of media content that is then uploaded, shared, and disseminated on social networks is becoming increasingly common. The intellectual and creative process inherent in media creation lends itself well to engaging people within their communities to discover, explore, contribute, and discuss issues around sustainability. This motivates participants to explore related topics in their local environment and consequently creates trust among government, people, and cities.

Box 17.1   Locast

Locast is an open locative-media platform (http://locast.mit.edu/) that combines web and mobile applications to allow geo-located media production and interaction. The Locast platform consists of three main components: Locast Web – the web-based interface; Locast Core – the backend and API; and Locast Mobile – an Android-based mobile application. Locast technology enables users to create individual and collective narratives, disseminate content, and generate community-related conversations. People produce their own media elements through Locast mobile and web applications and share their activities on a location-based map in real time.

This social platform helps people, communities, and other groups to explore new opportunities through social interaction in the Locast community and enables them to exchange ideas with decision-makers. The aim is to improve connections between people and their social, cultural, and physical spaces. This framework enables people to share their knowledge practices and collaborate in content generation to generate more democratic and collaborative environments.

17.3 Locast: location-based open platform

The Locast platform explores new ways to implement information and communication technologies in cities and urban areas (see Box 17.1). Locast technology developed by the MIT Mobile Experience Lab allows a realization of this aim through different ways of achieving sustainable urbanism: creating new cultural and social expressions, collaborative problem-solving abilities, and civic engagement.

Locast technology has been used to address various issues and provide insights into current practice approaches in sustainable urbanism: *civic engagement, capturing memories, and participatory learning.* As an example in *civic engagement as citizen journalism* practice, Locast Civic Media aims to engage citizenship in the process of collecting, reporting, and disseminating news and information related to the urban environment. The platform incentivizes citizens' proactive role through Locast open publishing tools, community self-regulation, social circulation of content, collaborative authoring as well as other production tools to improve the dynamics of an individual's work, conversations, and collaborations.

The emphasis is on bringing together urban conversations with civic knowledge-sharing practices for building information-based communities. Nelimarkka (2008) and Rheingold (2002) have stated that mobile communication is becoming an effective instrument to strengthen civic bonds through the empowerment of individuals, the creation of ad-hoc networks, and the proliferation of information. Locast mobile application enables the user to create street reports (casts) through video and audio content and decide whether to produce them individually or to involve peers in large-scale reports on a specific topic and/or urban area projects. Casts and projects are created, collected, and shared in real time on Locast websites where the entire members' community can join the conversation with comments and further casts.

The Locast Civic Media project has been deployed in Porto Alegre, Brazil, with 25 media and communication students and 11 reporters. The participants were encouraged to use Locast freely to explore as many urban scenarios as possible according to personal interests and relations with the city spaces. The list of topics included social and cultural aspects of city neighborhoods, local communities, ongoing grassroots activities, subcultures, and popular events. Various media forms were created, from live capture, reports, interviews, and breaking news to coverage, point-of-view narrations, investigations, and sequential narrations. The participants had the opportunity to report news in their local area in real time and share problems with policy-makers and other citizens.

Another practiced approach to *citizen as street smart mapper* is the Locast Youth Mapping project, which explores mobile and web tools to help youth in Rio de Janeiro to build impactful, communicative digital maps reporting problems in their communities. The MIT Mobile Experience Lab collaborated with UNICEF's Social and Civic Media Section and the Public Laboratory for Open Technology and Science (PLOTS) to develop the mapping tools.[1] The project uses traditional media combined with new technologies, including social networking tools, SMS, and digital mapping, to empower the youth to play an active role in society.

Through a mobile phone application, youth produce a real-time portrait of their community, creating geo-located photos and videos, organized as thematic maps. As a result of deploying the project in Rio de Janeiro in a one-week time frame, the main issues to emerge were: 374 reports on walking hazards, accumulation of garbage, sewage problems, collapse risk, power-line problems, and faulty stairs. This is an example of participative actions resulting in requests for governmental action leading to community benefits.

The mapping exercise enabled young people to contribute to raising awareness about the vulnerabilities they face in their community and to preventative planning. Participants played an active role in identifying and communicating risks to local officials, thereby taking ownership of the process. The project showed that youth-led digital mapping is a compelling tool to articulate adolescents' concerns on social and environmental topics to local officials.

The initiative generated positive outcomes that directly impacted the lives of young people in the favelas. It increased the advocacy capacity of community actors, drew visibility to existing challenges and created offline community changes. In addition, it contributed to more inclusive, secure, and participatory actions aimed at reducing risks and disparities in the city.

Another approach to improve sustainability patterns in an urban environment is to enable learning and develop awareness on local issues. In collaboration with the Museum of Science in Trento, Italy, Locast H2flow illustrates how a locative participatory media platform has the potential to strengthen connections between people, places, and information on local and regional environmental issues. The project was designed around the specific circumstances and context of this region, which features glaciers that are melting at an alarming rate. The area is rich in natural water resources as well as high-quality tap water, yet the consumption of bottled water is widespread and the fabrication of the plastic bottles and their transport by road mean that a great deal of fossil fuel is burned, a contributor to global warming.

Students used a mobile application to create geo-located video content. Investigating the prospect of using mobile devices for guided video production, this application moderates the learning process by providing tasks to complete and video templates that structure the individual video content. The tasks were designed to be experienced by a student sequentially, progressing through the content in a way that is meant to aid in their understanding of the overall topic of water use and sustainability in their community.

In completing the task, a student is guided through video creation, and is given the opportunity to communicate their own interpretation and understanding of a topic, ultimately producing individual scenes of a larger narrative. The students cooperate in groups of four to five, and conduct interviews with the public. They additionally participate in role-playing scenarios, taking the role of reporter, environmental activist, or private water company owner. Through this process, students study the topic from multiple perspectives using media generation templates: private versus public water; greenhouse gas emission; overall climate change; the melting glaciers; as well as the cultural value of water for their local community. The application could be extended into an educational curriculum in a school's academic calendar.

Memories are yet another aspect of resilient cities. A city without a memory is like a 'dry city' without a soul. Expressing and discovering memories in the city reveals the spirit of the historical, cultural, and social values as well as identity. Memories sprout throughout the city and reflect emotional attachments to places. The Memory Traces project, in collaboration with the Italian Consulate of Boston, allows storytellers to describe their experiences and memories in a narrative approach. The potential of storytelling through new interactive media combines the digital environment with the physical urban environment. The project is an interactive collection of stories of Italian immigrants who live in Boston. One hundred and fifty episodes of experiences and memories have been captured in an open source platform where geo-located video stories overlaid on a map of the city can be filtered by person, time, period, or theme on the project's website (http:// locast.mit.edu/memorytraces/).

17.4 Conclusion

'Better' cities will emerge through participation of people, facilitating socio-technological change through the convergence of industry, government, and community for more sustainable outcomes.

In this chapter, some examples have been given through application of user generated and practice-based applications directed towards developing more resilient and sustainable cities. Here, new information and communication technologies and their applications represent key ingredients for future change in major urban sectors as well as cities and their built environments. Innovation is achievable through collaborating, engaging, participating, and creating synergies.

Cities have evolved in different forms throughout the years depending on social, cultural, economic, and environmental factors. Culture, global economy, climate, and social issues have changed the places where we live from skeleton skins to physiological cities.

It is true that cities now have a nerve system, so it is important to explore new strategies, approaches, and tools to involve residents and encourage them to participate in the decision-making process, developing awareness related to the environment in which they are living, acting, producing, and consuming. However, a more holistic approach, benefiting from innovative uses of ICT platforms, can embrace shared media production and consumption practices fostering social connections, sparking citizen participation, and improving the sense of community belonging at a range of scales – from citywide to local neighborhood.

It should be possible in the twenty-first century for everyone to participate in the process of sustainability through learning, civic engagement, and participatory urbanism so that cities can be livable and environmentally sustainable, as well as competitive, productive, socially inclusive, and resilient.

Note

1   Rio environmental mapping is part of the Social and Civic Media Section's global Digital Empowerment and Advocacy (DEA) initiative. The local implementing partner, Centro Desenvolvimento Apoio Programa Saúde (CEDAPS), is a civil society organization that aims to develop the autonomy and capacity of impoverished communities by promoting equity and better health and quality of life.

References

Boyd, D. 2009. Taken out of context: American teen sociality in networked publics. Doctoral dissertation, University of California, Berkeley.

Federconsumatori. 2008. Acqua in bottiglia: l'affare dell'acqua 2008. Retrieved March 2011 from: http://www.federconsumatoripisa.it/29-09-2008/acqua-bottiglia-laffare-dellacqua.

IPCC. 2007. Summary for policymakers. In *Climate Change 2007: The Physical Science Basis*. Cambridge: Cambridge University Press.

Mitchell, J.M. and Casalegno, F. 2008. *Connected Sustainable Cities*. Cambridge, MA: Mobile Experience Lab Publishing.

Nelimarkka, M. 2008. The use of ubiquitous media in politics: How ubiquitous life effects into political life today and what might happen in the future. In *MindTrek '08, Proceedings of the 12th International Conference on Entertainment and Media in the Ubiquitous Era*. New York: ACM Press.

Rheingold, H. 2002. *Smart Mobs: The Next Social Revolution*. New York: Perseus.

Shirky, C. 2008. *Here Comes Everybody*. New York: Penguin Press.

World Wide Fund for Nature. n.d. Going, going, gone: Climate change and global glacier decline. Retrieved March 2011 from: http://assets.panda.org/downloads/glacierspaper.pdf.

CHAPTER 18

(Re-)designing resilient, sustainable precincts

Urban armatures

Shane Murray and Lee-Anne Khor

18.1 Introduction

Successful urban places are self-perpetuating. They are in a constant state of flux, adapting and evolving to accommodate changes in populations, activities and technologies. They are resilient (Walker and Salt 2006), inclusive (Manzi *et al.* 2010) and each has a distinctive character. Small city-systems, or urban ecosystems, continually negotiate each other and their extended contexts to maintain an urban equilibrium within the economic, political, environmental, social and technological influences that constitute our cities (Newton and Thomson forthcoming; Douglas 2011). We now know this 'urban flux' has been destabilized. As discussed elsewhere in this book (see Chapter 2 for challenges, and other chapters in Part Three for sector-specific issues), significant areas of our existing cities as well as new suburban developments are failing to meet the contemporary challenges of rapid population growth, urbanization and intensification, resource constraints and climate change.

In Australia, Canada and the US, energy consumption generated through building and transport use can contribute more than half of total greenhouse emissions (Calthorpe Associates 2011). To reduce the environmental burdens generated by our cities, it is critical that we formulate new strategies for accommodating growth that do not rely on the expansion of low-density development on the urban fringe. The uniformity of housing typology in these areas, combined with low service and amenity levels, has failed to meet the dwelling needs of both an ageing population and diversifying contemporary households. These areas are also failing to provide first-home buyers and the low waged with affordable housing alternatives in locations with access to employment, education and other public services. Conventional development patterns are no longer sustainable; altering the business-as-usual model for urban growth is now essential to enable both new and established suburbs to re-emerge as resilient and dynamic urban places.

Current low-density suburban expansion and piecemeal, individuated regeneration of existing suburban areas are inadequate to the task of achieving the scale of transformation necessary for sustainable transitioning. We need to find models that enable effective, structural urban change to provide the armatures from which resilient cities can grow, new economies can flourish and healthy societies can evolve. It is at the scale of a precinct that we can begin to engage with these challenges in a comprehensive manner.

By 'precinct' we mean the consideration of an area of urban regeneration or development of sufficient scale to support a balanced mix of programs, housing diversity and shared public space connected through a walkable open space network. In addition a precinct ideally is able to support networked systems for energy distribution, sustainable water management, and effective waste handling. While typically a precinct is considered as a bounded entity in a similar way to our understanding of 'quartier' or 'neighborhood', precincts may also be disaggregated. These types of precincts emanate from acupuncture-like infill of an existing urban area in a non-contiguous manner whereby the combination of strategic redevelopment with the existing context can form an overall precinct solution. Precincts offer a regenerative potential unavailable to individual building proposals (Newton *et al.* 2011). The scale and type of development contained in the precinct model provides opportunities for integrative design approaches capable of delivering performance enhancements and collective benefits across several urban arenas. For example, considerable performance enhancements can be achieved with innovative district-wide servicing, or building social capital through neighborhood design and local programs. This chapter presents a range of best-practice models for precinct redevelopment and offers a critical discussion of the innovations they have achieved, the 'urban armatures' being affected and the principles driving their implementation.

18.2 Precinct redevelopment models

Existing approaches to precinct design vary in scale, location and context. They can include new masterplanned communities, eco-towns or neighborhoods in greenfield locations (BioRegional and CABE 2008) as well as urban renewal strategies for obsolete industrial areas (brownfields), surplus government facilities or underperforming business/retail centers (greyfields) (Dunham-Jones and Williamson 2009; Newton and Thomson forthcoming). These types of precincts are generally large, consolidated sites that can be redeveloped as new mixed-use urban centers incorporating effective infrastructure, services and technology, or involve the renewal of failing urban centers, commercial strips and activity corridors requiring better pedestrian links and transit connections integrated with more appropriate building designs and public open space amenity.

The redevelopment of Stapleton Airport, USA (Calthorpe Associates, Wolff Lyon Architects, Aecom; see http://www.calthorpe.com/stapleton) is an example of large-scale precinct renewal comprising a range of design initiatives for enhancing the environmental, economic and social armatures for Denver County. Located ten minutes from downtown Denver, the 1,900-hectare site is the largest urban infill redevelopment in America and is expected to accommodate 12,000 new dwellings, 8 schools, 7.8 million square feet of office space and 4.3 million square feet of retail area.

The masterplan is designed around a regional open space network enabling the reinstatement of important natural habitats and waterways for Denver, the most notable being the 85-acre Westerly Creek Corridor. The open space environments constitute about a third of the development area and provide extensive pedestrian and bike connections from Stapleton to surrounding districts. The open space amenity, integrated with a commuter rail system, bus network and a series of walkable community destinations, provides public space and transit arterials that stitch together a number of smaller urban neighborhoods.

The design and distribution of public amenity and common facilities are the backbone for community building and social integration, a distinctive feature of the new development. Employing the principles of New Urbanism, the residential neighborhoods comprise a mix of compact dwelling typologies, local retail facilities and pedestrian-friendly streetscapes. While largely constituting single-family accommodation, the residential building forms are four times denser than typical development patterns in Denver. Importantly, the dwelling mix is accessible to a range of income levels, enabling an inclusive neighborhood structure within Stapleton and greater social equity for the inner-urban Denver region.

The Stapleton redevelopment began concept design in the mid-1990s and is due for completion in 2020, demonstrating the time needed to implement a successful urban precinct and the importance of a strong design framework for the evolution of such a development. It exemplifies how careful spatial distributions, as well as the physical design of buildings, spaces and environments, can positively influence the way urban communities grow and mature. These benefits are most pronounced at the scale of a precinct, and Stapleton takes advantage of its large redevelopment area to optimize the convergence of urban and natural environments.

By contrast, E-Gate (Fender Katsalidis Architects, Aurecon; see http://www.majorprojects.vic.gov.au/our-projects/our-current-projects/e-gate) is a smaller urban renewal precinct proposed on an under-utilized public transport site on the fringe of Melbourne's central business district. The proposed redevelopment intends to demonstrate a new model for high-quality, future urban living in Australia. It will accommodate 3,700 new dwellings at a density of 185 dwellings per hectare, 2 schools, 20,000 square meters of retail/leisure facilities and 78,600 square meters of commercial space. The project aspires to be the first carbon-zero, self-water-sufficient, 'car-free' development in the city.

The 20-hectare island site is bounded by an existing rail yard, regional train line, natural watercourse and major road arterial. At an urban level, the new precinct provides a crucial connection between a major train station and several activity areas lying beyond the transit barriers. By providing the 'missing link' between activity areas, the design takes advantage of the existing topography and creates a new car-free ground terrain over the rail lines and roads. Service vehicle and parking access is gained at lower levels of the site.

Mid- and high-rise buildings are distributed at the precinct's periphery, flanking the new terrain and creating a range of public plazas, laneways and pedestrian streetscapes. A diversity of innovative dwelling designs responds to contemporary household make-ups, enabling a greater social mix and flexible options for future urban living. The landscaped terrain forms a green spine of open space amenity and community facilities constituting 45 percent of the overall precinct. A water treatment train also runs along this spine filtering stormwater for potable uses and enhancing the quality of the public open space environment. Other precinct-wide technology provides renewable energy and collects and treats black and grey water for reuse by the residential and commercial tenancies.

E-Gate was the last remaining land parcel of its size in inner Melbourne to have undergone strategic planning (VicTrack 2009). An increasing challenge for effective precinct redevelopment is, and will continue to be, the assembly of suitable consolidated sites in established urban areas, particularly in the middle regions of our cities. Middle suburbs are characterized by highly atomized distributions of private property ownership, low-density building forms, dispersed services and facilities and high car dependency (typical of post-Second World War development patterns). Assembling individually owned allotments suitable for consolidated redevelopment is often unfeasible. While infrastructure and servicing are beginning to fail, the age and quality of existing building stock varies and existing communities are now well established. The logic of demolishing and rebuilding large swaths of land in these areas is less convincing from an environmental and economic point of view and, more often than not, is undesirable from a social perspective. Newton (2010) identifies this challenge as a new urban arena requiring alternative development pathways for the regeneration of 'residential greyfields'.

Responding to this distinctive challenge, the following precinct design model proposes redevelopment of several smaller, non-contiguous allotments as a cohesive and integrative infill design strategy for the sustainable transformation of established suburbs (Murray *et al.* 2011; Monash Architecture Studio; see http://www.artdes.monash.edu.au/architecture/research.php#). A diversity of building forms and flexible dwelling designs made possible through the precinct approach could accommodate a broader range of household types and occupations and respond to societal shifts emerging in pressured housing and rental markets, as shown in Figure 18.1. This might include multi-generational families, home offices, shared ownership or leasing options. This is particularly pertinent in relation to the 'baby-boomer' cohort who are looking for more equitable opportunities to downsize, relocate in place and still retain some liquidity to fund their retirement.

Infill precinct redevelopment offers management and construction advantages relating to increases in operational scale and proximity. These include the use of prefabricated elements and alternative supply chain processes, the cost of which can be borne across the entire precinct redevelopment. Linking off-site manufacture and on-site modular assembly reduces many negative impacts of a traditional construction site, reduces time to 'construct', reduces cost of delivery and increases quality to more closely align with a manufactured product.

The potential for shared facilities and open space enhancements are significant benefits of a coordinated approach to infill redevelopment over several sites. Facilities and equipment could be 'pooled', offering cost savings to residents and encouraging social interaction. For example, workshops and recreation facilities along with tools and equipment could be shared by a community rather than duplicated by individual households. Other advantages might include informal child-minding arrangements in common spaces or concentrating car parking to prioritize pedestrian and bicycle movement throughout the remainder of a precinct.

District-wide sustainable systems relating to energy production, water capture and reuse and waste management are more effective on a collective level and more viable at this scale of development. Benefits such as these could also extend beyond the boundary of a precinct redevelopment whereby new infrastructure upgrades,

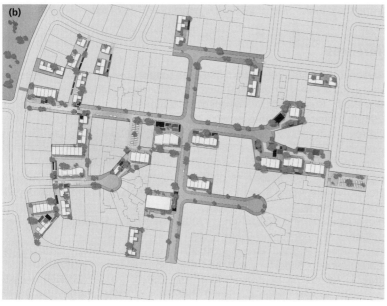

Figure 18.1 Speculative design for a dispersed precinct in Melbourne's suburbs
Source: Monash Architecture Studio

community programs or open space enhancements are utilized by surrounding residents and businesses. With appropriate community engagement, the precinct-scaled infill model could increase buy-in and support for sustainable urban change. This type of regeneration may also warrant sponsorship from local authorities or organizations, creating further opportunities for innovative financing arrangements and community capital initiatives.

18.3 Conclusion

The compounding pressures of climate change, resource limitations and population growth are challenging conventional strategies for urban growth. Expediency and economic viability are no longer credible arguments for our continued reliance on business-as-usual development approaches. Enduring solutions to the complex challenges we face require sophisticated, whole-of-system thinking and a reevaluation of the tenets upon which we develop and operate our cities.

Precinct-scaled design approaches provide opportunities for us to get right the fundamental armatures for urban resilience and sustainability. The examples discussed here provide insights into some of the strategies that could instigate sustainable change, including the physical design and distribution of spaces and buildings, technological innovations and integrative urban systems, as well as the careful integration of new redevelopments with existing social and environmental landscapes.

Encouragingly, several models for precinct redevelopment are emerging around the world. However, when compared with the majority of development taking place, they are still too few and far between. Existing barriers to effective and sustainable transformations, such as inhibitive governance structures and erroneous economic models that underestimate the value of social and environmental capital, must be addressed to enable long-term urban solutions to unfold rather than allowing the current cycle of ineffective, reactionary 'quick fixes' to continue.

References

BioRegional and CABE. 2008. *What Makes an Eco-town? A Report from BioRegional and CABE Inspired by the Eco-towns Challenge Panel*, industry report, London. Retrieved from: http://www.oneplanetcommunities.org/wp-content/uploads/2010/03/What-makes-an-eco-town-2008.pdf.

Calthorpe Associates. 2011. *Vision California: Charting Our Future: Statewide Scenarios Report*. Retrieved from: http://www.visioncalifornia.org/Vision%20California%20-%20Charting%20Our%20Future%20-%20Report.pdf

Douglas, I. 2011. 'The analysis of cities as ecosystems', in Douglas, I., Goode, D., Houck, M. and Wang, R. (eds), *The Routledge Handbook of Urban Ecology*, New York: Routledge.

Dunham-Jones, E. and Williamson, J. 2009. *Retrofitting Suburbia: Urban Design Solutions for Redesigning Suburbs*, New Jersey: Wiley and Sons.

Manzi, T., Jones, T. L. and Allen, J. (eds). 2010. *Social Sustainability in Urban Areas: Communities, Connectivity and the Urban Fabric*, London: Earthscan.

Murray, S., Newton, P. W., Wakefield, R. and Khor, L. 2011. 'Greyfield residential precincts: A new design model for the regeneration of the middle suburbs', paper delivered at the State of Australian Cities National Conference, Melbourne.

Newton, P. W. 2010. 'Beyond greenfields and brownfields: The challenge of regenerating Australia's greyfield suburbs', *Built Environment*, 36(1), 81–104.

Newton, P. W., Murray, S., Wakefield, R., Murphy, C., Khor, L. and Morgan, T. 2011. *Towards a New Development Model for Housing Regeneration in Greyfield Residential Precincts*, Final Report No. 171, Australian Housing and Urban Research Institute. Retrieved from: http://www.ahuri.edu.au/publications/p50593/.

Newton, P. and Thomson, P. Forthcoming. 'Urban regeneration in Australia', in Roberts, P., Sykes, H. and Granger, R. (eds), *Urban Regeneration: A Handbook* (rev. edn), London: Sage.

VicTrack. 2009. *State Government Annual Report*. Retrieved from: https://www.victrak.com.au/~/media/0BB795D45E9044E8AC8868744109B7D2.ash.

Walker, B. H. and Salt, D. A. 2006. *Resilience Thinking: Sustaining Ecosystems and People in a Changing World*, Washington, DC: Island Press

CHAPTER 19

Social inclusion and cohesion through housing tenure

Kathy Arthurson

19.1 Introduction

The global trend of increasing inequality in many high-income societies is represented spatially by disadvantaged groups concentrated in particular neighbourhoods. Given this situation, it is not surprising that the issue of neighbourhood diversity has become a burning topic. One focus of this debate has centred on diversity as represented by housing tenure and in particular the contemporary problems of large-scale mono-tenured social housing estates constructed in the post-Second World War period. Over time, due to progressively tighter eligibility criteria to access social housing, which now limits access to the most high-need groups, as well as social and economic changes, social housing estates increasingly experience a variety of issues. These include incidents of antisocial behaviour, concentrations of residents receiving welfare benefits, poor reputations attached to the locations and assumptions about the existence of 'neighbourhood effects'. The latter term refers to the supposition that residing amongst concentrations of similarly disadvantaged people creates additional negative effects over and above the experience of poverty. For instance, it is sometimes argued that a lack of role models of others in work or appropriate exemplars of virtuous citizens leads to the development of a culture within these neighbourhoods whereby residents are more likely to accept or support irresponsible and feckless behaviour. In turn these factors are recognised as precursors for the occurrence of social exclusion from mainstream society, which is regarded as a threat to social cohesion and inclusion.

Efforts to diffuse the concentrations of social housing on estates have involved rebalancing housing tenure mix through urban renewal projects that attract home-owners to purchase in the neighbourhoods and permanently relocate some social housing tenants to other areas. There are expectations that rebalancing housing tenure mix will create more socially cohesive and inclusive communities. 'Housing tenure mix' in this context refers to the balance between different housing tenures in a spatially defined area encompassing home-owners (housing owned outright), home purchasers (housing owned with a mortgage), private renters (renting from landlord or family member) and social housing renters (renting from government housing authority or non-profit agency). The success or otherwise of tenure mix strategies within contemporary urban renewal projects is still being determined. Aside from re-engineering the tenure mix within existing social housing neighbourhoods, there are also older, well-established mixed tenure neighbourhoods that include substantial levels of social housing amongst the housing mix.

These neighbourhoods were planned with tenure diversity from the start and have remained socially inclusive and cohesive as they have evolved over time often due to past housing and urban planning policies.

It is critically important that residents of these mixed tenure communities view them as pleasant places to live and enjoy living there. Otherwise residents with the most resources and greatest propensity to move, such as middle-income home-owners or -purchasers, may choose to relocate to other neighbourhoods. Compared to other tenures, social housing tenants are more constrained by the requirements of waiting lists and limited opportunities for transferring to other neighbourhoods. If those with choice move out of the mixed tenure neighbourhoods, leaving behind only the most disadvantaged residents, then in effect these actions work against safeguarding the housing tenure mix or supporting long-term residency, and in turn the development or maintenance of social cohesion.

This chapter is concerned with housing tenure mix as a type of neighbourhood diversity. It identifies some common principles that appear to enhance the planning, development and maintenance of mixed tenure neighbourhoods that have the potential to support social cohesion and inclusion.

19.2 Some case studies of successful mixed tenure neighbourhoods

Where do we find these long-established neighbourhoods that have a housing tenure mix (including social housing in the mix), which are also viewed as popular, successful and vibrant places to live by residents, policy-makers and other stakeholders? Box 19.1 includes five neighbourhoods in the UK that appear to meet these criteria, and in support of their success they have been extensively researched

---

Box 19.1   Five successful communities with housing tenure diversity

Bowthorpe (located on the western edge of Norwich)

Bowthorpe was planned as a mixed tenure housing estate from its origins largely as a reaction to the stigma that was attached to large pre- and post-war council estates. Fifty per cent of the land was allocated for council housing and the remaining 50 per cent was sold to private developers, housing associations and individual purchasers. In 1988 the local government council abandoned its original intention to use half of the land solely for council housing, choosing instead to balance the tenure mix with rented and owner-occupied housing (Further informations Allen *et al.*, 2005).

Coulby Newham (located on the south side of Middlesbrough)

In 1974 Coulby Newham encompassed a council housing estate, a private estate and an integrated council and private housing estate. Planning for the tenure mixing aspects of the development commenced in 1978 and included a commitment to quality design and a shared equity scheme between council, self-build and housing cooperatives. Part of the success of the neighbourhood is attributed to the difficulty in visually identifying the council housing from other tenures due to the design of the housing and estate. (Further information Allen *et al.*, 2005.)

Middlesbrough (located on south bank of the River Tees, north-east England)

Initially there was some opposition to the proposal for developing mixed tenure housing in Middlesbrough. This was mainly due to concerns about the potential negative impact of social housing on the value of private housing in the area. Despite this opposition, the local government council remained committed to achieving social balance and integration. The community includes residents from different housing tenures and across a mix of age groups, socio-economic backgrounds and ethnic origins. (Further information Holmes, 2006.)

Bournville Estate (located on the south side of Birmingham)

Bournville Village was conceived by the British Quaker and chocolate maker George Cadbury and commenced development as a mixed housing tenure estate in 1895. Even today the neighbourhood is viewed as a success as it has remained an attractive and sustainable community. This seems partly due to the high-quality housing and favourable location with close proximity to work opportunities and public transport. Key aspects thought to contribute to the success of mixed tenure are the high architectural quality of the built environment, housing that is not high density, and the positive involvement of the community in management of the neighbourhood. (Further information Bournville Residents, 2012, and Groves *et al.*, 2003.)

Milton Keynes (located in Buckinghamshire)

A balance between housing and employment was a major objective of this development, which commenced in 1969. New social housing residents were required to prove that they had employment or connections with the local community. Milton Keynes is designed on a grid with a 'chessboard' of residential housing and businesses (1 km grid squares), with major roads running between rather than through communities, and includes an extensive network of cycle tracks. Data and regular surveys were used to ensure that the type of housing matched people's needs, especially for students, the aged and the disabled. (Further information Cambridge City Council and South Cambs District Council, 2011, and Jupp, 1999.)

and evaluated. Another important factor in selecting these case studies was that the urban planning and renewal policies adopted in Australia more closely resemble those of the UK than the US or other countries, which arguably makes the lessons learned from within the former milieu more applicable.

19.3 What are some of the common elements that make these communities a success?

Some of the key elements that appear to enhance the success of the case study neighbourhoods and other mixed housing tenure communities include:

- architectural quality of the housing;
- level/percentage of tenure mix;
- scale at which the tenure mix is implemented;
- socio-economic balance of residents and housing tenure mix;
- availability of quality services, especially schools; and
- application of the social housing letting policies.

Each of these aspects is discussed in turn.

Architectural quality of the housing

Mixed tenure appears most successful in terms of social cohesion within the neighbourhood where there is little or no difference in the quality and appearance of social housing as compared with other housing tenures (Arthurson, 2012; Baker and Arthurson, 2007). In other words it is important to design the housing to blur the distinctions between the tenures so that the social housing blends into the neighbourhood and is not readily identifiable as such. It seems that the pertinent mechanism at work here is that designing social housing that blends into the existing environment helps to accentuate similarities between residents rather than differences. In turn this counters the potential for prejudice to occur against social housing tenants on the basis of their tenure.

Level/percentage of tenure mix

In the case studies and from the findings of other research there appears to be no magic percentage or ideal level of tenure mix that will make a community successful (Bailey *et al.*, 2006; Graham *et al.*, 2009). In the US there have been some attempts to identify 'tipping points' whereby once a certain level of concentration of residents experiencing poverty is reached whether this has adverse 'neighbourhood effects' in terms of facilitating negative consequences for individuals. These effects include, for instance, increased crime levels and dependency on welfare provisions. The pertinent body of work has largely involved statistical modelling, making it difficult to provide a nuanced understanding of what particular mechanisms and processes are at work.

It is important to remember that every locality is different in terms of its neighbourhood dynamics. What seems most effective is to provide a range of housing within the neighbourhood to cater for the needs of different household types and across a range of age groups (see Galster, 2010, for further insights).

Scale at which tenure mix is implemented

The scale of the housing tenure mix may also vary in the way it is implemented within the neighbourhood (Beekham *et al.*, 2001). The social housing might, for instance, be 'pepper potted' amongst home-owners and private renters or clustered in one block of flats or there might be a mix of flats and houses where one part is rental and the other shared ownership. Alternatively, social housing tenants might be placed mainly in houses that are located in different parts of the neighbourhood to home-owners or rental tenants or just on one side of a street. In the case study of Bournville Village (Groves *et al.*, 2003), which is widely regarded as socially cohesive, part of the success was attributed to the integrated form of tenure mix whereby private and social housing were indistinguishable from one another and situated side-by-side. However, another part of the neighbourhood in which there was no conscious attempt to integrate tenure mix was also regarded as socially cohesive.

Certainly, where there is street-level mixing of different housing tenures, the potential exists for higher levels of cross-tenure contact to occur between residents. It appears, though, that often a little exclusion between different housing tenures is a good thing for social cohesion. Sometimes an overly fine-grained housing tenure mix is linked to conflict occurring rather than the anticipated social cohesion. This is more likely to occur where there are large differences between the comparative incomes, values and lifestyles of home-owners and renters and raises issues about the relationship between tenure mix and the socio-economic mix of residents, as explicated below.

Socio-economic balance of residents and housing tenure mix

'Housing tenure mix' is often used interchangeably with 'social mix', with the inference that housing tenure mix equates to the socio-economic mix of residents. It is important to note, however, that implementing policies to rebalance housing tenure mix in a neighbourhood does not necessarily lead to changes in the socio-economic mix of residents. In the UK, for instance, under the 'Right to Buy Scheme', social housing tenants were given the opportunity to purchase their homes, and many did. While this changed the tenure mix on social housing estates through increasing the proportion of home-owners, it did not alter the socio-economic or income mix. It is important to recognise this factor in planning for mixed tenure communities (see Arthurson, 2012, for more on this).

Availability of quality services, especially schools

The availability of quality services within the neighbourhoods is also an important aspect of social cohesion and inclusion. Where generic services cater to the needs of different population groups within the neighbourhoods they provide occasions for meeting and interacting and opportunities for social integration between different housing tenure groups (see Allen *et al.*, 2005; and Holmes, 2006, for further insights). Schools appear to be an especially important factor as accessibility to high-quality schools helps to attract and retain a mix of younger families with children within the neighbourhood. If middle-income residents are unhappy with the local schools or feel that they are of poor quality then they may move to other neighbourhoods, or choose to send their children to schools outside of their immediate neighbourhood. If schools are of good quality they can facilitate more social inclusion in terms of encouraging mixing across different housing tenure groups. Children's interactions and play is acknowledged as important in bringing together different income groups, which is more likely to be facilitated when home-owners and renters send their children to the same local schools.

Application of the social housing letting policies

Selected letting policies by social housing organisations have been used in some neighbourhoods so that only tenants across a limited range of incomes are housed or whereby tenants who have been disruptive in the past are barred. Often neighbourhoods where such letting policies have been adopted are popular with residents even though they could be considered somewhat exclusionary. This situation points to a tension between the ideals of social cohesion and social inclusion as in some instances cohesion might be strengthened through exclusion from socially cohesive neighbourhoods of particularly disruptive or difficult tenants who engage in antisocial behaviour. It raises the important question of how to meet the needs of disadvantaged special-needs individuals and households and their social inclusion while at the same time paying heed to important issues about wider neighbourhood social cohesion.

The imperative is to be mindful of utilising letting policies in order to ensure that disproportionate levels of disruptive tenants are not concentrated in particular areas and at the same time make sure that these policies are not utilised in ways that further disadvantage complex high-need tenants (Holmes, 2006).

19.4 Conclusions

The case studies illustrate the importance of planning for diversity at the very beginning of urban development. Where housing tenure mix is implemented from the start and gradually evolves over time it seems more successful than when deliberate and complicated interventions to change and rebalance housing tenure mix are introduced into long-established neighbourhoods.

There is unlikely to be a simple formula for facilitating successful mixed tenure neighbourhoods due to different histories and contexts. What works in established neighbourhoods that were planned with diversity from the start may not necessarily work when applied to other sorts of neighbourhood. Nevertheless, some common elements in the case studies of successful mixed tenure neighbourhoods appear to contribute to their success.

These include: high-quality housing where the social housing blends into the neighbourhood and is not obviously identifiable as social housing; attention to the level or percentage of tenure mix and scale at which the mix is implemented; recognition that changes to housing tenure mix do not always result in a reordering of the socio-economic balance of residents within the neighbourhood; the availability of high-quality generic services that have across-tenure appeal, especially schools; and applying social housing letting policies in ways that ensure that there are not disproportionate concentrations of disruptive tenants in particular areas while at the same time making sure that lettings policies do not further disadvantage complex high-need tenants.

References

Allen, C., Camina, M., Casey, R., Coward, S. and Wood, M. 2005. *Mixed Tenure, Twenty Years on: Nothing out of the Ordinary*, York: Joseph Rowntree Foundation. Available at: http://www.jrf.org.uk/sites/files/jrf/190501807x.pdf.

Arthurson, K. 2012. *Social Mix and the Cities: Challenging the Mixed Communities Consensus in Housing and Urban Planning Policies*, Sustainable Cities Series, Melbourne: CSIRO Publishing.

Bailey, N., Haworth, A., Manzi, T., Paranagamage, P. and Roberts, M. 2006. *Creating and Sustaining Mixed Income Communities: A Good Practice Guide*, York: Chartered Institute of Housing and Joseph Rowntree Foundation.

Baker, E. and Arthurson, K. 2007. Housing, Place or Social Networks: What's More Important for Relocating Tenants? *Australian Planner*, 44(4), pp. 28–34.

Beekman, T., Lyons, F. and Scott, J. 2001. *Improving the Understanding of the Influence of Owner Occupiers in Mixed Tenure Neighbourhoods*, Edinburgh: ODS Ltd for Scottish Homes.

Bournville Residents. 2012. Bournville Village: The Latest News, Pics and Chat from Bournville in Birmingham. Available at: http://bournvillevillage.com/.

Cambridge City Council and South Cambs District Council. 2011. *Balance and Mixed Communities: A Good Practice Guide*, Cambridge: Cambridge Horizons. Available at: http://www.cambridgeshirehorizons.co.uk/documents/publications/horizons/balanced_and_mixed_communities_brochure.pdf.

Galster, G. 2010. The Mechanism(s) of Neighborhood Effects: Theory, Evidence, and Policy Implications, presentation at the ESRC Seminar, St Andrews University, 4–5 February.

Graham, E., Manley, D., Hiscock, R., Boyle, P. and Doherty, J. 2009. Mixing Housing Tenures: Is It good for Social Well-being?, *Urban Studies*, 46(1), pp. 139–165.

Groves, R., Middleton, A., Murie, A. and Broughton, K. 2003. *Neighbourhoods that Work: A Study of the Bournville Estate, Birmingham*, Bristol: The Policy Press. Available at: http://www.jrf.org.uk/publications/neighbourhoods-work.

Holmes, C. 2006. *Mixed Communities, Success and Sustainability*, York: Joseph Rowntree Foundation. Available at: http://www.jrf.org.uk/sites/files/jrf/0176.pdf.

Jupp, B. 1999. *Living Together: Community Life on Mixed Housing Estates*, London: Demos. Available at: http://www.demos.co.uk/files/livingtogether.pdf?1240939425.

CHAPTER 20

Urban design

The future looks familiar

Lewis Knight

> A great city is not to be confounded with a populous one.
>
> (Aristotle, 384–322 BC)

20.1 Introduction: sustainability and resilience

The purpose of this book is to highlight critical issues of sustainability and resilience and bring them to the fore when considering our settlement patterns. Whereas sustainability is in essence about 'doing more with the resources we have', resilience requires that we address (from a holistic systems standpoint) a changing baseline. Resiliency thinking requires that we reconceive our notions of environmental baselines to adapt to higher levels of energy acting on our biosphere. The symptoms are evident: in the storm surge in New York created by Hurricane Sandy; in the materials price spikes following Cyclone Yasi in Australia; and in myriad local instances of greater environmental dynamism unsettling our communities. The critical challenge is that we treat the affliction rather than band-aid the many maladies that act at local scales.

Design matters

In China, mass migration is driving rapid and dense urbanization, but also an immense investment in the infrastructure to support it. Concurrently, cities like Detroit, Michigan, designed to support more than 6 million lives, are now home to less than a million and are confronting aged infrastructure that needs to be contracted in response to reduced demand. In India, lacking a strong central government, hotels like the Gardenia in Bangalore are achieving very short payback periods on the investment in sustainable infrastructure (LEED Platinum under the Indian Green Building Council was achieved in less than four years), which is significantly less than the anticipated payback period in the United States. And in London, the 2012 Olympics are seen as a highlight of a sustainability movement for construction in Europe (see Box 20.1 for more details).

Our settlements are neither sustainable nor resilient unless they embrace the ability to inspire. But we are living at a moment when the collective heritage of city making is being questioned, and we are given a moment to wonder . . . so what does the future look like?

Box 20.1   The Olympics as metaphor

It is in the Olympics that we see cues about how the planning and design of the places we visit daily could evolve over the next two generations. For England, a country that has suffered during the global financial crisis, and whose cities outside London have been subject to multi-generational decay, the 2012 Olympics offered optimism for the future. There is symmetry between 2012's Games and the last Olympics to be held in London, in 1948, which helped the country rise from the shadows of the Second World War. The host cities that followed – Helsinki, Melbourne and Rome – fostered national pride and catalysed urban transformations of infrastructure, buildings and public open space. Each contributed to making quality urban environments, ensuring that these cities continue to rank among the most livable and sustainable places.

In Tokyo, venues and housing created for the 1964 Olympics are still in use today. So too is the 'Bullet Train' system, the first sections of which were part of an ambitious transportation modernization effort sparked by the Games. All subsequent host cities have used the Olympics as a catalyst for urban and social transformation to varying degrees and levels of success. Each time the Olympics visited a smaller city (Munich, Montreal and Barcelona), the urban legacy has proved to be one of design execution, renewed venues, and better infrastructure and landscapes that have positioned each city high in global livability rankings. Admittedly, Barcelona still struggles with adapting the venues it created, but the neighborhoods built near the port have transformed that part of the city and influenced regeneration practitioners globally.

Like Barcelona, Sydney (2000) sought to redevelop the geographic center of the city, but added sustainability as an aspiration. Sydney's Olympic housing raised the bar for housing throughout the city. Today, 50 percent of Sydney-siders live in multi-family apartments that are well designed and a great advance on the three-story brick walk-up flats that had been the norm throughout the 1970s and 1980s. Mid- and high-rise apartment life – near transit, in places of great design, with strong urban amenities – is now part of Sydney's urban landscape.

For both Athens (2004) and Beijing (2008), the Olympics led to a much-needed upgrade in infrastructure, and the Games were critical to repositioning each city in a global world. Their legacies will be found in the manner in which each city husbands the catalytic effect and the aspirations the Olympics provided. The most successful Olympic cities are those that have a stable urbanity and understand that they are in need of a dose of positive energy to reincentivize the urban regeneration industry.

When the London Docklands Development Corporation was established in the early 1980s as a tool of renewal for London's East End, it addressed the regeneration of obsolete docks, housing, open space, transportation, and the then-impending commercial land shortage in the City as the last sites left vacant after the Second World War were taken up. The insight of the 2012 Olympics is the city's belief that the East End can become highly sustainable, with a diversity of amenities, parks, housing and communities that will be an epicenter for renewing and improving a place that for many generations has been the working center of Greater London.

20.2 Changing paradigms of planning

The apparent root of our questions about the form of our cities is nothing new. Every time over the past 500 years we have confronted health issues in our cities, we have developed new professional approaches to dealing with those issues.

In response to the Black Death and other urban health concerns of the time in Europe, architecture and engineering symbiotically rose to the fore in London and Paris. Where stagnant and dirty water was defined as the root of illness, engineers built new sewers (the Embankment in London, and a citywide system in Paris) and architects restored and renewed the urban fabric with new environments that were more democratic. They included consistent facade treatments, street trees, the creation of sidewalks, and an improved public domain.

At the turn of the twentieth century, in response to health concerns about overcrowding in Europe's cities and a need to parcelize and establish new towns in the US's west that were ordered, democratic and healthy, planning and the landscape professions began their rise. Like the earlier genesis, a technical profession arose in parallel to a soft science. The results were familiar to many in the production of urban environments that had a strong public domain.

Fast forward a century. We are again concerned with basic aspects of the health of our settlements. But now we have big data and parametric modeling, as well as uncertainty over the stability of our collective future owing to the potential impact of climate change.

Urban trends

The nineteenth century was one of colonization from a city-making standpoint, with new cities established and existing cities renewed with greater public space. The twentieth century was one of mobility, which layered infrastructure and roads onto the public domain. What will the twenty-first century be in terms of city making and urban design? And what will our cities look like?

Unfortunately, the answer doesn't reside in any of the significant indices that guide sustainability at the built scale: LEED, BREEAM and the Living Building Challenge in multiple countries; SEEDA and BRE in the United Kingdom; GB Tool in South Africa; Greenmark in Singapore; Green Star in Australia. All are ranking tools that anticipate building performance, which may impact design, but they provide little guidance on design qualities that are sustainable and resilient.

At the next scale, that of the urban system, there are several areas of enquiry and practice that have evolved concurrently over the past three decades. These may generally be grouped into seven thematic groupings. Each can, and indeed does, influence the others at various times, and so none should be considered independently.

The Planned City

This emphasizes policy and urban planning in shaping our environments as logical, connected places with sufficient delivery of public services, energy and water. For Planned City advocates, the public domain and the qualities attributed to it are seen as a framework around which populations may grow, remain static, or contract.

Traditional Urbanism

Whether it's New Urbanism in the US (guided by the Congress for the New Urbanism), Neo-Traditionalism in Europe (touted by the Prince of Wales), or a second-generation movement such as Smart Growth, Traditional Urbanists respect and seek to learn lessons from urbanism as it existed prior to 1945: low-rise, mixed-use, walkable neighborhoods clustered around retail services and schools. In many ways, these lessons still resonate for communities that are more residential in nature, but like traditional planning, they are not readily scaled up to meet the demands of Chinese-like mega-development or the more commercially minded downtown cores common to modern cities.

Landscape Urbanism

This and other forms of design that engage with the landscapes and infrastructure of our cities and regions – including transportation, drainage and the nascent agricultural urbanism – provide a valuable systems-based counterpoint to other broad movements. They preface the landscape, biophilia and passive engineering of landscape defenses to cities and settlements. At a range of scales, Landscape Urbanism-based solutions are impacting reestablishment of the Gulf Coast wetlands around New Orleans and the revitalization of the High Line in New York (see Figure 20.1), a disused elevated rail line that is now a vibrant social and open space connector. More recently, the impact of food has been added to this discourse, and cities including Oakland and San Francisco have passed domestic agriculture ordinances.

Index Cities

With the growth of 'big data', a range of ranking and information-centric equivalency indices seeks to describe the successes or failures of cities at every scale. Each one – from sustainability to innovation to happiness, and many more – takes physical characteristics into account and seeks to use these in a reliable manner to gauge the comparative competitiveness of cities. While not actually a design response, the ability of data to inform more meaningful decisions about the future design of our cities and regions cannot be overlooked.

Figure 20.1 The High Line in New York, reuse of old elevated rail infrastructure for health and wellbeing and green infrastructure
Source: Robert Wright/ *New York Times*/Redux; http://graphics8. nytimes.com/ images/2012/08/02/ garden/02HIGHLINE_ SPAN/02HIGHLINE_ SPAN-articleLarge.jpg

Smart Cities

Touted as the hyper-connected and hyper-efficient urban future, Smart Cities are being promoted by many of the major players in digital systems, including IBM and Siemens. The promise is that 'smart' (i.e. wired and networked) infrastructure will contribute to greater efficiency in the use of natural resources, whether in transit controls or water and electricity distribution. As with Index Cities, there is little that the Smart City will provide that significantly impacts the design of our public domain. Yet being able to respond immediately and intelligently on a regional and district level may provide real advancement in the ways we occupy space.

DIY Cities

This term encompasses a range of guerrilla tactics by socially based arts, design and place-making organizations. Perhaps the most successful of this form of urban activism is 'Parking Day', which began in San Francisco and has grown into a global event in which parking spaces in cities are coopted for a day with the purpose of making accessible public space. Pop-up retail, container stores, tactical urbanism, and many other trends are indications of global concern over the future of our cities and the desire to 'make a difference'. DIY Cities pose a simple pair of questions. Does urbanism need to be so concrete? And, if not, what other spatial and physical devices may be used to enhance community building?

Hypothesis Cities

In a fertile environment where digital online game playing, the environments required to support that play, parametric modeling and advanced software are being developed concurrently – like the Renaissance as the translation of perspective drawing influenced city design and planning – we find a rich palimpsest of hypothetical city designs. While many are founded in reality, some are outright fiction, but, like the Tricorder in *Star Trek* and the now ubiquitous Apple iPad, convergent evolution may occur. Apart from hypotheses such as the 'high-rise city', with 1,000-meter interconnected mixed-use towers and architectural mega-structures akin to proposals frequently published in the 1960s, many show human-scale communities and robust public domains. Like DIY Cities, the message is very clear: more people are now engaged in a dialogue about the future form of our cities.

20.3 Case studies

How do we confront the issues associated with a growing global urban population?

In order to define how we will shape our places of residence in 2050, it's useful to give ourselves a simple set of lenses for understanding the following case studies. These are common to many of the indices used to drive increased sustainability and resilience and should be nothing new: a positive impact on community; benign impacts on ecology and personal health; and careful consumption of water, energy and materials in buildings. For ease, we might consider them Growth Cities (usually in the developing world), Mature Cities (usually in the developed world), and Cities in Decline (such as Detroit).

Growth Cities

Among Growth Cities, many important projects are being done by US- and European-based companies in the developing world. Those of most interest occur in second-generation urbanization, where the initial capacity building has been completed and cities are being pushed to consider the social and environmental impacts of a new, rapidly created urbanization.

In China, Peter Calthorpe and Associates has published a series of masterplans, including components of the Tianjin Ecocity. These plans seek to establish quantifiable changes to current practice that define a low-carbon community in the context of rapid urbanization. Calthorpe identifies eight principals, rooted in traditional urbanism, that he believes will produce a more carbon-sensitive development pattern. With the exception of residential tower placement and orientation, which in China is governed by laws on access to daylight, the urban form is similar to what Europeans and Americans have become accustomed to in medium-density communities: strong street walls, walkable street patterns and access to open space, as well as human-scaled public domains.

By contrast, in the Middle East, a radically different climate zone, new schemes are under way for advanced city pilot projects that challenge the verticality of Dubai and Abu Dhabi. Foster and Partners' Masdar City is envisaged as a sustainable city that is also a seat of economy and commerce. The plan seeks to use significant solar power and establish a water- and energy-efficient city that borrows its form in part from Islamic cities of the past. Significantly, the car is subjugated to below-grade levels in order to maximize pedestrian comfort and connections. The scale of Masdar City is highly pedestrian in nature, and, like Tianjin, if successful it will produce a public domain that is human-scaled and rich in pedestrian environments.

China and the Middle East are examples of second-generation city building in developing nations where the cities are envisaged not purely as capacity for a growing population, but as statements of a strong central government's societal vision. By contrast, in India, the planning and design of new communities is hampered by an arduous land acquisition and assembly process; compounded with lax fire codes and simple concrete construction, the results are urban environments of poor quality. This is exacerbated by the comparative lack of a public domain tradition in Indian society.

Mature and Declining Cities

For Mature Cities, the discussions and trends are not of rapid growth, but of careful planning and design of environments that are intended to be socially, environmentally and economically sustainable. Three trends appear to translate across nations.

Eco-districts offer great promise to capture efficient synergies across mixed-use environments and create environments that are sustainable across the triple bottom line. Early key examples have been completed over the last decade or more and are now being used as baseline projects to confirm the claims when designed are being met. One of the more notable projects is the Western Harbor in Malmö, Sweden, the large-scale sustainable development of a 25-acre brownfield site created as part of the 2001 European Housing Expo. Also in Sweden, Stockholm's Hammarby Sjöstad uses advanced techniques to gather and separate the waste stream. The overall urban environment created by these projects is one of pedestrian-scaled development that seeks to create an urban form at the community scale. Streets and alleys are designed to be pedestrian friendly and are supported by robust transit and bicycle-sharing programs, with a six–eight-story environment punctuated by signature towers at key points. In North America, British Columbia has established a leadership role, with projects including Dockside Green in Victoria, a 15-acre mixed-use project that plans to be the continent's first 'greenhouse gas neutral' large neighborhood development.

More recently, the cities of Portland, Oregon, and San Francisco, California, are experimenting with eco-districts at a policy level as well as a design level. These initiatives, which seek to produce mechanisms that establish eco-districts in existing city environments, should be monitored closely, as they seek to establish a policy and design basis for establishment of eco-districts. If successful, these mechanisms may offer a policy basis by which existing cities can be retrofitted to promote a more cellular structure to the provision of public domain and amenities.

Eco-districts, however, are being pursued in relatively wealthy communities in temperate climate zones. What are the approaches at the margins of our communities, what one might call our *eco-edges*?

Here, the penetration of sustainability and resilience thinking is less clear. San Jose, California, has borrowed a leaf from the establishment of greenbelts in Europe and North America by establishing a very clear growth boundary to the city as part of its 2040 General Plan update. In less well-off communities, including some of California's bankrupt cities, the lateral consumption of agricultural land threatens to continue should the American housing market rebound. Unfortunately, this is a familiar scenario the world over, where car-oriented greenfield development is apparently more cost-effective than denser, walking- and transit-based urban opportunities.

The American urban strategist Christopher Leinberger contends that the US housing market has missed a significant opportunity to build more multi-family housing, and he claims that denser transit-oriented environments also hold their value better than the single-family suburb. One example of a potential solution that addresses the increased carbon emissions and damage to agriculture and ground water supplies, and addresses almost forty years of homogeneous attitudes to community development, is the Preserve in Stockton, California, a planned community considering application as a One-Planet Community which seeks to establish high goals on site for water efficiency and reuse, energy generation on site and community satisfaction (see Figure 20.2).

The discussion about the edges of traditional suburban development is repeated in a different fashion in Declining Cities, for which Detroit is the poster child. Here, a city designed and planned for many millions has contracted to under a million in population, so the central question becomes: how do you maintain community scale and organization physically while converting former urban areas to alternative uses? Again, the outcomes of these activities will be informative, but the likely

Figure 20.2 The Preserve in Stockton, California, is considering a One-Planet Living application. This table compares 'business-as-usual' planning with a more far-reaching plan based on OPL principles
Source: Gensler for AG Spanos Companies

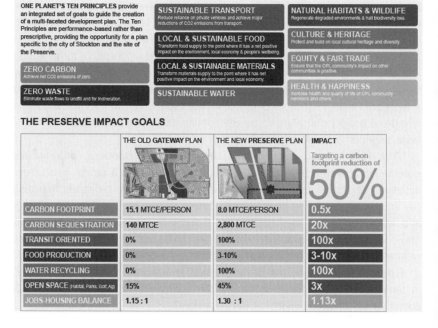

THE PRESERVE IMPACT GOALS

	THE OLD GATEWAY PLAN	THE NEW PRESERVE PLAN	IMPACT
			Targeting a carbon footprint reduction of 50%
CARBON FOOTPRINT	15.1 MTCE/PERSON	8.0 MTCE/PERSON	0.5x
CARBON SEQUESTRATION	140 MTCE	2,800 MTCE	20x
TRANSIT ORIENTED	0%	100%	100x
FOOD PRODUCTION	0%	3-10%	3-10x
WATER RECYCLING	0%	100%	100x
OPEN SPACE (Habitat, Parks, Golf, Ag)	15%	45%	3x
JOBS-HOUSING BALANCE	1.15 : 1	1.30 : 1	1.13x

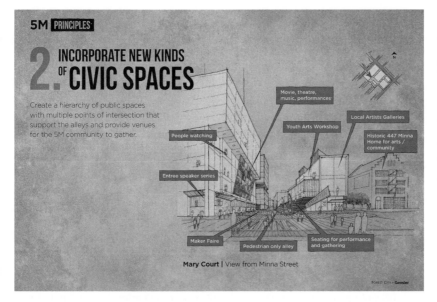

Figure 20.3 The 5M Project in San Francisco envisions a new type of mixed-use development specifically targeted at finding and inspiring breakthrough innovation in the knowledge sector. It is founded on strong place-making principles that marry spatial characteristics with programmed uses
Source: Gensler for Forest City

physical form will be a return to a set of urban villages containing the neighborhoods that are more socially sustainable.

And so, finally, to a San Francisco project that seeks to reframe how development relates to community value. The 5M Project, the revisioning of a 4-acre newspaper production site with heavy transit at the edge of San Francisco's downtown, proposes almost 1.85 million square feet of mixed-use development. Currently under review, this effort may be a new type of urban redevelopment in the manner of becoming a *social engine*. 5M is changing the discussion about the public benefits of a development project and is based on the hypothesis that a deeply researched development that builds community connections will have a much higher, and better, impact on the surrounding community than the usual stand-alone project. The community art organization Intersection for the Arts and the social equity non-profit Policy Link are working with the landowner, the developer, local artists, innovative creators of new products (makers) and community organizations to review the usual fee structure mechanisms of the project. While proposing to breach many of San Francisco's generation-old planning and zoning regulations, the project itself looks very familiar.

20.4 Conclusion: a short note about the future

Our future urban form will be very familiar. Making cities relies, and will continue to rely, upon collaborative approaches between a great many experts (all of whom claim to be urban designers), including planners, architects, infrastructure engineers, landscape architects, transportation engineers, and more. In many ways, the form of our cities will be shaped by the way those active in making our cities choose to collaborate and help define a new profession of sustainable and resilient place-making.

Our city of tomorrow will be denser and more compact than cities today, will likely limit itself to less than ten stories in height, and will be constructed of intimate networks of urban space (potentially on multiple levels). It will be pedestrian oriented and will make greater use of transit options. It will be mixed use, rather than divided by separate land uses. It will incorporate significant open space appropriately distributed throughout the community.

In short, much of what we are familiar with will be repeated, but improved, at a planning level. I believe our environmental design responses will matter even more than in the past and will help shape places of great sustainability and resilience for future generations.

. . . And a postscript

There may be evolutionary changes to urban form, but these will be carefully researched and conceived. In my opinion, the keys will be:

- *Design.* The design of our public domain and its architecture will be more malleable and important. Our cities will seek to be better designed than those that are constructed simply to house a growing population. See Chapter 18 for more insights.
- *Biophilia.* The links between nature and public health are increasingly understood, and open space and agriculture may be more deeply incorporated in the city of 2050. See Chapter 10 for more insights.
- *Social resilience.* The potential to establish deep collective resilience by creating strong communities that embrace education, the arts and 'do-it-yourself' movements that sit at the crossroads of art, technology and social activism – the makers. Embracing these new communities will challenge traditional notions of public benefit, and may support migration to a more resilient urban form. See Chapters 5 and 21 for more insights.
- *Devaluing the commute.* The cost of commuting will be valued more appropriately and thus impact land use and transportation planning. See Chapter 12 for more insights.
- *Clean city.* The center of economic activity is the city, and clean technologies will allow traditionally dirty industries to return to the city and reduce the burden of distance on infrastructure and emissions. See Chapter 9 for more insights.

Reference

Leinberger, C. 2009. The Option of Urbanism: Investing in a New American Dream, Washington, DC: Island Press.

PART FOUR

GOVERNANCE AND LEADERSHIP FOR RESILIENT, SUSTAINABLE CITIES

CHAPTER 21

Governance for resilient, sustainable cities and communities

Concepts and some cases

Peter Roberts

21.1 Introduction

This chapter provides a brief overview of some of the basic conceptual models available for the governance of resilient, sustainable cities and communities, and, in addition, it illustrates the strengths and limitations of these models as they have been applied in practice.

At the heart of the material covered in this chapter is a concern with ensuring that the governance of ownership and engagement (and the limitations which inhibit its achievement) is understood fully. This is especially important given the context of continuing uncertainty regarding the scope and content of changes outlined elsewhere in the book, many of which are highly contested. The point that most of the key concepts in this field of enquiry are contested will not be lost on the reader, because one of the dominant themes of the debate on resilience and sustainable development is inherent uncertainty regarding the precise nature of the basic model itself (Redclift, 2005; Lafferty, 2004). Although these contested spaces of resilience and sustainable development can be seen, on the one hand, as potentially disruptive and problematic, they can also be viewed as helpful because they present a genuine opportunity for experiment and for active collaboration in the creation and application of 'steering capacity' (Bressers, 2004, p. 286) that can be used to plan and implement policies that are intended to enable cities and local communities to be (or become) resilient, sustainable places.

By using the term 'steering capacity', Bressers is suggesting an active, rather than a passive, role for governance at all spatial levels. This, in turn, suggests that governance for resilient, sustainable places should be at the inclusive end of the governance spectrum; that is, it should be governance which seeks to involve and engage citizens in their neighbourhoods in the management of what has been described as 'collective affairs or public realm' (Healey, 1997, p. 8). Such an approach has much in common with the 'citizen power' end-point envisaged by Arnstein (1969) in her ladder of citizen participation. As a consequence, this chapter places emphasis on the various ways in which governance for resilience can be linked to processes and procedures designed to encourage and support participation and engagement. This relationship between governance for resilience and participation also reflects aspects of the core principles of the Brundtland Report (World Commission on Environment and Development, 1987), which placed considerable weight on the desirability of securing effective citizen participation in decision-making alongside a clear commitment by governments at all levels to deliver sustainable development.

All of the three main elements of sustainable development, as identified by Lafferty and Langhelle (1999), can be seen to be related to each other through a shared concern with various aspects of regulation (Baker et al., 1997) and governance. The three elements are:

- physical sustainable development – this reflects the requirement to protect and manage resources to satisfy human need;
- generational equity – this requires sustainable development to ensure that future needs are satisfied; and
- global equity – this requires sustainable development to be managed so as to give priority to the essential needs of the world's poor in preference to the less essential desires of the wealthier nations.

The following sections of this chapter explore further the concept and nature of governance – as distinct from government – as it is applied at various spatial scales. Following this, attention is then focused on the use of governance as a means of achieving resilient, sustainable cities and communities. Both of the preceding debates are illustrated by reference to a number of brief case studies. A final section of the chapter offers some tentative conclusions and guidelines for future practice.

21.2 The governance of cities and communities

As already noted, governance is about the management of collective matters in the public realm – this offers a spatial perspective which is allied to the need to manage public affairs in a way which generates and ensures inclusion (Healey, 1997). It can alternatively be defined as about 'the control of an activity by some means' (Hirst and Thompson, 1996, p. 184). These definitions offer a control and regulation perspective on the topic. Other definitions abound, but a recurring theme is what Hirst and Thompson (1996, p. 183) describe as the emergence of a political world characterised by 'complexity and multiplicity of levels of types of governance'. In many ways this increasingly varied and complex model of governance can be seen to reflect both the range of problems implied by the sustainable development approach and the difficulty of assigning fixed or particular roles to any individual organisation in a rapidly evolving and open global 'village'.

The above observations are important considerations for cities seeking to embed resilience in their structures of governance, and this is especially the case if cities are seeking to embed a model of good governance that can deal with the complex mosaic of activities encompassed by the adoption of a sustainable development approach to city development and management. By way of contrast with freestanding private companies – even if they are large in terms of their financial base and range of products – cities and communities face myriad additional challenges in designing and implementing governance structures and procedures. Whilst in part these additional challenges reflect the inherent difficulties experienced when dealing with spatially variegated issues, they also represent the complexity of ensuring that democratic legitimacy is embedded in any arrangements that may be put in place. As a consequence of the need to deal simultaneously with the above-noted issues, governance structures and procedures need to reflect the requirements of:

- the sustainable development triad of environmental, social and economic concerns coupled to the requirement that both intergenerational and intra-generational equity should be considered (Roberts, Ravetz and George, 2009);
- the various levels or layers of governance that are involved in order to regulate and manage cities and communities effectively – it can be argued that this implies governance from the supranational to the neighbourhood (Tewdwr-Jones and McNeill, 2000); and
- the various dimensions of democratic legitimacy and especially the implications in communities that have been or are the subject of 'political exclusion' (Geddes, 1997, p. 209)

What results from the simultaneous consideration of the above requirements is a model of governance which resembles a Rubik's cube; each cluster of requirements is itself represented as a mosaic of concerns and the pattern on each of the faces of the cube changes over time. Therefore, governance must be fit for purpose and accepted as an essential component of a resilient city or community.

However, in order to be able to make progress in such a complex and contested arena, it is necessary both to distil the lessons from prior experience of dealing with such matters and to develop some general principles that can be used to guide future thinking and practice. In terms of previous experience, the principal lessons that can be identified relate to the design and operation of systems of citizen parti-cipation and governance in general, and especially the application of such systems at various scales: the city-region, conurbation or metropolitan region; the city or town; the district, quarter or urban community; and the individual neighbourhood, urban 'village' or city block. Whilst the governance of place displays certain generic characteristics, the issues of scale and context would also appear to be important determinants of success or failure. As Garner observed when editing a special edition of *Town Planning Review* dedicated to comparative perspectives on public participation, constitutional provisions vary from nation to nation, as do socio-economic circumstances and the traditions of communities, and, as such, 'it is not surprising that public participation has made a varying impact' (Garner, 1981, p. 258). However, despite these considerable variations in legal, socio-economic, constitutional and other circumstances, it is possible to elicit some general observ-ations and lessons. These include:

- the importance of establishing governance structures which have a clear democratic mandate and a firm legal basis – this may be provided through a specific constitutional requirement or could be the outcome of a less formal collaboration agreement, but the basis must be explicit, sufficiently detailed and accepted by all parties (Jessop, 1997);

- the need to create an open, transparent and accountable system (or systems) for engagement and participation – such systems may vary in terms of the methods of election, selection or engagement which are employed, but all systems should be inclusive and be subject to scrutiny (Dobbs and Moore, 2002);
- the requirement that those directly engaged in the various processes of governance should be supported in the performance of their duties of governance – this support may take many forms, including the provision of technical, legal and other professional help, the payment of expenses and allowances, and the provision of training and personal development facilities (Baker *et al.*, 2003);
- the provision of leadership at all spatial levels and in all major areas of governance activity – this is an essential part of a resilient governance system and it implies both selecting and nurturing leaders, as well as the need to understand and support leadership dynamics (Collinge *et al.*, 2010);
- the creation, support and management of community capacity, again at all spatial levels – such capacity may, for example, take the form of advice and other support services, or, in more active mode, provide the necessary technical and organisational facilities to enable such activities as participatory budgeting (Clarke, 2012);
- the need to involve professionals, politicians and the wider public in governance arrangements – this also implies the need to work across the public, private and voluntary sectors (Heywood, 2011); and
- the desirability of linking governance structures to wider partnership networks and other forms of collaboration – such networks can help individuals and organisations to sustain each other and to respond to changing circumstances and rapidly emerging challenges (Chatterton and Style, 2001).

These characteristics and features of resilient governance reflect the experience of many metropolitan regions in different countries. The lessons that have been elicited are valid in both advanced and less developed nations, and, as Brundtland observed, the essence of good governance is the presence of 'a political system that secures effective citizen participation in decision making' (World Commission on Environment and Development, 1987, p. 65).

Some illustrations of what can be achieved, often under difficult or tumultuous circumstances, are provided by two very different cases: Ontario in Canada; and Knowsley in the United Kingdom. The regional case of Ontario reflects the challenge of providing a full and integrated range of health services within the fields of community development, social services and health. In this model governance is provided through what Heywood (2011, p. 259) describes as a functional mix with service levels that draw 'together into governance boards caregivers and service providers, representatives from government departments together with consumers and clients from hinterlands defined by accessibility catchments'. This regional-cum-provincial arrangement provides a context for local boards 'representing both providers and consumers of services irrespective of whether they are in the public, private or voluntary sectors'. The Ontario case demonstrates, in particular, the importance of ensuring effective democratic control and forging collaborative arrangements across policy areas.

The second case is set at the district and neighbourhood level and reflects the experience of the metropolitan district of Knowsley, located in Merseyside. A key actor in Knowsley is the First Ark Group, consisting of a community-based housing association and a number of social enterprises. First Ark was originally established in 2002 (following the transfer of municipal social housing stock to an independent community-based housing association) and from the outset it has embedded strong governance at all levels of activity. Overall governance is provided by a group board consisting of tenant, nominated and independent members; this board acts as the custodian of the group's mission and ethos. Separate boards for the housing association and social enterprise components reflect the inclusive composition of the group board. A further, more local, level of governance is provided by neighbourhood area boards, which bring together tenants, elected representatives and other partners. The group, as a whole, provides training, financial and skills support for all elements of the governance structure, and reports its wider activities annually through a set of social accounts (First Ark, 2012). This case demonstrates the importance of involving local people from the outset in governance and of linking grass-roots engagement with real powers of policy determination and decision-making.

These brief case studies substantiate the general observations and lessons provided earlier, and they illustrate the considerable range of responses to the challenge of providing effective governance for resilient, sustainable cities and communities. As the present author (Roberts, 2007) has observed elsewhere, places need to be considered in the round and over time through a 'whole of place, whole of life, whole of community' approach, which places emphasis on inclusion, resilience and the integration of function. The following section reflects further on these matters.

21.3 Resilience and governance

For Torjman (2007), resilience, when applied to places and communities, is about the relationship between four clusters of activity: sustenance, adaptation, engagement and opportunity. These four activity clusters are seen as components that can be combined in different ways to provide resilience, which in Torjman's analysis can be characterised as having different applications. Thus, for example, an ecological application would combine sustenance and adaptation: here resilience is seen by Torjman (2007, p. 9) to be 'the ability of a system to maintain its structure and function when subject to disruptive force'. Another application or interpretation of resilience might be in relation to health. Here the challenge of illness – the threat or disruptive force – compels people to engage actively and to seek opportunities to improve their wellbeing. This implies that 'resilience is the capacity to thrive in a changing context' (Torjman, 2007, p. 13). Bringing the four clusters together and applying them to cities and communities, this implies that governance is about both ensuring that the core characteristics of resilience are in place and utilised to guide and govern actions related to the planning and management of places, and that the processes of governance themselves also reflect the characteristics of the four clusters.

Torjman's model neatly encapsulates many of the key concepts of resilience and, by definition, the governance of places in order that they might be, or become, resilient. However, because of the need to isolate the necessary preconditions of governance for resilience in sustainable communities, it is also important to recognise the significance of individual resilience as the fundamental building block (Norman, 2012) and the need for the contributions of individuals to be channelled through community-based organisations in order to 'make strong, resilient places for the future' (External Advisory Committee on Cities and Communities, 2006, p. xviii). These additions to the standard list of resilience components are also related to the fostering of wellbeing at city and community level (Mguni *et al.*, 2012), and this additional consideration provides an extra dimension of governance because it suggests that a wider agenda needs to be addressed.

A further fundamental consideration with regard to the development and implementation of governance for resilience is the importance of place. As Ashby *et al.* (2008) observe, although there is no one 'recipe' for resilience, there are common factors and components that can be used to guide the provision of resilience at a metropolitan to local level. Indeed, the international comparative work of Ashby *et al.* (2008) demonstrates that each governance for resilience model needs to be tailored to fit the requirements of an individual locality. In turn, this implies that the 'tailored to fit' approach offers many of the advantages of both 'bespoke' and 'one size fits all' approaches, without the respective disadvantages of either high cost or rigidity that are associated with these alternative models.

Moving beyond these initial considerations, it is evident that governance for resilient cities and communities should be framed within the wider theory and practice of engagement, participation and what Springett and Foster (2005) refer to as 'deliberative democracy'. This latter term was used to analyse the role of trade unions in delivering sustainable development in New Zealand. It demonstrates the importance of establishing widely dispersed ownership of the policy system in question, and the special requirement that governance should proceed as part of an evolving discourse on the structure and content of sustainable development (and its overall resilience), through an 'open, fair, transparent and democratic process' (Springett and Foster, 2005, p. 279).

The notion of 'deliberative democracy' is also central to other conversations on city and community (and wider place) resilience. It is, for example, a fundamental underpinning element which can be seen to determine the achievement (or otherwise) of Diamond's three essential tasks or functions of metropolitan governance: research and intelligence gathering; strategy, vision or the provision of a sense of direction; and leadership (Diamond, 1997). Equally, 'deliberative democracy' is a basic requirement for the operation of legitimate decision-making at sub-metropolitan level (Roberts *et al.*, 1999) and as a means of justification for interventions that may limit the rights or abilities of an individual in the interest of the welfare of society as a whole.

This line of argument leads to the penultimate element of consideration in this section – the extent to which a governance model for resilience is able to go beyond its principal mission of ensuring that a city or community has a structure of governance which is fit for purpose now and in the future. One additional task that a governance model for resilience might be expected to perform is the provision of a means of integrating the various strands of policy that guide and deliver sustainable places. If, by definition, resilience is concerned with creating a common thread that links policy strands together in order that they might be better able to cope with pressures or threats (Torjman, 2007), then policy integration can be considered to be an integral part of resilience. Thus, it can be argued that the development and delivery of an integrated spatial policy system is an important accompanying attribute of governance for resilience.

A final consideration is concerned with the evaluation and assessment of the success, or otherwise, of systems of governance for (and of) resilience. In part this consideration relates to the standard agenda of citizen and community engagement, and especially the extent to which engagement has resulted in enhanced governance which enables a city or community to become resilient or more resilient. Dobbs and Moore (2002) have argued that the structure and operation of an evaluation system can itself be used to assess the extent and quality of participation and engagement. They point to innovations in policy development and delivery, including evaluation, that place emphasis on engagement and empowerment, and conclude that 'participatory evaluation' can add to institutional capacity and, as a consequence, will enhance the ability of a city or community to respond to change events. This facet of governance for resilience is also evident in the literature on community cohesion and inclusion (Commission on Integration and Cohesion, 2007), the environmental dimension of resilience (Lombardi et al., 2012) and the economic aspect of local resilience (Ashby et al., 2008).

Summarising the key points from this section of the chapter, it is evident that governance for resilient cities and communities should:

- be robust and able to cope with the demands of both the present and the future;
- be accessible and inclusive in order to ensure the widest possible participation and engagement through both formal governmental structures and other organisations that perform the role of managers of collective affairs;
- be able to reflect the requirements of sustenance, adaptation, opportunity and engagement;
- be capable of operating at all relevant spatial levels and especially from the scale of the metropolitan region to the individual neighbourhood or locality;
- be able to demonstrate formal democratic legitimacy, which itself will reflect the specific characteristics of national and sub-national democratic arrangements, and encapsulate the wider functions expected of a governance system as a means of fostering and supporting 'deliberative democracy';
- be capable of developing integrated approaches to the delivery of policy – this may both be through structures of partnership and collaboration, and through other forms of cooperation and integration, such as joint delivery organisations; and

- be subject to scrutiny, evaluation and review, and be open and transparent across all aspects of policy and practice.

21.4 Conclusions and guidelines for future practice

This chapter has identified that governance for resilient places needs to be capable of coping with complex and rapidly changing urban systems. Even when considering this issue solely from an environmental and construction sector perspective, Lombardi et al. (2012) identify complexity and the range of difficult choices to be made. In their assessment the tensions between intended benefits and unexpected impacts suggests the need for solutions that cross spatial scales and embrace widespread social ownership and engagement. This conclusion is confirmed from other perspectives, including those that reflect the requirement of human wellbeing (Mguni et al., 2012) and economic development (External Advisory Committee on Cities and Communities, 2006).

A second, tentative conclusion reflects the long-established need for governance for resilient cities and communities to be valid at all spatial scales. Almost a century ago Geddes (1915) argued the case for a continuum of governance across the classic 'valley section' and this remains as an essential characteristic of effective governance for resilient places. The problems which confront cities and communities do not respect administrative boundaries and the governance arrangements associated with solutions to these problems should equally cross boundaries and be consistent at various scale levels. This is an established principle of metropolitan planning and development (Roberts et al., 1999) and it can be translated directly into the governance of resilient places.

Equally important as validity at all spatial scales is validity across sectors. As illustrated earlier, actions to ensure effective engagement and governance may emanate from all sectors and types of organisation. The case studies showed how both top-down and bottom-up inputs can contribute to the common cause, and this mutually reinforcing behaviour can help ensure that solutions are both robust and resilient (see, for example, Power et al., 2012).

The two preceding points contribute to a fourth conclusion and guideline: a governance system for resilient, sustainable places needs to encompass all relevant elements of both policy-making and implementation. As has been vividly demonstrated by environmental management approaches aimed at enhancing resilience, you cannot expect a half measure to provide a resilient platform for present or future performance. Whilst a resilient solution may comprise many small components, it is important to contextualise the system as a whole (Dandy et al., 2008). The same is true with regard to the social, economic and governance dimensions of resilient, sustainable cities and communities.

A fifth conclusion and guideline relates to the desirability of meshing together the traditional, elected democratic structures for the governance of places and the wider instruments and agencies of governance. The concepts and practices of partial and full territorial governance have been explored in greater depth elsewhere (Roberts, 2000) and they demonstrate the need to create and manage places through the medium of integrated territorial coalitions. Such territorial coalitions provide greater resilience than formal government, chiefly because they are inclusive and can extend governance to aspects that are outwith the competence of formal democratic structures. In addition, given the often lengthy processes involved in adjusting formal structures, the wider apparatus of governance allows for a rapid response to new challenges, threats and opportunities.

The final conclusion relates to the need for education, training and support of all those involved in the governance of cities and communities. The very essence of resilience is that it is about responding to both known and unknown events, and this implies the need continually to update and upgrade both intelligence and skills in order to provide 'willingness to act' (Cook and Ng, 2001, p. 69). In the United Kingdom, this dual requirement led to the creation of a special central government agency – the Academy for Sustainable Communities – which provided skills and knowledge for professionals and others involved with sustainable communities (Rogerson et al., 2011). As Heywood (2011, p. 201) argues, 'human learning flows continuously fresh to enliven each new generation', and this insight may provide the key to unlock effective and lasting governance for resilient cities and communities. That this is a universal requirement would appear to be a truism, but it is a truism which is neither fully acknowledged nor always accepted. Perhaps the acknowledgement that cities and communities are 'places of political empowerment' (Seixas and Albet, 2012, p. 10), and that this understanding can provide for better and more resilient urban governance, offers a positive pathway to the future.

References

Arnstein, S.R. 1969. A Ladder of Citizen Participation, *Journal of the American Institute of Planners*, 35(4), 216–224.

Ashby, J., Cox, D., McInroy, N. and Southworth, D. 2008. *Delivering Economic Success: An International Perspective on Local Government as Stewards of Local Economic Resilience*, Norfolk Trust. URL: http://www.cles.org.uk/publications/delivering-economic-success-an-international-perspective-on-local-government-as-stewards-of-local-economic-resilience/ (accessed 24 May 2013).

Baker, M., Roberts, P. and Shaw, R. 2003. *Stakeholder Involvement in Regional Planning*, Town and Country Planning Association, London.

Baker, S., Kousis, M., Richardson, D. and Young, S. 1997. *The Politics of Sustainable Development*, Routledge, London.

Bressers, H.T.A. 2004. Implementing Sustainable Development, in W. Lafferty (ed.) *Governance for Sustainable Development*, Edward Elgar, Cheltenham.

Chatterton, P. and Style, S. 2001. Putting Sustainable Development into Practice? The Role of Local Policy Partnership Networks, *Local Environment*, 6(4), 439–452.

Clarke, S. 2012. *Participatory Budgetary in Byker*, Your Homes Newcastle, Newcastle upon Tyne.

Collinge, C., Gibney, J. and Mabey, C. 2010. Leadership and Place, *Policy Studies*, 31(4), 367–378.

Commission on Integration and Cohesion. 2007. *Our Shared Future*, Commission on Integration and Cohesion, London.

Cook, A. and Ng, M.K. 2001. *Sustainable Communities: The Wanchai Experiment*, University of Hong Kong, Hong Kong.

Dandy, G., Walker, D., Daniell, T. and Warner, R. 2008. *Planning and Design of Engineering Systems*, Taylor and Francis, London.

Diamond, D. 1997. *Metropolitan Governance: Its Contemporary Transformation*, Floersheimer Institute for Policy Studies, Jerusalem.

Dobbs, L. and Moore, C. 2002. Engaging Communities in Area-based Regeneration: The Role of Participatory Evaluation, *Policy Studies*, 23(3/4), 157–171.

External Advisory Committee on Cities and Communities. 2006. *From Restless Communities to Resilient Places*, Infrastructure Canada, Ottawa.

First Ark. 2012. *Social Accounts 2012*, First Ark Group, Prescot.

Garner, J.F. 1981. Comparative Perspectives on Public Participation: Editorial Introduction, *Town Planning Review*, 52(3), 257–258.

Geddes, M. 1997. Poverty, Excluded Communities and Local Democracy, in N. Jewson and S. MacGregor (eds) *Transforming Cities*, Routledge, London.

Geddes, S. 1915. *Cities in Evolution*, Williams and Norgate, London.

Healey, P. 1997. The Revival of Spatial Planning in Europe, in P. Healey, A. Khakee, A. Motte and B. Needham (eds) *Making Strategic Spatial Plans*, UCL Press, London.

Heywood, P. 2011. *Community Planning*, Wiley, Chichester.

Hirst, P. and Thompson, G. 1996. *Globalisation in Question: The International Economy and the Possibilities of Governance*, Polity Press, Cambridge.

Jessop, B. 1997. Capitalism and its Future: Remarks on Regulation, Government and Governance, *Review of International Political Economy*, 4(3), 561–581.

Lafferty, W. 2004. Introduction: Form and Function in Governance for Sustainable Development, in W. Lafferty (ed.) *Governance for Sustainable Development*, Edward Elgar, Cheltenham.

Lafferty, W. and Langhelle, O. 1999. *Towards Sustainable Development: On the Goals of Development and the Conditions of Sustainability*, Macmillan, London.

Lombardi, D.R., Leach, J.M. and Rogers, C.D.F. 2012. *Designing Resilient Cities*, IHS BRE Press, Bracknell.

Mguni, N., Bacon, N. and Brown, J. 2012. *The Wellbeing and Resilience Paradox*, Young Foundation, London.

Norman, W. 2012. *Adapting to Change: The Role of Community Resilience*, Young Foundation, London.

Power, A., Herden, E., Provan, B. and Lane, L. 2012. *Bigger than Business*, London School of Economics, London.

Redclift, M. 2005. Sustainable Development (1987–2005): An Oxymoron Comes of Age, *Sustainable Development*, 13(4), 212–227.

Roberts, P. 2000. *The New Territorial Governance*, Town and Country Planning Association, London.

Roberts, P. 2007. Social Innovation, Spatial Transformation and Sustainable Communities: Liverpool and the Eldonians, in P. Drewe, J.L. Klein and E. Hulsbergen (eds) *The Challenges of Social Innovation in Urban Revitalization*, Techne Press, Amsterdam.

Roberts, P., Ravetz, J. and George, C. 2009. *Environment and the City*, Routledge, London.

Roberts, P., Thomas, K. and Williams, G. 1999. *Metropolitan Planning in Britain*, Jessica Kingsley, London.

Rogerson, R., Sadler, S., Green, A. and Wong, C. 2011. Learning about Sustainable Communities, in R. Rogerson, S. Sadler, A. Green and C. Wong (eds) *Sustainable Communities: Skills and Learning for Place-making*, University of Hertfordshire Press, Hatfield.

Seixas, J. and Albet, A. 2012. Introduction, in J Seixas and A. Albet (eds) *Urban Governance in Southern Europe*, Ashgate, Farnham.

Springett, D. and Foster, B. 2005. Whom is Sustainable Development for? Deliberative Democracy and the Role of Unions, *Sustainable Development*, 13(4), 271–281.

Tewdwr-Jones, M. and McNeill, D. 2000. The Politics of City-Region Planning and Governance, *European Urban and Regional Studies*, 7(2), 119–134.

Torjman, S. 2007. *Shared Space: The Communities Agenda*, Caldon Institute of Social Policy, Ottawa.

World Commission on Environment and Development. 1987. *Our Common Future*, Oxford University Press, Oxford.

CHAPTER 22

Economics and governance for city bounce

Neil McInroy

22.1 Introduction

'I don't know what the future will be for the city, but it has a good future', so said a city official of Tallinn, Estonia, as I chatted to him over dinner. This has always stuck in my mind, as it neatly sums up the enduring history of cities and the optimism we have in them – a history which (in Tallinn's case) is one of many changes in fortune, but which eventually comes good, in periods of stress. All cities, young and ancient, are in some ways characterised by adaptability and resilience in the face of social, technological and environmental change.

   However, we live in unprecedented times, with many challenges. Cities stand at a crossroads and for their future to be 'good', we need to start thinking through two issues: firstly, the detailed make-up of this intrinsic historical capacity for resilience; and secondly, how we build more of it. In this chapter, I shall look at how we can develop this capacity, a capacity which enables cities to 'roll with the punches' and 'bounce back' quickly from any adversity, remaining flexible to take advantage of opportunities.

22.2 The challenge

There are many challenges for cities, as outlined in Chapter 2, and the five main ones discussed here together form an unprecedented 'perfect storm'. Firstly, recent economic events have shown us that cities are dependent upon the global economy and that all cities are interdependent, with adverse or buoyant economic conditions in one city causing ripple effects in another. Therefore, there is a challenge to reposition and reset cities in relation to global economic forces, whilst creating more independent and self-sustaining local economic activity. Secondly, environmental change and an increase in threats are creating instability and uncertainty. This means there is a need for cities to plan and adapt, so they can mitigate the effects of environmental change and develop new ways of sustainable living. Thirdly, migration and demographic shifts, in particular ageing, have already and will continue to create new pressures on public resources and will change the nature of how we live together and use cities. Fourthly, city finances are under pressure. The fallout from the economic crisis, plus a seemingly ever-increasing demand on public services, means we must find ways to reduce the pressure on public finances. Finally, a range of political and cultural forces, including new forms of citizenship and social movements, are resulting in an increasing demand for people and civil society to do more to shape and make cities.

This ongoing economic, social, cultural and environmental change is now the new normal. This is no passing phenomenon. As such, we should not be complacent about the need to tackle these challenges. Therefore, our city plans and approach to governance should reflect this new normality.

Now and into the future, the extent to which these challenges result in neutral, damaging or energising consequences depends upon the abilities of cities to adapt and respond. No city can rely solely on past approaches to succeed in the future. We know from history that areas which become locked into a singular economic sector, fail to plan for environmental adaptation or misread the scale of social and cultural shifts may well be left behind, as the changes swamp and erode the city and the way it operates. Therefore, it is essential that we plan for cities which can 'bounce back' from these challenges, and in turn learn, create a memory, and develop knowledge of how to strengthen the city for the future and the additional challenges to come (see Box 22.1). Key to this is working with the notion that cities are networks.

22.3 Cities as networks

Cities are both parts of and in themselves networks. For the most part, city governance, whilst aware of networks, does not strategically assess the myriad connections and networks which operate within cities. However, these networks and connections are the 'DNA' of cities. They are its lifeblood. Yet these networks and connections are brittle (Edwards, 2009). For instance, in an area where networks are routinely assessed – transport – it is well known that a traffic accident can cause traffic mayhem and affect the lives of business and citizenry in many ways. However, when it comes to the economic, social and cultural life of cities, we are much less network savvy. For instance, take the economic crisis. The failure of the sub-prime mortgage market in the US, and the complex

---

Box 22.1 Resilience: the 'boing' factor

Resilience is about the ability to respond to challenges. It refers to a quality that enables some cities to respond effectively to shocks, or respond quickly to opportunities, be they economic, social, political or environmental, whilst other cities falter, decline or miss such opportunities.

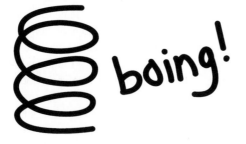

and opaque connections between this and the banking system around the world, had significant ramifications for city finances and numerous national economies.

Networks are important for resilience, which is why many researchers are increasingly interested in networks and how cities operate as systems. System thinking is about how different things in a network influence one another. In nature, an example is a typical ecosystem – including air, water, animals and plants and how they work together. In cities, we need to look at different people, structures and processes, and the efficient or inefficient ways in which they work together, depending on the effectiveness of the whole system.

Perhaps the most important element in a good system is that it is not about independent individuals and organisations going off in their own directions to create change in their own ways. Such a system, demonstrating a lack of connectedness and an un-joined-up approach, will suffer through lack of coherence and unintended consequences. An illustrative example comes from quantum physics (Wheatley, 2010). There are no independent entities at all at the quantum level as it is all about the relationships which make up the 'whole'. It is the same for the city. It's not the housing, or the transport, or business, or social life which is most important, but rather how they relate to one another as a whole.

Inspired by initial global research (Ashby *et al.*, 2009), the Centre for Local Economic Strategies (CLES) has been thinking of places and cities as systems for a number of years now (McInroy and Longlands, 2010) – defined by how they respond and adapt to new challenges, whether these are economic, social or environmental. Those systems which are able to exude these qualities are those which are generally the most resilient. System thinking underpins our resilience model.

22.4 A resilient future

Coming from its traditional use in relation to natural disasters (Hill *et al.*, 2008) and ecosystems (Pimm, 1984; Holling, 1986), resilience has gained ground in social and economic contexts. Indeed, it is now growing and attracting more attention across academia and policy (Pike *et al.*, 2010; Adger, 2000; Swanstrom, 2008) and within the fields of psychology (Kaplan, 1999) and engineering (Vale and Campanella, 2005).

Generally, resilience is about the capability of a system to be flexible and agile enough in response to forces or change. Brian Walker, from CSIRO, defines resilience as 'the capacity of a system to absorb disturbance and reorganise while undergoing change so as to retain essentially the same function, structure, identity and feedbacks' (Walker *et al.*, 2004). Thomas Homer-Dixon writes, 'resilience is an emergent property of a system – it's not a result of any one of the system's parts but of the synergy between all its parts. So, as a rough and ready rule, boosting the ability of each part to take care of itself in a crisis boosts overall resilience' (Homer-Dixon, 2006, p. 284).

Interestingly, the concept of 'resilience' differs from 'sustainability' in that it focuses on the proactive capabilities of a system. Thus it is not about protecting but developing the innate qualities which make a system survive and flourish. Instead of embracing stasis, as sustainability implies, resilience embraces the norm of change, flexibility, rapid unpredictability and networks.

Resilience also rejects the notion that systems change in a linear way. In resilience, elements within a system are in constant flux, unpredictable and highly complex. Many changes and events occur at very different time frames and speeds. Traffic jams occur over minutes, stock markets crash over days and weeks, housing markets change over months and years. All of this challenges the mechanical and linear approach to city making and shaping. Cities need to be understood as an interconnected system and the policy application and governance of resilience involve a search for qualities and attributes of place which make it adaptable and able to thrive on change.

Given the challenges we face, we need to think about how to make places more resilient – a resilience which recognises the importance of connections and relationships. In doing so, we would hope that some connections and relationships can be strengthened and made less opaque, thus equipping places to be more adept at both responding to shocks and exploiting opportunities.

22.5 The CLES approach

The CLES resilience model (Figure 22.1) has been designed to provide a conceptual framework of how a city is structured and the relationships that influence it and how we govern cities. The model moves beyond traditional 'linear' and 'silo' thinking about cities, taking a whole-systems approach that looks at the key agents and linkages operating within cities.

The framework has been designed to ensure all parts of the economy are represented: the social, commercial and public economies. The commercial economy is often seen as the priority for cities, but the resilience model demonstrates that the public sector can have considerable influence on a locality through procurement spend, planning and employment opportunities. Likewise, the social economy does not regularly feature in economic thinking and strategies, but plays a crucial role in providing the foundations for any healthy and effective economy both directly – through local employment, local supply chains, volunteering and social enterprise – and indirectly – through development of social capital and promotion of civil engagement and participative democracy.

What makes the resilience model stand out is that whilst it focuses on traditional elements of 'the economy', it homes in on the relative strength of the reciprocal relationships between the public, private and social economies. I believe these relationships and connections help to generate resilience within an area. Stronger mutual relationships allow a locality to be more flexible and reactive if faced with an economic or environmental change.

CLES has been working with a number of local authorities and their partners across the UK and in Greater Dandenong, Australia, over the past few years as part of our Place Resilience research programme. This has incorporated assessing the resilience of systems at a range of geographical levels – including city, county, sub-regional, district, town centre and individual neighbourhoods. The model's principal assumption is that, through improving the quality of the multitude of relationships

Figure 22.1 The
resilience model for
governance

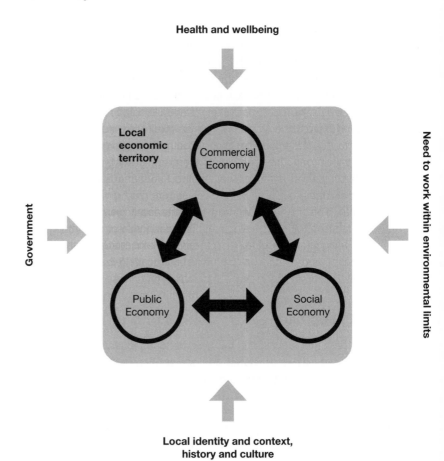

Figure 22.1 The resilience model for governance

within a city, that synergies and innovative responses to the key challenges can be generated. The CLES resilience model is unique in that it explores all of the assets and resources within a locality to ensure future positive change, and it is predicated on the resilience being achieved by a place having the systems in place which help both individuals and institutions to collaborate effectively in developing solutions to challenges.

Using the CLES resilience model, CLES develops a qualitative assessment of the strength of relationships between the sectors and the impact that these relationships have on city resilience. To do this, we use qualitative research techniques to explore the relationships between the three core spheres of the economy (the public, social and private sectors) through a lens of ten core measures of city resilience (see Figure 22.2). These measures relate to the different relationships which exist within a city. An implicit assumption within the model is that city resilience develops as a result of the strength and effectiveness of these relationships, so if they are strong, a city is more likely to be resilient.

For example, in Manchester, our work served to highlight some of the good work undertaken by the city. Using the assessments for each of the ten measures of the CLES resilience model, we concluded that Manchester can best be described as

The shape of your local economy		
Measure 1 **The commercial economy** The strength of the commercial economy is defined as economic wealth creation generated by businesses that are privately owned and profit motivated.	**Measure 2** **The public economy** The public economy consists of services delivered on behalf of government organisations whether national, regional or local, and funded by the public purse.	**Measure 3** **The social economy** The social economy embraces a wide range of community, voluntary and not-for-profit activities that try to bring about positive local change.

The relationships which influence your economy		
Measure 4 **Commercial economy's relationship with the public economy** Explores the existence and effectiveness of partnerships between the commercial and public sectors and the level of interaction between the two parts of the economy.	**Measure 5** **Public economy's relationship with the social sector** Explores the existence and effectiveness of partnerships between the public and social sectors.	**Measure 6** **Social economy's relationship with the commercial economy** Explores the existence and effectiveness of partnerships between the commercial and social sectors.

The wider relationships in a local economic territory			
Measure 7 **Broad health and wellbeing and the relationship to the local economic territory** How local health and wellbeing issues relate to the local economy. This includes ill health, quality of life, travel to work and leisure patterns, and the economic geography of the area.	**Measure 8** **Relationship between the local economic territory and working within environmental limits** Explores how the climate change agenda has been integrated into the economy of the local economic territory. This looks at both climate change mitigation and adaptation strategies.	**Measure 9** **Relationship between the local economic territory and local identity, history and context** The extent to which an area is shaped by and manages its identity, history and culture.	**Measure 10** **Relationship between the local economic territory and governance** How national and local governance has affected the local economic territory.

lying somewhere between 'resilient' and 'stable'. The strong relationships between the public and commercial and the public and social, and the evidence of joint working, are somewhat restricted by a more 'vulnerable' relationship between the commercial and social economies.

Figure 22.2 The ten resilience measures

There are, however, areas where there is room for improvement and further means by which the public, commercial and social economies can respond to inherent conditions and emerging opportunities:

- enable a stronger role for commercial and social economies in place stewardship;
- step up the role of employers in policy, strategy and delivery;
- assess the vulnerability of Manchester's leadership and vision;

- work more effectively with SMEs;
- support the joining-up of social sector infrastructure; and
- use the public economy as a driver of commercial–social economy relations.

This work was fed into ongoing city strategy and approaches to the governance of the city.

22.6 Developing strong systems

Our work on resilient cities has allowed us to determine a number of key concepts for the governance of cities.

Collaboration

The strongest and most resilient city systems are those with strong leadership that is not based purely on a top-down approach, but encourages and inspires self-determination from a range of sectors and innovative collaboration and crossover between networks. This increases synergy and the potential to develop innovative solutions to address challenges and grasp opportunities.

Adaptability

Adaptability involves making the decisions to leave a path that may have proven successful in the past and moving towards new, related or alternative structures and processes. In terms of cities, some localities are more effective than others at this. The ability to adapt can depend on individual and institutional behaviours, and the rigidness or flexibility of organisations to accept and then instigate change.

Synergy

This is a central element of a successful city system, and those cities which display strong synergy across different sectors highlight that a cohesive group is greater than the sum of its parts. It is particularly important in cities, as those with high levels of synergy are often able to overcome barriers quickly due to shared and common objectives. Organisational synergy on its own is fine, say within a local council in which all departments work as a cohesive machine, but without linkages to the business community and the social sector development of a wider synergetic structure will be inhibited.

Social capital

Of course, it is important to have the human and institutional capital in order to develop city systems, but social capital is equally important. Social capital is defined as the features of social organisation within a locality that facilitate cooperation and coordination for mutual benefit, such as networks, norms and trust. It relates to community and voluntary groups, social enterprises and resident groups. Cities with strong social capital will have a strong social sector and will be places where considerations of social benefit are pervasive.

Co-production

'Co-production' has recently become a widely used term among a range of practitioners and commentators. It is a vision for public services which focuses on designing and delivering services *with* public sector professionals, rather than *for* them. CLES has been arguing for such approaches for a number of years now, and indeed co-production is a core component of our resilience model, with different sectors and individuals coming together to address the challenges faced by cities. Co-production is therefore an important concept underpinning a strong and fluid system (McInroy and Blume, 2011).

22.7 Conclusion

This chapter has outlined an approach in which the city can be understood in terms of its resilient capabilities. It has sought to outline the importance of creating a quality within the city and in city governance which enables cities to be flexible in the face of adverse change and take advantage of opportunities. Elements of resilience, or city bounce, are already within all cities. The task for city governance is to understand resilience more, harness it and promote those elements.

References

Adger, W. N. 2000. Social and ecological resilience: Are they related? *Progress in Human Geography*, 24: 347–364.

Ashby, J., Cox, D., McInroy, N. and Southworth, D. 2009. Delivering economic success: An international perspective on local government as stewards of local economic resilience. Norfolk Trust. Available at: http://www.cles.org.uk/wp-content/uploads/2011/01/An-international-perspective-on-local-government-as-stewards-of-local-economic-resilience.pdf.

Edwards, C. 2009. *Resilient Nation*. London: Demos.

Hill, E., Wial, H. and Wolman, H. 2008. *Exploring Regional Economic Resilience*. IURD working paper. Berkeley: Institute of Urban and Regional Development, University of California.

Holling, C. S. 1986. The resilience of terrestrial ecosystems: Local surprise and global change. In W.C. Clark and R.E. Munn (eds) *Sustainable Development of the Biosphere*. Cambridge: Cambridge University Press.

Homer-Dixon, T. 2006. *The Upside of Down: Catastrophe, Creativity and the Renewal of Civilisation*. London: Souvenir Press.

Kaplan, H. B. 1999. Toward an understanding of resilience: A critical review of definitions and models. In M. Glantz and J.L. Johnson (eds) *Resilience and Development: Positive Life Adaptation*. New York: Kluwer Academic/ Plenum.

McInroy, N. and Blume, T. 2011. The quest for co-produced community. *Local Government Chronicle*, 19 August. Available at: http://www.lgcplus.com/briefings/services/economic-development/a-quest-for-co-produced-communities/5032701. article.

McInroy, N. and Longlands, S. 2010. *Productive Local Economies: Creating Resilient Places.* Manchester: CLES.

Pike, A., Dawley, S. and Tomaney, J. 2010. Resilience, adaptation and adaptability. *Cambridge Journal of Regions, Economy and Society*, 3(1): 59–70.

Pimm, S.L. 1984. The complexity and stability of ecosystems. *Nature*, 307: 321–326.

Swanstrom, T. 2008. *Regional Resilience: A Critical Examination of the Ecological Framework*. IURD working Paper. Berkeley: Macarthur Foundation Research Network on Building Resilient Regions, Institute of Urban and Regional Development, University of California.

Vale, L. J. and Campanella, T. J. 2005. *The Resilient City: How Modern Cities Recover from Disaster*. New York: Oxford University Press.

Walker, B., Holling, C. S., Carpenter, S. R. and Kinzig, A. 2004. Resilience, adaptability and transformability in social–ecological systems. *Ecology and Society*, 9(2). Available at: http://www.ecologyandsociety.org/vol9/iss2/art5/.

Wheatley, M. 2010. *Leadership and the New Science*. San Francisco, CA: Berrett-Koehler.

CHAPTER 23

Leadership for sustainability and sustainable leadership

Edward J. Blakely

23.1 Sustainable leadership for sustainability

We learned in Rio I and II that we cannot look to the world's political leadership for all the answers. This is especially true as the global economic crisis deepens. Unemployed workers are viewing environmental measures as costing them their jobs. Social political alterations in the course of human action will have to come from other forums and processes than political discourse. The direction of nations, industries and individuals will have to be changed to generate a continuous intelligent and robust movement towards more resilient, sustainable communities. With the horrors of Hurricane Sandy on 30 October 2012 in New York and the US eastern seaboard, we saw political blame more than realistic assessments of agendas for change (Blakely, 2012). Elected political leadership is far too distracted by short-term issues like budgets, political fragmentation, elections, rising terrorism and racism to deal with longer-term, deep, complex, amorphous notions like global sustainability. This is not to say elected leaders are dismissive of the issues, but they feel powerless to deal with them. In addition, the extremists have conflated issues of stagnant economic performance and immigration with global warming science and environmental actions to curb carbon emissions. Finally, the ups and downs of national governments suggest that new forums for carrying on global mandates must be grown from a new stream of information that breeds a new cadre of leaders. Where to start?

23.2 Communicating resilience and sustainability sustainably

Creating resilient communities capable of adapting or mitigating long-term climate and other risks is not an issue a government can solve by itself. Government mandates only go so far. Human behaviour is far more important. The SARS epidemic that swept the world in the early 2000s is an excellent example of how people got the message and changed what they did and where they did it and made intelligent sacrifices for all humanity (World Health Organization, 2003). They took action because the problem was laid out clearly and graphically by credible sources and pushed through every medium on the planet persistently. Similarly, cigarette smoking is dropping among most people around the world. There are differences among cultures and nations, but the overall trend is clear. As Marshall McLuhan said, 'The medium is now the message' (McLuhan, 1964, p. 9).

Resilience is a longer-term issue since it takes step-by-step action with reinforcing messages of praise for good behaviour. Media presentation of good, healthy living with not so subtle anti-smoking messages is leading to worldwide change. Similarly women's movements are altering female roles through persistent, resilient pressure.

McLuhan (1964, p. 68) said, 'If the work of the city is the remaking or translating of man into a more suitable form than his nomadic ancestors achieved, then might not our current translation of our entire lives into the spiritual form of information seem to make of the entire globe, and of the human family, a single consciousness.'

We need a single human consciousness, in McLuhan's term, to guide daily decisions of how we, each of us, use our precious planet. While it can be argued that a poor slum dweller in Africa has no time for subtle ways of obtaining and using resources, this is simply not true. Many slum dwellers crowd round the TV to see their favourite footballer or basketball star and wear apparel imitating those distant demigods. In essence, most of the world knows 'what is cool' from a relentless media that saturates the globe and tells people what kind of life and lifestyle are preferred. Remarkably, it is this constant messaging that spawned and continues to fuel the 'Arab Spring'. The constant march to democratic systems is viral and no regime can resist it. As Francis Fukuyama, formerly director of policy for the US State Department, put it so eloquently,

> The triumph of the West, of the Western idea, is evident first of all in the total exhaustion of viable systematic alternatives to Western liberalism. In the past decade, there have been unmistakable changes in the intellectual climate of the world's two largest communist countries, and the beginnings of significant reform movements in both. But this phenomenon extends beyond high politics and it can be seen also in the ineluctable spread of consumerist Western culture in such diverse contexts as the peasants' markets and colour television sets now omnipresent throughout China, the cooperative restaurants and clothing stores opened in the past year in Moscow, the Beethoven piped into Japanese department stores, and the rock music enjoyed alike in Prague, Rangoon, and Tehran.
> (Fukuyama, 1992, p. 212)

In the same vein, Thomas Friedman, of the *New York Times*, says the 'world is flat', a dictum that traces the convergence of global ideas as the major force for shaping tomorrow, not global armies (Friedman, 2007).

There is no clear communication of what sustainability is, or indeed what it is not. I am calling for a *Sustainability CNN* that broadcasts the sustainability message day and night around the globe by tracking stories and highlighting successes and failures and presenting courageous leaders while fostering debate and carrying a consistent message across all media, from social networks to pay and free television, radio and even blog internet radio with the core of a sustainability movement which is not a 'one-off fix'. All the world's social movements know this, from al-Qaeda to the soccer World Cup. They have to fix your mind with their message. Simple propaganda will not do. Sustainability has to be a movement that causes actions, not just passive thoughts and inactivity. It has to spawn tree plantings and river cleaning as spontaneously generated acts across the planet.

How is this possible?

Global foundations spend billions annually on worldwide projects to do many good things. Some of this money might be directed at creating the equivalent of an international *Sustainability BBC*. It could attract advertising and prominent people to lend their brands and names to programmes and media efforts around the world to showcase sustainability issues of both local and global proportions: for example, neighbourhood videos of elephant poachers and celebrations of slum clearance. It would be courageous journalism aimed at global transformation. There are already some responsible networks filling this space, such as National Geographic and CNN. But they have many issues to cover. I am suggesting a network so powerful that world leaders would want to appear on it or feel compelled to address messages from it. I am not discounting print media here. Bloomberg appears in print and online and so would this approach. It might be seen as bold or dangerous in some quarters, but the truth about government green efforts and green washing has to be told. It would give scientists a place to present solid information on a regular basis, covering all sides of the issues. High-quality debate is valuable in ensuring the truth is shown clearly.

How resilient is communication?

There is no guarantee for this approach. But we certainly have good gut instincts that tell us we cannot change individual or collective behaviour until we have a message outside politics. Yet building resilience is based on collective action toward the use of all resources and protection of vital systems. The Japanese have created resilient neighbourhoods across the nation's urban areas by building into each community a five to ten-day supply of fresh, drinkable water, underground cisterns and solar-powered generators. This approach builds local resilience and moves away from dependent, centralized utility infrastructure.

23.3 A sustainable institutional framework to generate leadership for business, community and science

Sustainability is more than a set of ideas. It has become a large-scale business. Sustainable business comes in so many forms that it is hard to catalogue all of them. We have sustainably produced foods, energy and myriad other products and services. At this point, anyone can use the word to promote almost any-thing. Sustainability is not an issue that governments can define and regulate simply, like toxins. At this point, we need a new international-level institution to sit outside UN and international agency politics, a global sustainability institute to certify and accredit 'green', 'sustainable', 'climate', 'carbon', etc. goods, products, services and concepts, and provide training. This seems a monumental task, but if we are to shift the debate, we have to have an apolitical institutional organization that lives only on the trust it generates by dealing with science, technology and information, in the same way as international food and drugs agencies do. These globally trusted bodies are (for the most part) not controlled by governments, even though they are government funded. They have developed deep credibility over many years. It would be wonderful if parallel, equally well-funded national sustainability certification and training institutes were to arise.

However, even the most committed governments have faced problems in this sphere. Australia, which has implemented a carbon tax, has recently eviscerated its climate agency in the wake of political attacks (Franklin, 2012); and James Hansen, who headed the US Goddard Institute for Space Science, faced pressure from the Bush administration to edit his reports on climate change (Revkin, 2006). If even the strong are folding or under attack, it does not bode well for any national body assuming responsibility for assessing the myriad goods, services and ideas that are offered up as solving sustainability dilemmas.

Clearly there are many good green institutions on the ground now, such as the Green Building Councils. But their job is to advocate, not to assess. Moreover, each Green Building Council lives in its own political environment and is subject to the pressures of that environment. It is unlikely that Green Councils in many Asian and African nations will be deeply or intensively critical of their governments. None-theless, most of these bodies act as weak or strong advocates of green building. But there is more to greening than buildings. There is energy development and delivery, bio-products and a host of good and bad carbon reduction schemes, ranging from various forms of 'cap and trade' to permitting systems. Technical analysis of these approaches is currently conducted by politically inspired 'think tanks' that come up with whatever result their masters want to hear. So, no matter what comes out of their research, there is scepticism. The International Panel on Climate Change has to stay close to its mandate of monitoring what is; it cannot judge all of the notions of what might be. Creating an independent organization for sustainability assessment might find support among global industry. Large firms need to *show* they are green. It is not enough for them merely to say they are. So, they would have an interest in promoting this approach and forming the organization from a voluntary membership or tax on themselves.

I am suggesting a new *Global Sustainability Products and Services (GSPS) Laboratory* which would act like US consumer agencies by investigating products and claims and issuing reports based on its own independent analysis. These reports would be in the public realm so anyone could read and assess them. Firms could use them to promote their goods and services, but no firm could demand a report. The GSPS would review entire ranges of products, comparing them across many dimensions. Products and services would have to be registered and companies would have to pay registration and subscription fees to be among those assessed in most instances, but the GSPS would conduct as wide a search as possible of organizations marketing products or offering services.

Why is this a leadership issue?

It is a leadership issue because 'if you don't know where you are going, any road will do'. Leaders need facts to use as a foundation for their stances. The data emerging from a body like this would breed new leadership in firm management, boards and investors, so consumers find leadership that is institutionally robust and accountable. Having an objective base from which to build leadership will be transformative because it is harder to attack a system than a person. Jared Diamond, the author of *Collapse* (2005), Hansen, and others currently suffer relentless attacks for proposing their ideas about social and societal change. In a sense, we need an honest broker so that thought leaders such as Diamond can speak their minds. However, this is not to suggest that schools and universities cannot or will not continue to advance important sustainability ideas. We must continue to support them, too, because they will spawn people by hosting scholars with differing views and developers of much basic and applied science. But it is important, perhaps vital, to have a neutral establishment with the globe's sustainability health as its sole mandate, much like the Centers for Disease Control and the World Health Organization have their respective mandates.

Getting started

This is an idea that seems to be ripe. There is talk at many conferences, including the most recent Rio conference in 2012, to have some form of independent institution of this type. A global champion, someone like Brundtland, will need to be asked to form such an organization and then promote it. There are many potential candidates who possess the necessary global credibility. Once the name is announced, the door would open for serious funding to commence the project and find the right home for it. One possibility would be Strasbourg, the second and currently under-utilized home of the EU.

A global sustainability training and development institute would also be part of the agenda of the GSPS, dedicated to training both current and future leaders for sustainability roles. The institute's mission would be to develop leadership across all dimensions for sustainability managers in the public and private sectors, with residential courses held at key centres around the world and at the home campus. It would not replace the fine work going on in many universities, but rather would act as a trainer of trainers to build global capacity, much like Harvard, Oxford and many other world-renowned universities offer short leadership programmes using case study and action learning modes of delivery.

The combination of teaching and technical analysis of products, ideas and services would keep the learning fresh and provide opportunities to have multiple return sessions. Costs for students would be at the market rate, with fellowships and scholarships available through a variety of sources, including funds earned by product assessments along with UN, World Bank and large international organizations, ranging from the Red Cross to Global Vision, as co-sponsors.

The right person in the right place can bring the resources together to make this happen, as Brundtland did.

23.4 Building sustainable leadership roots at the grassroots

Local communities see and feel the problems of climate change and unsustainable living. So it is understandable that organizations like C-40 have emerged to promote sustainable practices. The big-city leaders who comprise C-40, with or without national support (or even recognition), are forging strong, smart agendas across the globe. But leaders in forty mega-cities cannot and will not change the face of the earth. At the moment local leaders are more likely to run against or away from climate change and sustainability than to show a willingness to address them.

Nonetheless, local communities are fertile grounds for forming new leaders and building leadership that in time can ascend to higher levels. In some countries local Green Parties attempt to perform this role. Unfortunately, though, in too many instances the local Green candidate is working on a national agenda with modest or even no relevant local implications. In other cases Green might be the party label but community greening is not on the agenda. So we have to think of ways to develop local leaders who will work in the community to generate new projects outside local politics. My preference is to craft non-partisan leadership; that is, no party allegiance but a commitment to certain principles.

This could be achieved through *local sustainable leadership academies.* These would be modelled on the very successful Mayors' Institute for City Design. The base for the mayors' programme is collective – mayor-to-mayor and peer-to-peer learning working on problems with people from selected communities. In the academies the approach would be similar, with each participant required to be part of a community team of three to five people who would bring local issues to the academy. At each three–five-day academy leading professionals would be on hand to work with the selected communities and develop options and leadership strategies to deal with the issues. All the selected communities would be cross-trained with other communities to gain skills in solving a variety of issues, not just what they brought to the academy.

In effect, these academies would be learning labs. The participants would be community leaders, but not necessarily elected officials. At least two unrelated, locally sponsored people from each community would come to the academy (screening for gender and racial/ethnic balance) with a widely acknowledged problem that has some physical and social dimensions. The problems in the group would form the core of the curriculum. There would be few lectures, rather observations by experts from relevant fields such as engineering, urban planning, architecture and social/community development who would operate as input generators – not as masters of dogma but as resources offering a range of best-practice options for consideration by the participants. Each community would have to tailor its own solution from the information it received from the experts and other community peers. The intention would not be to solve problems in the academy but to demonstrate the various ways problems might be solved using sustainability templates. Selected community leaders would return home with new tool kits thus growing a new cadre of associate community professionals along with a new peer network within communities with similar issues, as well as national and international databases via webinars and web information along with periodic one-day or web-based update seminars and workshops. All manner of reinforcing learning could and would be used.

Who should run the academies?

I believe local colleges and universities are best placed to host these academies, but they may not have the reserves of staff to conduct them. So local expertise from real estate, architecture and related fields would have to be recruited. Since such ventures require good facilitation and strong message, staff running the pro-gramme would attend the aforementioned international academy or similar institutions, where they could gain training and certification. There are myriad ways to maintain quality control, but ultimately the academies would have to undergo the same kind of review and accreditation process that is required of university degree programmes.

The idea is to grow leaders with an agenda at the grassroots. Some of these leaders might eventually enter politics, but the main aim is to prepare leaders with sustainability problem-solving skills who are apolitical and non-partisan.

How might the academies be funded?

The best way to fund the academies would be to impose a surcharge on property insurance premiums in each province or state in advanced nations. The World Bank has the capacity to mount a similar effort in the developing world. Some other international organizations, such as the Clinton Foundation, might also see the academies as the ideal way to leverage the green agenda around the world at a modest cost.

23.5 Conclusion

What I have tried to do here is come up with sustainable leadership systems for sustainability. I have not attempted to discuss personal characteristics of good sustainability leaders as this is too vulnerable to cultural bias and stereotyping. I have made the approach global in nature, with sustainability problems, not platitudes, at the base of my three systems.

First, we have a sustainable information platform to keep ideas growing and flowing. Next, we have an institution outside politics to inspect and assess sus-tainability tools, approaches, products and concepts, and to mentor sustainability management. The proposed organization would not be a generator of science but an examiner of products and ideas with its role being to report findings openly to all. It will also have an education mandate to train based on the best knowledge available to current leaders across all fields, from business to religion, using a case/information-based knowledge-delivery approach. Just one bias would be inherent in delivery – climate and sustainability. Finally, we have to grow new leadership roots. Local leadership academies would be formed to develop skilled resilience leaders. Resilience is a mission, a belief, a movement, a philosophy, a way of life and a way of thinking and seeing the world. People who have led such missions historically have been ridiculed in their time (Jesus, Mohammed, Gandhi, Abraham Lincoln, Martin Luther King and more). Self-sacrifice and living the example formed the essence of their leadership, not popularity in the moment.

There is no silver bullet in this proposal. These are ideas I advance for further inspection and deliberation. Only one thing is certain – time is running out and we need many leaders, not just one person, to guide us out of this wilderness.

References

Blakely, E. 2012. Take your heads out of the Sandy. *New York Observer*, 11 November, p. A2.

Diamond, J. 2005. *Collapse*. New York: Viking.

Franklin, M. 2012. Labor takes axe to green bureaucrats to bolster surplus. *The Australian*, 4 March. Available at: http://www.theaustralian.com.au/national-affairs/climate/labor-takes-axe-to-green-bureaucrats-to-bolster-surplus/story-e6frg6xf-1226318042678.

Friedman, T. 2007. *The World is Flat*. New York: Picador.

Fukuyama, F. 1992. *The End of History*. New York: The Free Press.

Lovins, E. 2012. *Reinventing Fire: Bold Business Solutions for the New Energy Era*. White River Junction, VT: Chelsea Green.

McLuhan, M. 1964. *Understanding Media: The Extensions of Man*. Cambridge, MA: MIT Press.

Revkin, A. 2006. NASA chief backs agency openness. *Science Section*, *New York Times*, 6 February, p. C1.

World Health Organization. 2003. *Severe Acute Respiratory Syndrome (SARS): Multi-Country Outbreak – Update 6*. Geneva: World Health Organization.

CHAPTER 24

The plan and the policy

Who is changing whom?

Rob Roggema

24.1 Introduction

A future that is more sustainable and where everyone is happier is a noble goal but, for one reason or another, it is difficult to achieve. It is not the case that there is no common agreement about what this beautiful future might include. When we limit ourselves to the more technical sustainability indicators, it means a higher biodiversity, zero emissions of GHGs, clean air and water, and sustainably produced food, evenly spread over the globe. No one opposes these goals.

Policy stands in the way; or, more accurately, the institutions, such as governments, large (energy) companies, the economically driven platforms for growth and job creation, to name a few, that together form the establishment of power. Most of these institutions are old, have a long history and are based on unwritten agreements about how the future needs to be perceived. Namely, these futures are based on the past, implying a linear development. But many of the currently encountered changes, and especially the disruptive and unexpected ones, such as the impacts of climate change, are *non*-linear.

Therefore, if the current policy constellation is incapable of providing adequate responses to these non-linear changes, a reverse approach might be advisable. What would happen if we did *not* start by letting the established institutions define the policy for the future? Can we achieve a more sustainable future when plans (or spatial interventions in the landscape) are defined first, which then subsequently will lead to adjusted policies? Two elements are crucial: what is the plan? Or: what are the needs for spatial interventions, defined as an innovation niche that is capable of changing (Geels, 2002, 2005, 2011), and how do we get there? What is the transformational pathway?

24.2 Backtracking

The first questions concern what a sustainable future might look like and where the fundamental strategic interventions that initiate that future should be located. The answers depend strongly on the local environment, and earlier chapters in this book have outlined some essential criteria. As a result of urbanisation, the natural environment became hidden under concrete and asphalt, but it has not disappeared. It becomes apparent in extreme weather circumstances. For instance, the natural water system reappears in a city when it rains heavily. The places where flash

Figure 24.1 Forecasting, backcasting and backtracking
Source: Roggema (2009)

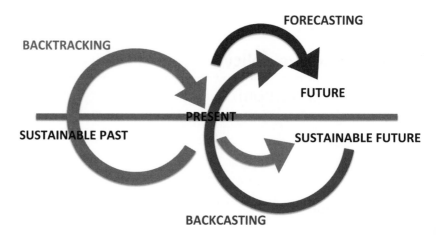

flooding occurs today are the areas where space was available to store excess rainwater in the original system.

The way to identify the features of this underlying natural system in urban environments is backtracking. In this methodology, contrasting with backcasting or forecasting (Figure 24.1), a sustainable future is based on a historical time when there was sustainable equilibrium. This is then used as an inspiration to define the desired long-term future. Subsequently, the strategies and measures which are needed to achieve this future in a step-by-step way can be identified. This methodology has been used, for example, in the hotspot Groningen, the Netherlands, to create long-term climate-proof scenarios (Roggema, 2009).

Once the desired future is defined, the next step is to envision the change that is required to reach this future.

Transformations

When looking back in (recent) history, changes in (urbanised) landscapes often take place after a specific spatial intervention. First there was the rail line or road and afterwards towns and cities developed. Illustrative is the western move in the early days of the United States. For instance, on the map of the northern Pacific country (Cohen, 2002, pp. 198–199) the transcontinental railroad is represented together with a development zone around it, attractive to farm or build a house.

Similar to this is the expected (economic) change that will happen after realising the magnet rail line in the Netherlands, connecting the northern provinces with Schiphol Airport. Quiet country towns, such as Heerenveen and Lemmer, are suddenly transformed into economic hubs of the future, at least in the minds of the authors of diverse underpinning reports (Oosterhaven and Strijker, 2000; Regionale Stuurgroep Zuiderzeelijn, 2005; Ministerie van VROM and Ministerie van EZ, 2006).

Not every change is transformational. Roggema et al. (2012) identify three types of change: incremental change, transition and transformation (see Box 24.1).

Box 24.1   Incremental change, transition and transformation

- *Incremental change.* A small adjustment made toward an end result. In a business environment, making an incremental change to the way that things are done typically does not significantly threaten existing power structures or alter current methods (http://www.businessdictionary.com/ definition/incremental-change.html#ixzz2Eo6mNOSD).
- *Transition.* A transition is defined as 'a gradual, continuous process of societal change, changing the character of society (or a complex part) structurally' (Rotmans *et al.*, 2000, p. 11).
- *Transformation.* The capacity to transform the stability landscape itself in order to become a different kind of system, to create a fundamentally new system when ecological, economic, or social structures make the existing system untenable (Folke *et al.*, 2010).

(Based on Roggema *et al.*, 2012)

Transformation is described as disconnected processes of growth (Ainsworth-Land, 1986): the next 'forming' cycle (phase 1) starts while the previous 'integrating' stage (phase 3) is still ongoing (Figure 24.2).

The new forming phase interferes with the existing regime. At the crossroads, the new phase one can only start operating through innovations outside the existing regime: niches. At the second crossroads, a new regime overtakes the existing one. Geels (2002, 2005, 2011) describes this process using the multilevel perspective of niches (the locus of radical innovations), socio-technical regimes (the locus of established practices and associated rules that stabilise existing systems) and the exogenous socio-technical landscape, representing the nearly unchangeable values and biophysical features. Change (or the new forming phase) starts in niches, where novel configurations appear (Geels, 2002). The effectiveness of the change, e.g. whether a regime shift (or transformation) will occur, is determined by reinforcements at the regime and/or the landscape level (Kemp *et al.*, 2001). Hence, this reinforcement determines whether a novelty fails, modifies the regime or transforms the landscape.

The process of transformation consists of several elements (Figure 24.3). The existing regime is dynamically stable (point 2), which means that it is potentially open for change. However, it will only open up if the pressure from the landscape level creates a window of opportunity (point 1). Both levels then externally influence the niches (points 3, 4), which supports the development of novelties (point 5). Once these novelties are developed and aligned towards a dominant design (point 6), they are capable of breaking through the existing regime (point 7) and enforce adjustments to the old regime, which will then transform into a new regime. Eventually, when regime shifts are profound, they may even influence the landscape level, changing the set of values and/or biophysical properties (point 8).

Figure 24.2
Overlapping growth
cycles
Source: Ainsworth-Land
(1986)

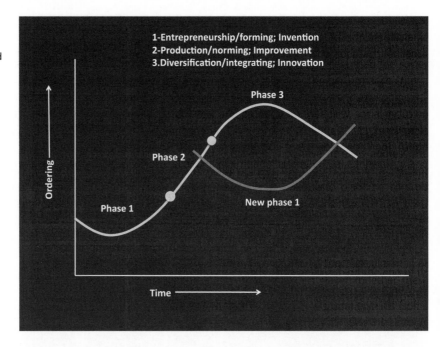

Figure 24.3 Interaction
between the levels of
the multi-level
perspective
Source: After Geels
(2002, 2005, 2011)

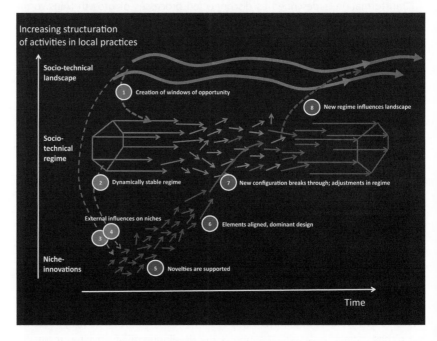

In a spatial sense the places where these niche innovations have the biggest chance to break through the existing regime can be found in two ways. The first way is through a detailed analysis of the water, energy and transport network, in which the most dense, intense and connected nodes form the most likely points for an effective intervention (Roggema *et al.*, 2012; Roggema and Stremke, 2012). The other way is to focus on the most likely places for the most severe climate impacts, such as the weakest point in a coastal defence (Roggema, 2011) or the obvious direction from which a bushfire will come (Newman et al., 2011).

24.3 Application

An early example of using disruptive interventions in spatial planning is the Groningen impulses (Roggema, 2008). Within the framework of developing a regional plan for the province of Groningen, strategic interventions were identified, which supposedly had the ability to enforce a transformation in the entire province, aiming to increase resilience for the impacts of climate change. The 'Windows of Groningen' show these opportunities, where tight and normative planning regulations are abandoned, enabling the area to anticipate and increase its preparedness, and allowing an easy return to its original state after a disaster. The interventions are simple, capable of reshaping the landscape while retaining the same landscape elements as before.

Example one: floodable landscape

The area of the Eemsdelta, in the northern part of the Netherlands, is a landscape under threat of sea level rise and storm surges.

As far as incremental change is concerned, the current regime is responding by strengthening the dikes (defending seawall system). It is reinforcing the current system while new properties to deal with future change are required. Instead of copying the current system A to a slightly improved system A*, a transformational change can only happen when B–, the announcer of a fundamentally new system B, is found or created (see Roggema et al., 2012). B– is a spatial intervention, transforming the system in order to enhance the resilience of the area for future climate impacts. In the case of the floodable landscape the proposed design intervenes through two disruptive spatial measures: seawater enters the hinterland; and land forms through wooden structures.

Instead of increasing the height of the dike, the niche innovation is to create an opening in it. This causes a slow and controlled entry of sea water into the hinterland: it follows the pace at which the sea level rises. Because water enters the landscape in moderate, incremental steps, there is plenty of time to anticipate and adjust the area's way of living (housing on and next to water-rich environments) and working (new ways of agriculture) to continuous change. This is very different from a sudden and unexpected amount of water in your back garden as a result of water breaking through a dike.

Once the first intervention is understood, the second niche innovation is introduced, further constructing the landscape. At the edge between the highest expected sea levels (1.2 m) and the lower-lying landscape, long wooden structures (historically well-known techniques in the area) are projected. These odd elements are provided with tall poles attached to them, which make them even stranger in the currently dry landscape. However, when sea water enters the landscape and reaches these structures they begin to function as sediment catchers and places where floating houses can be attached. A natural process of land forming starts, increasing the ground level of the area above future sea levels. This results in a landscape where houses start floating in deeper water and new land is formed between the wooden structures, on which new agriculture or housing can be developed.

The two disturbing interventions start a process of landscape transformation, which results in a landscape that over time is capable of adjusting itself to future, even unprecedented, change. Hence its resilience increases. The spatial interventions, at first disturbing, create a landscape that cannot be foreseen initially. Space is occupied in a manner that cannot be planned for in great detail. This approach is contrary to the traditional policy approach, where policy is initially formulated and then translated into plans followed by implementation, most likely to deliver a landscape that is not prepared for change because it is based on predicting the unpredictable and does not give the landscape the chance to change according to future demands. Therefore, in this case, the spatial intervention needs to occur *first*, followed by a process of landscape self-organising, after which spatial policies can accommodate the resulting spatial configuration.

Example two: bushfire resilient landscape

The regional town of Bendigo, in Victoria's western central area, Australia, is vulnerable to bushfires. After a bushfire, such as the one happening on Black Saturday in 2009, the current regime reacts by implementing incremental change in the form of improved resistance of rebuilt houses. This approach places the houses back in vulnerable positions. They may be built of more resistant materials, but the increased impacts of climate change imposed on the buildings will far outstrip any improvements in their construction. Similar to the case of the floodable landscape, this incremental change only improves the current system A to a slightly better A*. What is required is a fundamental change to a system B, a complete transformation of the urban system so that it becomes truly resilient against future impacts. The niche innovations, or disturbing spatial interventions, proposed for Bendigo are twofold: do not rebuild; and introduce sand dunes.

The first intervention is simple: a once-burned house cannot be rebuilt on the same spot. Instead, it should be replaced by a monumental pillar. Over time the placing of these pillars at the most vulnerable, northwest side of the town will form a protective shield (see Figure 24.4).

The second spatial intervention will provide sand dunes at the less vulnerable, southeastern side of town. Local micro-climatic differences in moisture and wind, following the laws of nature, will cause dunes to form, although their precise shape is difficult to predict. Once the dunes have taken shape in a more or less stable form, the bottom zone will be planted with pig face, an 'unburnable' plant, then houses will be built by local citizens in the most sheltered spots, followed by bike paths and other infrastructure. Over time the dunes, plants and housing will occupy the whole southeastern side of town.

The entire urban 'system' will reorganise itself: the northwest side of town will have no new housing, while the opposite side will be incrementally developed.

As a result the whole town will slowly 'move' towards less vulnerable landscapes in the southeast and will become increasingly protected at its most vulnerable northwestern side.

    The two interventions, once implemented, will transform the Bendigo landscape, although it is hard to predict exactly how it will look. The traditional approach, as in the floodable landscape example, fails to encourage this kind of development because the unpredictable cannot be predicted by policymaking. By contrast, once the interventions have been implemented, the spatial impacts can be drawn and subsequently laid down in policies.

Figure 24.4 Artist's impression of Bendigo's protection zone
Source: Newman *et al.* (2011)

24.4 Conclusion

Policymaking is framing the future in a particular way. Future events are, to a certain extent, predicted and then used to design policy. Because the majority of predictions are based on extending recent history in combination with probable climate impacts, the future is seen as an improved version of the present. When unknown, new and fundamentally different problems are expected but cannot be predicted, these policies are almost certainly wrong. The most probable future never happens. When future policy is based on the past combined with most probable climate impacts, making spatial plans can prove a risky business. When detailed spatial propositions and measures are used to solve former weather extremes, they are preparing our cities and landscapes for the wrong impacts, because they are based on incorrect premises of continuation and incremental change.

New and fundamental impacts require transformation; and, as we have seen in this chapter, a spatial transformation is more likely to occur after a spatial intervention, which can sometimes be very disturbing. In transformation terminology, a niche innovation is required to break through the current regime and eventually change the overarching socio-economic landscape (another 'landscape', in addition to the more familiar spatial physical landscape). These interventions will impact the current city and landscape and change the way they appear. The new and emerging land use and spatial configuration of elements in the city and the landscape are the result of self-organising principles and will be more resilient against (even unknown) future climate impacts.

Although it is counter-intuitive to let individual spatial interventions determine the configuration of city and landscape, it would certainly be ineffective to develop a spatial policy that inhibits these resilient and sustainable developments. Under the influence of extreme, unprecedented climate impacts, spatial interventions can be defined that increase the resilience of the landscape as a whole, which will form the basis of future spatial policy. Operating planning and policy processes in this way, areas will be able to adjust and adapt in the most sensible way, and will not be constrained by restrictive and counter-innovative policies.

References

Ainsworth-Land, G.T. 1986. *Grow or Die: The Unifying Principle of Transformation*. New York: John Wiley & Sons.

Cohen, P.E. 2002. *Mapping the West: America's Westward Movement 1524–1890*. New York: Rizzoli International.

Folke, C., Carpenter, S.R., Walker, B., Scheffer, M., Chapin, T. and Rockström, J. 2010. Resilience thinking: Integrating resilience, adaptability and transform-ability. *Ecology and Society* 15(4): 20. Available online: http:// www.ecology-andsociety.org/vol15/iss4/art20/ (accessed 15 December 2010).

Geels, F.W. 2002. Technological transitions as evolutionary reconfiguration pro-cesses: A multilevel perspective and a case study. *Research Policy* 31: 1257–1274.

Geels, F.W. 2005. Processes and patterns in transitions and system innovations: Refining the co-evolutionary multi-level perspective. *Technological Forecasting and Social Change* 72: 681–696.

Geels, F.W. 2011. The multi-level perspective on sustainability transitions: Responses to seven criticisms. *Technological Forecasting and Social Change* 1: 24–40.

Kemp, R., Rip, A. and Schot, J.W. 2001. Constructing transition paths through the management of niches. In Garud, R. and Karnoe, P. (eds) *Path Dependence and Creation*. Mahwah, NJ: Lawrence Erlbaum.

Ministerie van VROM and Ministerie van EZ. 2006. *Structuurvisie Zuiderzeelijn*. Den Haag: Ministerie van VROM and Ministerie van EZ.

Newman, J., Al-Bazo, S., Kendall, W. and Newton, J. 2011. *Re-burn*. Melbourne: Design Studio KINDLE, Landscape Architecture, School of Architecture and Design, RMIT University.

Oosterhaven, J. and Strijker, D. (eds). 2000. *Effecten Magneetzweefbaan Randstad-Noord-Nederland. REG 23, Ruimtelijke Economie Groningen*. Groningen: RUG.

Regionale Stuurgroep Zuiderzeelijn 2005. *Zuiderzeelijn – de kansen in kaart Gebiedsvisie Groningen, Fryslân, Drenthe, Flevoland*. Groningen: Regionale Projectorganisatie Zuiderzeelijn.

Roggema, R. 2008. The use of spatial planning to increase the resilience for future turbulence in the spatial system of the Groningen region to deal with climate change. Paper presented at the UKSS Conference, Oxford, 1–3 September.

Roggema, R. 2009. *DESIGN, Final Report Hotspot Climate Proof Groningen*. Groningen/Wageningen/Amsterdam: Province of Groningen and Climate Changes Spatial Planning.

Roggema, R. 2011. Swarming landscapes, new pathways for resilient cities. Paper presented at the Fourth International Urban Design Conference, 'Resilience in Urban Design', Surfers Paradise, 21–23 September.

Roggema, R. 2012. Swarm planning: Development of a spatial planning methodology to deal with climate adaptation. Ph.D. thesis, Delft University of Technology/Wageningen University and Research Centre.

Roggema, R. and Stremke, S. 2012. Networks as the driving force for climate design. In Roggema, R. (ed.) *Swarming Landscapes: The Art of Designing for Climate Adaptation*. Dordrecht/Heidelberg/London: Springer.

Roggema, R., Vermeend, T. and van den Dobbelsteen, A. 2012. Incremental change, transition and transformation? Optimising pathways for climate adaptation in spatial planning. *Sustainability* 4: 2525–2549.

Rotmans, J., Kemp, R., van Asselt, M., Geels, F., Verbong, G. and Molendijk, K. 2000. *Transities en Transitiemanagement: De Casus Van Een Emissiearme Energievoorziening*. Maastricht: ICIS.

CHAPTER 25

How to move from talking to doing

Creating sustainable cities

Gil Penalosa and Leonie J. Pearson

25.1 Change is hard, but it offers wonderful opportunities!

Just two or three decades ago there was not much talk or concern regarding the creation of sustainable resilient cities. We saw multiple cases, like Mexico, whose nine largest cities on average doubled their population but increased their footprint by seven times between 1982 and 2012. How can governments provide transportation, sewage, water, hydro, education and multiple other services to seven times the area? How can this be sustainable?

Similar situations have been witnessed across the world. In the last forty years the world's population has more than doubled, going from 3 billion to over 7 billion; fortunately, the rate of growth has decreased substantially and is projected to increase by 'only' another 3 billion over the next forty years – roughly 50 per cent growth as opposed to more than 100 per cent. Nevertheless, this means that we not only have to improve the cities that we have today but are responsible for the creation of great cities for another 3 billion people. More than half the world's population already lives in cities, and that is where most of the growth will take place. Many estimates show that by 2050 over 80 per cent of the world's population will reside in urban areas.

Now there is much talk amongst decision-makers about many crises, as if we are approaching a 'perfect storm': population growth, traffic congestion, global warming, the obesity crisis and other public health issues, as well as economic crisis. All these seem to be taking place simultaneously, ultimately leaving us overwhelmed.

There are clear challenges, then, but also magnificent opportunities in the future. In order to improve the current situation substantially, we *must* move from thinking and talking to doing.

Most decision-makers seem reluctant to be pioneers, perhaps due to the misconception that those who act often get 'shot in the back'. Fortunately, though, a significant number of exemplar cities worldwide have overcome seemingly insurmountable challenges and created utterly successful spaces.

This book has focused primarily on the thinking and talking parts of achieving sustainable resilient cites. The cities we want will improve the quality of urban life for all and promote the synergies of bicycling, walking, parks and trails, with better overall health, improved transportation systems, equal opportunities for recreation, economic development and a greener environment. Everyone wants to live in these types of cities, whether they are eight or eighty years old! This chapter moves from the thinking and talking to showing how people have achieved, and are achieving, the changes that are necessary to produce resilient, sustainable cities.

There are certainly many barriers to change. One of those we most commonly hear is: 'We are not like Melbourne, Copenhagen or New York; we are unique.' That brings to mind a quote from Margaret Mead: 'Always remember that you are absolutely unique – just like everyone else.' While it's not about copying any other city, it is evident that cities do not have to invent what has already worked in other places. They can adapt and improve certain elements and create their own model to suit their specific circumstances.

Another often-cited barrier to change in cases relating to mobility is climate: 'It is too hot in Phoenix/too cold in Stockholm/too wet in Vancouver/too variable in Melbourne to change how we move around our city.' Yes, there is something unique about every climate, and it has affected the way we move, how we design our cities and what is convenient in making our lives better. But the reality is that this is not a barrier: climate is changing and weather is dynamic. A Danish street philosopher stated in relation to the weather and walking or riding a bicycle that 'There is no such thing as bad weather . . . only bad clothing.'

The last common barrier to changing our cities is: 'It's not part of our culture.' People claim that pedestrian streets are for Italians who enjoy strolling and chatting in public spaces; while cycling is for Danes who behave like Vikings. The reality is that all cultures are different, weather is different, but people are the same: we are social animals who inherently enjoy being around other human beings. All over the world, what people enjoy most in public spaces, such as parks, plazas and streets, is the presence of others.

These barriers are encountered in every city, and they result in every city having a unique approach to delivering a sustainable and resilient future. When considering what your city's future will look like, do not think in terms of 'cutting and pasting'. We need to consider all the issues, think and talk about what has been discussed in the previous chapters of this book, and ask ourselves: 'How can we adapt and improve this for my city to deliver the best possible city now and into the future?'

Copenhagen has been considering, developing, planning and implementing a resilient, sustainable city for over forty years. It has faced all of the barriers mentioned above, but has proved that you can effect change through continuous refinement, discussion and movement.

So, how do we advance our cities from thinking and talking about resilient, sustainable futures to actually doing it?

25.2 Making the change in cities

I (Gil Penalosa) have been thinking about this for a long time, while working for the mayor of a large city and during my time at an NGO that advises cities of all sizes and on all continents. Before emigrating to Canada, I was Commissioner of Parks, Sport and Recreation for the City of Bogotá, Colombia, where I led the design and development of over 200 parks, of which Simón Bolívar, a 360-hectare park in the heart of the city, is the best known. Here we created the Summer Festival, with over 100 events over 10 days and more than 3 million people attending, making it

Box 25.1 Copenhagen's cycle tracks

In the 1970s Copenhagen went through a major oil crisis and chose to reassess how people lived and its city design, and focus all future design on its citizens. This has resulted in improvements in lifestyle, health and wellbeing, economic prosperity, community cohesion and is said to have delivered a future that is sustainable now and resilient to the future pressures of more people and increasing environmental impact. The aim was to reduce cars and traffic in the downtown city and increase people's ability to walk, cycle and access public space. The perceived barriers included (but were not limited to): 'the city has bad weather (too cold in winter and too hot in summer)' and 'we are private people – it is not part of our culture to walk the streets'.

The result was that there were transformations all over the city, considering pedestrians first, then cyclists, then transit users and finally car drivers. As far as age is concerned, the priority has been children and older adults first, as these are the most vulnerable citizens. An example of the changes was the Nyhavn street along the docks, which previously supported parking for ninety-three cars. Pedestrianizing the street was not supported unanimously, but then no innovative proposal ever is. Some merchants thought pedestrianization would ruin their businesses. As it turned out, they could not be more wrong, as those ninety-three cars were replaced with over 10,000 people daily, who buy far more of the merchants' food and services.

Another major change has been the increased use of bicycles. From the 1950s to the 1970s the car took over Copenhagen, as it did in most cities around the world. However, things changed radically during the oil crisis of the 1970s, when car use was severely restricted, including an outright ban on Sundays. Copenhageners soon realized how great the two-wheel, non-motorized alternative could be and usage more than doubled in just ten years. Moreover, it has doubled again in the past decade. Now almost 40 per cent of all trips in the city are made by bike, and in winter most cyclists (70 per cent of those who ride in summer) just keep riding through the snow. Much car-parking space has been removed to provide space for safe cycle tracks that are physically separated from the cars.

Yet another example of the new culture has been the transformation of eighteen former car-park areas into pedestrianized spaces, plazas and paths that are enjoyed by all.

the main annual recreational and cultural event in the country. We also initiated the 'New Ciclovia' – a programme which sees over 1 million people walk, run, skate and bike along 121 kilometres of Bogotá's city roads every Sunday. Today, it's recognized and emulated internationally.

Now, as Executive Director of the NGO 8–80 Cities, I have had the honour of working in over 130 cities around the world and learning from the people in every one of them.

These experiences have led me to conclude that our cities need five elements in order to generate change:

- a shared sense of urgency;
- political will;
- leadership;
- doers in the public sector; and
- citizen participation.

Usually we need to start with a shared sense of urgency: we need a critical mass of decision-makers and/or citizens sharing the desire to change, the vision of where to go, and the sense that it must start now. Once we have achieved this first element, the other four must be present, too, but not necessarily in any specific order. Each city is different and the combination of elements and the level of intensity of each is unique. Ideally, all should be part of the mix to create change; but if one or more are absent, the others must compensate to ensure that change still happens.

Shared sense of urgency

The first step to change is to realize that the way we are creating communities is unsustainable and to accept that we need to change. We are facing traffic congestion, climate change, an obesity crisis, economic crises and many other issues directly and/or indirectly related to the built environment.

We need to develop a shared sense of urgency. Everywhere we find symptoms that we do not have much time to think about; we need to act now. One key element is population growth: metropolitan areas like Toronto and Melbourne will increase their populations by over 50 per cent over the next twenty years; the USA will increase by a third by 2040; and the world's population will have an additional 3 billion people by 2050. Each month an additional 5 million people arrive in cities in developing countries.

All of this means that we not only need to improve the cities that we have today; we must create vibrant and healthy cities for millions of people all over the world.

The key question we must ask is: how do we want to live? Once we develop a shared vision on this key issue it will become easier to make the decisions on densities, modes of mobility, even size of schools. Everything is related to everything else.

One of my brothers, Enrique, was Mayor of Bogotá, and he initiated some major transformations, especially relating to sustainable mobility and public spaces. He made it clear that, although we have been building cities for over 5,000 years, over the last sixty to eighty years this process has focused more on car mobility than on people's happiness. The two concepts are simply not compatible.

By the way, no city of over half a million inhabitants has adequately solved the issue of mobility exclusively through the use of private cars. If such a solution were feasible, we would have hundreds of examples by now, as almost every city has tried this option over the last century. None has succeeded. Therefore, public transit is a must for sustainability, both economic and environmental. However, since public transit will not pick us up in front of our homes and drop us off at our destinations, cities must also be walkable and bikeable in order to make links with public transit, in addition to being modes of mobility in their own right.

Political will (guts)

Change is hard, which is why it is almost never supported unanimously. Politicians cannot stop change because there is 'some concern', as there will always be apprehension. They must realize that deciding not to change is actually choosing to stay as they are.

The most important factor is to have clarity that the general interest must prevail over particular interests. This means that any discussion on any project must begin and end with a focus on the general interest.

As an example, when car parking is eliminated to widen the sidewalks or create safe cycle tracks, obviously car owners are likely to complain. But politicians cannot give in to particular interests who use pressure tactics. They must have the courage to do whatever is right. That is never easy, but it is essential.

When Mayor Delanoë in Paris implemented that city's very successful public bicycle system, Velib, he eliminated 7,000 car-parking spaces. The system had 20,400 bicycles distributed at 1,451 docking stations, and they had to find the space for those docking stations, hence the removal of the parking spaces. Initially, many business owners complained as they were set to lose two or three parking spaces in front of their shops. Nevertheless, Mayor Delanoë continued to prioritize the general interest over the particular and insisted that the parking spaces had to go to make way for the docking stations. Eventually, most business owners realized that a docking station housing up to forty bicycles was far better for business than parking spaces for two or three cars.

Politicians are not elected to make the easy decision, which usually involves doing more of the same, even if it's done a little better. They are elected to do things right, and to do the right thing.

Leadership

Leadership seems like a characteristic reserved for well-known figures, such as politicians and artists. But when the objective is to change mindsets, we need many leaders from all sectors of society: teachers, athletes, public sector staff, entrepreneurs and community workers, among others. Leadership does not always come at the global level. Everyone in our community has a responsibility to step up and take ownership of the problem and work out its solution. These leaders are the real change agents at the city scale.

Anne Fenton is a PE teacher at a local Ontario school. She was appalled that fewer kids were walking to school each year and could see the detrimental effect this was having on students, both physically and emotionally. After one school holiday she dressed up as a traffic cone and closed the school's car-parking lot. That meant parents had to drop off and pick up their kids at least 500 metres from the school building, guaranteeing that each child would walk at least a kilometre each day. The resulting impact is that now, instead of being driven to the drop-off zone, many kids choose to walk, bike or scoot the whole way to school. And they do so all year round, even in the winter, when temperatures can hit −24 degrees.

We need hundreds of Anne Fentons in all of our communities, playing different roles at schools, community centres, libraries, senior-citizen centres and businesses. A common denominator among these people is that they see something that is not working well in their community, they want to change it, and they don't take 'no' for an answer. They end up becoming experts at finding solutions to the problems (not problems with the solutions).

Doers in the public sector

It used to be a common topic of conversation among people interested in urban issues that nothing transformational could ever be achieved in New York City. The corruption, the mafia, politicians, even the taxi drivers all seemed like insurmountable obstacles.

However, over the last decade, under the leadership of Mayor Bloomberg and through the fantastic vision and work of Janette Sadik-Khan, Commissioner of Transportation, and Amanda Burden, Commissioner of Planning, the city has transformed itself into a people-friendly place. All of a sudden there are hundreds of thousands of people cycling; the sidewalks are wider; and new public spaces have been created, including magnificent large ones like High Line Park and a succession of small ones such as those along Broadway.

Sadik-Khan and Burden well understand that New York's citizens pay city staff to find solutions to problems, not to come up with dozens of excuses why things cannot be done. As ever, it has not been easy. These two women have employed knowledge, experience, creativity and a great deal of hard work to come up with several innovative solutions, crafting partnerships among private, non-profit and public sectors to fulfil projects that are improving the quality of life of all citizens.

Many people have ideas, and usually there is no shortage of them. But most cities lack champions, the 'doers' who can take idealists' 'impossible dreams', overcome all the obstacles and make them reality. Public sector staff must keep in mind that they have a magnificent opportunity to transform cities into vibrant and healthy communities and they must do whatever it takes to progress from talking to doing. Sometimes the stars are aligned and they will be able to move forward with relative ease. More often they will have to overcome envy, jealousy, personal interests and innumerable other hurdles, but the end result will make the effort worthwhile. After all, most people work in the public sector to improve the quality of life of citizens by doing whatever is right, not necessarily whatever is easy.

Public participation

The fifth and final element required to create change is public participation. Citizens can no longer be spectators, they need to participate: attending public meetings, writing letters to editors, calling up radio stations, and lobbying their elected officials.

If they are not participating, if they are not acting, then someone else will be, and that other someone will be setting policy.

Every city has a range of people who use the city and want it to be as good as it can be for their health, wellbeing and future prosperity. By engaging with the locals through meaningful processes – asking kids at school for their ideas on how to improve the city; asking older residents about the changes they would like to see – you will find both the impatiens and the orchids.

We ask participants who attend our community workshops to compile lists of these 'flowers'. Impatiens are small flowers that provide lots of bright, colourful solutions. They are low-cost, low-risk, high-visibility options, which means they play an important role in building trust and support for innovative action. Following this analogy at a workshop in Timmins, Ontario, a municipality with 43,000 inhabitants, one resident said that when she walked home at night she felt unsafe on the dark sidewalks. She asked for lighting to be improved to ensure the sidewalks are safe, which would then lead to them being used more. Initially, other participants argued that this would be a high-cost option, but then the proposer explained that, while the sidewalks were very dark, the streets were very well lit. Her idea was simply to rotate the existing street lights through 90 degrees so that they shone on the sidewalks, rather than the roads. She backed up her argument by pointing out that cars already have lights, whereas pedestrians don't. The total cost would involve paying an engineer to climb each post and turn the light around. Everything else would remain the same: post, cable, light bulb and energy use. Since hearing this proposal, I have found that most streets around the world are very well lit while most sidewalks are very dark. This is the result of decades of building cities that focus on car mobility rather than people.

Orchids, in contrast to impatiens, are beautiful statements of what is possible, but they need careful nurturing and plenty of growing time. These are high-cost, iconic or exemplar solutions that might require two to five years to come to fruition. They are also more expensive and complex than the low-risk options, but the rewards will be worth the investment.

Some of these actions, both short and long term, relate to infrastructure but others, which are just as important, are programmes and activities. Creating change requires plenty of the latter 'software' as well as the former 'hardware'.

25.3 Conclusion

In summary, it is evident that over the last forty years, during which time the world's population has more than doubled, most of this growth has taken place in cities in a way that is unsustainable. We see the symptoms of this deficient growth everywhere: traffic congestion, climate change, obesity and other public health issues, economic crisis. We need to change.

We have seen that change is a challenge but also that it presents marvellous opportunities. We have explained that five elements – shared sense of urgency; political will; leadership; doers in the public sector; and public participation – are vital to produce change at the city level. Although ideally all five elements should be present, the importance of each depends on context because each and every city has a unique past and present, and therefore a unique route to a resilient future.

These issues are neither technical nor financial. They are political, which is why the five elements are so important.

We need to approach the process as a three-legged stool. One leg comprises the elected officials at all levels – municipal, state and national. The second leg represents the public sector staff, and not just those involved in planning and transportation. Equally important are those engaged in public health, education, environment, economic development, parks and other departments. Finally, the third leg is the community: universities, businesses, non-profit organizations, unions, media and others. For the three legs to work in harmony, they will need to be glued together by a shared sense of urgency.

There have been many references in this chapter to walking, riding bicycles, using public transit, as well as to parks, sidewalks and streets, but we must be clear that all of these are means, not ends. The end is creating vibrant cities and healthy communities where residents will be happier through their enjoyment of great public spaces.

Our priorities must be our most vulnerable citizens: the children, the older adults and the poor. Imagine if everything we did in our public spaces benefited both eight-year-olds and eighty-year-olds. The end result would be great cities for *everyone*. And a magnificent bonus would be that we'd also end up with cleaner air, improved public health, superior economic development and better quality of life for all our citizens.

CHAPTER 26

Adaptation and transformation for resilient and sustainable cities

Leonie J. Pearson and Craig Pearson

26.1 Introduction

Historically, much attention has been focused on building the resilience of mega-cities (i.e. those with more than 10 million inhabitants) and urban sector sustainability, such as transport, design, service delivery, energy consumption and planning requirements. But little effort has focused on integrating the concerns of resilient cities and urban sustainability.

This book has sought to redress the balance by looking at the whole-system changes required to achieve a resilient and sustainable city. It has brought together practitioners' and academics' perspectives on two questions. What is a resilient, sustainable city? And how can it be achieved? The contributors have done this by showcasing cycle tracks in Copenhagen, precinct design in London, governance in Ottawa and many other real-life examples. The aim of this concluding chapter is to bring together and answer the two unifying questions of the book.

26.2 What is a resilient, sustainable city?

City sustainability has had numerous definitions, but we like the 1987 Brundtland definition: to 'meet the needs of the present without compromising the ability of future generations to meet their needs' (Brundtland 1987, p. 43). However, this lacks any teeth for application. Therefore, each chapter in this book has added to this definition in various ways. For example, a sustainable city system may be defined as 'an affordable, globally competitive economy that emits zero carbon, is less consumptive, more equitable, and provides personal fulfillment, longevity and reasonable health' (Pearson 2012, p. 223). The chapters in this book provide nuanced insights into this definition: community ownership of problems and solutions, caring for resources and increasing the efficiency of their use, innovative technology fixes and integrated co-produced design for multiple purposes are common elements that we, and many of the other contributors to this book, see as essential to achieve sustainability.

A sustainable city is achievable; it is a tangible goal. An outcome of the 2011 Oliphant Conference in Melbourne, which inspired this book, was a synthesis of goals (from four workshops) which participants felt were essential for a resilient, sustainable city. These goals are consistent with the themes arising from the chapters within this book and they are shown in the first column of Table 26.1. The goals

Table 26.1 Goals, opportunities and blockers of resilient and sustainable cities, cross referenced through the book

Goals	Opportunities to achieve goals	Blockers	Chapter cross-references where goals are explicit
Be dynamic	Collective visioning for low-carbon, equitable food, shelter, etc.	Public-policy caution associated with electoral cycle of all levels of government; media celebration of special-interest (usually status quo) pleas.	Chapters 1, 2
Start with people and place	Community participation in planning. Balance and compromise using examples.	No shared narrative: compartmentalization of views by stakeholders, compartmentalization within sectors, government departments.	Chapters 5, 8, 24, 25
Collaboration and social cohesion	Working with grassroots organizations, explicit policy objectives and support.	Inertia and desire to minimize risk especially political risk. Major critical role of media in politics.	Chapters 19, 21
Maximize equity, employment and justice	Housing tenure, change in governance and intuitions, leadership that is engaged with the community.	Lack of connection between community activism and strategic government action.	Chapters 4, 16, 22, 23
Design to address externalities, e.g. carbon pollution, waste, water	Integrated co-production design for multiple purposes, e.g. recreation, carbon sequestration, flood mitigation; design for low-carbon precincts that reduce material consumption.	Disconnect between short- and long-term evaluations, e.g. costs.	Chapters 7, 14, 15, 18, 20
Value and enhance greenspace	Green design: better integration of public and private green assets; remove barriers to access. Greening of urban buildings and space, using under-utilized land in short breaks, rethinking zoning and planning requirements.	No scaling procedures, public zoning and the time it takes to negotiate, land tenure and inability to introduce peppercorn leasing.	Chapters 3, 6, 10, 11
Technological innovation	Private and public interest through collaborative research.		Chapters 9, 12, 13, 17

support the currently held notion that sustainability is primarily about a process, rather than an end point or destination. They build on (but differ from) the nine 'design principles' enumerated by Walker and Salt (2006), who approach resilience and sustainability from a more ecological, and theoretical, perspective.

These goals recur throughout the book and, as shown in Table 26.1, every chapter references at least one of them and provides suggestions on how they might be achieved.

Table 26.1 also reminds us that there are many obstacles (or blockers) to achieving sustainability and resilience. Whilst this book is positive, it does address the elements in our current city systems which hinder the progression to a resilient and sustainable future. These blockers range from policy and planning controls (e.g. Chapters 5, 11 and 25) to technological limitations (e.g. Chapters 9 and 24) and lack of community engagement (e.g. Chapters 5, 21 and 23). The case studies that appear throughout the book show practical ways of working around these blockers and developing pathways to achieve resilient and sustainable cities.

26.3 How can we achieve a resilient and sustainable city?

This book has emphasized that we have rarely achieved sustainability, and many of the discussions have been about the paths, the processes, the journeys and the blockers with which we need to engage, rather than the achievable goal. Some of the commonly identified processes that represent opportunities for action are presented in column 2 of Table 26.1. From the theoretical (see Elmqvist et al., Chapter 3) to the practical (see Table 26.1), there are many pathways, and while some solutions are generic, many are specific to particular societies and environments.

It is helpful to characterize pathways as being adaptive, transitioning or transformative (Table 26.2). Some writers consider all three of these to be aspects of resilience (e.g. Elmqvist et al., Chapter 3), whereas others posit that the purpose and characteristics of transformation are different from, and sometimes likely to be opposite to, those that will achieve adaptation (Pearson and Pearson 2012). Importantly, this book has drawn on all three types of pathway to explore how a city could become resilient and sustainable. These three pathways contrast with coping (Elmqvist et al., Chapter 3), doing nothing or collapsing (see Diamond, 2005; Butzer, 2012), as a 'brittle' system might (Chapters 1 and 22). None of these pathways will deliver a resilient and sustainable city future, so they are not considered further.

Adaptive, transitioning and transformative pathways may all lead cities to resilient and sustainable futures. Whilst Table 26.1 has identified some opportunities for achieving these goals separately, we see that there are two unifying messages that recur throughout the book and as such are 'priority actions' for cities wanting to start on the pathway to a better future. These are:

- Desirability of reframing the city development issues into an issue of social desirability.
- Need for long-term co-produced (i.e. community, government and business) city design which accounts for full costs and externalities.

Table 26.2 The three pathways for change discussed throughout the book

Pathway for change	Definition	Amount of change required; and scope	Citation within the book
Adaptive	Adjustment in the urban system in response to actual or expected disturbances when frequencies tend to increase.	*Marginal change* focused on changes in technology, management practices and organizations. It does not typically threaten existing power structures or alter current methods: e.g. retrofitting local parks and gardens to improve water use efficiency.	Chapters 1, 3–9, 12, 18, 22, 24
Transitioning	A gradual, continuous process of societal change, changing the character of the city (or a complex part thereof) structurally.	*Incremental change* focused on changes in technology and governance practices to secure procedural justice: e.g. putting bushfire risk planning in community hands to deliver large built structures for protection, householder designed and built houses with responsibility.	Chapters 1, 3–9, 13, 24
Transformative	The ability to change the city system and its broader environmental context (e.g. political, societal, ecological) in order to become a different kind of system, to create a fundamentally new city and society.	*Reform change* focused on overarching change to social norms and political regime ensuring issues of equity and justice lead the process: e.g. designing towns for schoolchildren and the whole community, prioritizing bike paths and public gardens, focus on footpaths not roads.	Chapters 3–8, 15, 24, 25

So far in this chapter we have addressed the goals and pathways for achieving resilience and sustainability at a high or generic level. A handful of generic goals do indeed apply to all cities, as though they are all the same and all internally homogeneous. However, specific goals and priorities for action can be determined meaningfully only with reference to a specific system or, in our context, urban precinct (Allenby and Fink, 2005). This introduces the notion of community-specificity and scaling.

City communities and infrastructures exist at several scales, from the city-region (see Pearson and Dyball, Chapter 11), to the whole city, to numerous local government entities, to the neighbourhood or precinct. These are spatial and geopolitical scales, which are often the focus of planners. Equally important is the hierarchy of socially defined scales that may be distributed throughout a city but is not necessarily spatially contiguous.

To draw down from generic attributes (Tables 26.1 and 26.2) to specifics, we bring together three examples from different continents that show spatially contiguous precincts (e.g. suburbs and cycle tracks) or socially defined intra-city systems (e.g. parklets) (Table 26.3). These illustrate the importance of recognizing heterogeneity and uniqueness within, as well as between, cities.

26.4 The way forward

This book has covered a wide range of theory and practice for achieving resilient and sustainable cities. It has drawn on multiple disciplines and practice areas to

Table 26.3 Precinct examples of how three different cities are achieving a resilient and sustainable future

	Melbourne, Australia	San Francisco, USA	Copenhagen, Denmark
	Chapter 5	Chapter 11	Chapter 25
	Gentrification in Brunswick suburb, residential housing and greyfield light industrial sites undergoing densification	Establishment of 'parklets', conversion of 2–3 parking spaces or under-utilized land into mini-parks	Establishment and support of a connected, integrated cycle tracks to be the main source of urban transit
Goals addressed:			
• Be dynamic	Somewhat	Yes	No
• Start with people	Yes	Yes	Yes
• Collaboration & social cohesion	Yes	Mostly	Yes
• Maximize equity	Yes	Yes	Yes
• Design to address externalities	No	No	Yes
• Value & enhance greenspace	Yes	Yes	No
• Technological innovation	Yes	No	No
Pathway: • Adaption • Transitioning • Transformation	Adaption as incrementally changing current identity and use	Transformation of built infrastructure to green recreational space	Transitioning from roads used only by cars to specific bike spaces and now their own 'roads'
Blockers overcome	Public policy concern for zoning rules and current densification guidelines	Competing community values for a single space, e.g. bench seat versus edible garden versus café tables	Social norm of bike riding in winter
Priority actions	Reframed the precinct development from a social inclusive perspective	Reframed the suburb development from a social inclusive perspective	Integrated co-design approach to solving city traffic problems

provide an integrated, holistic perspective, rather than the traditional sector or single insight. In so doing it has come to the conclusion that a resilient and sustainable city is achievable, as many existing examples prove. Moreover, for cities, resilience and sustainability are not end points, but rather the continuing attainment of seven goals:

- be dynamic
- start with people and place;
- collaboration and social cohesion;
- maximize equity, employment and justice;
- design to address externalities;
- value and enhance greenspace; and
- technological innovation.

Multiple obstacles to achieving these goals have already and will continue to be put in place, but practice and theory provide numerous insights on how to overcome them using the pathways of adaptation, transition and transformation.

As has been said, this book is optimistic, but there is still much work to be done for our cities to achieve all seven goals both now and in the future. We have two recommendations for the best way forward. First, we need more trialling and testing of innovative ways to achieve a resilient and sustainable city in academia, practitioner and policy space – along with a need to share successes and failures. It would be nice to think that this book is a one-off, that in twenty years' time all cities will be so well versed in how to achieve a future that is better for people and the environment that there will be no need for another book of ideas, theories and examples. However, that dream will not come to fruition unless we start to test all the goals, minimize the blockers and initiate the pathways to a better future. A key to trialling innovation will be to encourage partnerships between emboldened policy-makers, precinct developers, designers and researchers, all working together to deliver technological innovation and better social environments: buildings and precincts that transform rather than simply 'cope' at the lowest cost.

Second, to quote Nike, 'Just do it!' Everyone has a role, an idea, an insight and the ability to participate in delivering cities where our children will *want to live*, rather than those where they will *have to work*. It is up to the community to use its power as a collective, as well as at the individual level, to make changes that deliver:

- better systems that use less resources, e.g. water-use-efficient precinct development or recycling in the household;
- institutions that truly provide equitable and procedural justice to all people starting with inclusive community; and
- governance structures that deliver decision-making and resources to societal preferences with collaborative leadership and innovative buildings and green space design that are dynamic and flexible enough to deal with the human and environmental stressors facing our society.

These are some of the many initiatives in which we can all participate to make our future cities resilient and sustainable.

References

Allenby, B. and Fink, J. 2005. Towards inherently secure and resilient societies. *Science* 309, 1034–1036.

Brundtland, G.H. 1987. *Our Common Future*. Brussels: World Commission on Environment and Development.

Butzer, K.W. 2012. Collapse, environment, and society. *Proceedings of the National Academy of Sciences, USA* 109: 3632–3639.

Diamond, J. 2005. *Collapse: How Societies Choose to Fail or Survive*. Melbourne: Allen Lane, Penguin.

Pearson, C.J. (ed) 2012. *2020: Vision for a Sustainable Society*. Melbourne: MSSI, University of Melbourne, p. 250.

Pearson, L. and Pearson, C. 2012. Societal collapse or transformation and resilience: Letter to editor. *Proceedings of the National Academy of Sciences*. URL: http://www.pnas.org/cgi/doi/10.1073/pnas.1207552109.

Walker, B. and Salt, D. 2006. *Resilience Thinking*. Washington, DC: Island Press.

Index

References in **bold** indicate tables and in *italics* indicate figures.